Sparks

GAMBETTA AND THE NATIONAL DEFENCE :
A REPUBLICAN DICTATORSHIP IN FRANCE

GAMBETTA AND THE NATIONAL DEFENCE: A REPUBLICAN DICTATORSHIP IN FRANCE

BY

J. P. T. BURY

FELLOW OF CORPUS CHRISTI COLLEGE, CAMBRIDGE

WITH ILLUSTRATIONS
AND A MAP

GREENWOOD PRESS, PUBLISHERS
WESTPORT, CONNECTICUT

Originally published in 1936
by Longmans, Green and Company, London,
New York, Toronto

First Greenwood Reprinting 1971

Library of Congress Catalogue Card Number 77-114490

SBN 8371-4818-9

10- 17- 74

Printed in the United States of America

FOREWORD

GAMBETTA's political career, which began in the 'sixties and lasted until his death in 1882, is a record of almost continuous activity. It passed through many different phases, but there is only one definite break, the break which occurred in 1871, when the ex-" Dictator " went into retirement at San Sebastian. Then many thought that he was a spent force, and that he could never again play an influential part in French politics. In this book I am concerned only with the first period of Gambetta's career, with the period before the withdrawal to Spain ; and for my purpose the success or failure of the statesman of the Third Republic is irrelevant for any judgment upon the politician of the Second Empire and the minister of the Government of National Defence.

In any study of this period the war of 1870 must necessarily bulk large ; it is the culminating point, and it occasioned the most spectacular part of Gambetta's whole career. The crowded events of a few months overshadow the normal political activity of years, and it may be urged that to attempt to combine a study of the politician of the 'sixties with one of the Dictator of 1870 must result in a work which has neither unity nor proportion. Nevertheless, understanding of the politician is quite essential to comprehension of the Dictator, for it was only because he was a Republican politician that Gambetta could become Dictator. In the history of French institutions September 4, 1870, may be said to mark the end of one chapter and the beginning of another, but in the history of the man Gambetta it is merely a more abrupt, unexpected development of an old argument. Although it forms little more than a prologue, I consider that a sketch of that argument is an indispensable preliminary. The narrative here is comparatively straightforward and simple. It is after September 4, and still more after October 9, 1870, that it becomes complex, for, although the war is the dominant preoccupation, military operations, diplomacy, and questions of internal politics and administration all interact, and Gambetta was concerned with all. It has been my object to emphasise this interaction, and while I have wished to make clear the essential points in the problem of the national defence as it presented itself to Gambetta, I have tried as far as possible to avoid the details of military operations except where they are essential to an understanding of the general situation, or for an appreciation of Gambetta's methods. On the other hand, I have given in the narrative itself a fairly detailed account of certain negotiations which seemed to me to shed a particularly clear light, not only upon his methods, but also upon his general purpose and his conception of the war he was waging.

I am very greatly indebted to Professor Harold Temperley for the advice and encouragement he has so kindly given me while I have been working on Gambetta, and I take this opportunity of thanking him. I wish also to thank my colleagues, Mr. Kenneth Pickthorn and Mr. P. E. Charvet, for their criticisms and for reading the proofs; Mr. J. M. Newton for his help in preparing the Index; and the Editors of the *Cambridge Historical Journal* for permission to reprint from the *Journal* of 1934 the substance of Chapters IV and V.

J. P. T. B.

CONTENTS

viii   CONTENTS

LIST OF ILLUSTRATIONS

ix

NOTE UPON THE PRINCIPAL SOURCES

By far the greater part of the material for a study of the earlier period of Gambetta's career and more particularly of his activities as a minister in the Government of National Defence has already been published. Apart from certain Foreign Office despatches in the Public Record Office [1] and from the despatches of Prince Metternich preserved in the State Archives in Vienna,[1] I have been unable to discover any unpublished documents of importance. The sources upon which this work is based are therefore, with these few exceptions, printed sources.

The following publications are primary sources of the greatest value :—

A. CORRESPONDENCE

1. P. B. Gheusi—Gambetta par Gambetta (14th edn., Paris, 1909—an English translation 1910)—a collection of Gambetta's letters to his family and friends, the majority written before the war of 1870.

2. J. V. Laborde—Léon Gambetta, biographie psychologique (Paris, 1898)—contains letters from Gambetta to his friend Dr. Fieuzal.

3. A. Lavertujon—Gambetta inconnu (Paris, 1905)—letters written by Gambetta to Lavertujon in 1869-70, found among his papers much later by friends and published at their instance with copious annotations by the recipient, who was intimately acquainted with Gambetta during the years 1867-70.

B. SPEECHES AND DOCUMENTS

1. Gambetta, Discours et plaidoyers politiques (3 vols., edited by J. Reinach, Paris, 1881).

[1] Extracts from these have appeared in Lord Newton, *Life of Lord Lyons*, and in H. Salomon's, *L'ambassade de Richard de Metternich à Paris.*

2. Gambetta, Dépêches, circulaires, etc., 4 septembre, 1870-76, février, 1871 (2 vols., ed. J. REINACH, Paris, 1886).

3. Enquête parlementaire sur les actes du gouvernement de la défense nationale (Paris, 1872-75). This monumental work was the fruit of the labours of the Commission of inquiry set up by the National Assembly. It contains 18 volumes which are divided into 3 sections :—

(A) *Dépêches Télégraphiques*—a selection of those telegrams which seemed to the Commission most interesting or important from a political, administrative, or military point of view, made from the vast correspondence of those officials who had the right to communicate with one another free of charge. The sources upon which the Commission drew were not, however, complete. Some of the archives of post offices were destroyed in the course of the war, others were removed by the Germans or were hidden or mislaid by the French at moments of fear or hurried evacuation. Thus very few of the despatches of thirty departments could be traced, and there is a much fuller telegraphic record of the doings of the Delegation after December 9 than before that date, for the archives of the post office at Tours disappeared, whereas those of Bordeaux were preserved intact. But, despite these lacunæ, it is possible to discern the general lines of the policy followed by the Government in the provinces, and these two volumes are invaluable for a study of the mentality of Republican administrators, for an estimate of the reactions of civil and military officials to the chief measures of the Government and to the chief events of the period, and for a general understanding of the administrative background of the national defence, of the methods of Gambetta himself and of the men with whom he had to deal.

(B) *Dépositions*—the evidence of witnesses interrogated by the Commission. The value of these depositions naturally varies considerably. Some of the witnesses supported their evidence with notes and documents, others relied solely upon their memories ; some were questioned much sooner than others ; some preferred to answer questions briefly, others (such as Trochu and Gambetta) to give a long continuous narrative which generally tended to be an apologetic of their own conduct ; some were freely communicative, others (Spuller for example) reticent and inclined to regard this Commission composed largely of " Notables " as a definitely hostile institution.

(C) *Rapports*—fully documented reports upon various special aspects of the national defence, such as foreign policy, the defence of Paris, the Ligue du Midi, the army of the East.   The tone of these reports tends to vary according to the prejudices of the *rapporteur* and none of them was prejudiced in favour of the Government of National Defence. But it is to be noted that the Commission rejected a report produced by one of its members as too violently anti-Republican.   The author, M. Callet, wrote as one who found himself " in a political arena opposed to the most detestable party that ever existed."   (His work was published posthumously in 1889 under the title—*Les origines de la troisième république.*)

4. A. DRÉO—Procès-verbaux des séances du conseil du gouvernement de la défense nationale (Paris, 1906).   These were private notes made by Dréo for the benefit of his father-in-law, Garnier-Pagès.   They are often scanty, but they are the only record of what happened at the sessions of a council which kept no official minutes, and they are none the less valuable for being unofficial.

5. La guerre de 1870-71—the great work published by the *Revue d'Histoire* and compiled by the " Section historique de l'État-Major de l'Armée " is more fully documented than the Rapport Perrot or the other reports of the parliamentary Commission of Enquiry dealing with military organisation and operations.   The narrative is also far more objective, and less prejudiced than those of the Commission's " rapporteurs."   For the military history of the war from the French point of view it is unquestionably the most valuable authority.   Unfortunately, however, one of the most important sections, that dealing with the campaigns of the army of the Loire has never been completed.   Two parts only have appeared and they carry the tale of operations no further than October 11.   They appeared in 1914.   Further publication seems to have been interrupted by the war.

C. CONTEMPORARY DIARIES AND NARRATIVES

1. Juliette ADAM—Mes sentiments et nos idées avant 1870 (1905).
   Juliette ADAM—Mes illusions et nos souffrances pendant le siège de Paris (6th edn., 1906). These books, the substance of Mme Adam's diaries, are invaluable for the light they shed upon Republican politics and personalities. The authoress, the chief Republican hostess of the time, was an exceptionally acute and intelligent observer.

2. A. CLAVEAU—Le 4 septembre in Revue de Paris, Sept. 1, 1911.

3. E. DRÉOLLE—La journée du 4 septembre au Corps Législatif (Paris, 1871).

4. L. HALÉVY—Le 4 septembre au Corps Législatif (Paris, 1904).

5. Comte G. D'HAUSSONVILLE—Mon journal pendant la guerre (Paris, 1905).

6. George SAND—Le journal d'un voyageur pendant la guerre (Paris, 1871).

7. Adolphe THIERS—Notes et Souvenirs (Paris, 1901).

Among the numerous German war diaries the following are of special value for their reflection of German or French opinion and for their comments upon the national defence :—

1. H. ABEKEN—Ein schlichtes Leben in bewegter Zeit (Berlin, 1898).

2. M. BUSCH—Graf Bismarck u. seine Leute während des Kriegs mit Frankreich (2nd edn., Leipzig, 1878).

3. Frederick III—War Diary (tr. A. R. ALLINSON, London, 1927).

4. Frédéric Charles, Prince—Mémoires (tr. et rés. par le Commandant CORTOYS).

5. Count Paul HATZFELDT—Letters to his wife (tr. J. L. BASHFORD, London, 1905).

D. In addition there are various publications by the principal actors in the national defence ; works which are naturally more or less apologetic in tone, but which contain numerous documents not always accessible elsewhere. The chief of them are as follows :—

1. A. CRÉMIEUX—Le gouvernement de la défense nationale. Actes de la délégation de Tours et de Bordeaux (Tours, 1871). This together with

2. Al. GLAIS-BIZOIN—Dictature de cinq mois (Paris, 1873), reveals much about the elder Delegates and the general atmosphere in which the business of the Delegation was conducted.

3. J. FAVRE—Le gouvernement de la défense nationale (Paris, 1871-75).

4. C. DE FREYCINET—La guerre en province (Paris, first published 1871, 14th edn., 1894). The first presentation of his defence for the conduct of the war. Able, but not always convincing, it was written immediately after the war and the greater part of it was read by the author to Gambetta at San Sebastian before it was published.

   C. DE FREYCINET—Souvenirs, vol. 1 (written long after and first published in 1912), in part abridges the narrative of " La guerre en province." Its tendency is to be more dramatic, but there are also some interesting modifications of the case presented in the earlier book.

5. J. SIMON—Souvenirs du 4 septembre (Paris, 1874).

   J. SIMON—Le gouvernement de M. Thiers, 1871-73 (Paris, 1878).

The French secondary sources may conveniently be divided into two classes :—

A. The numerous histories and accounts of the war or of different incidents connected with it by contemporary writers. The majority of these books are the strongly biased products of political partisans concerned either to glorify or to discredit the Third Republic. Roughly there are three viewpoints, two hostile and one favourable to the men of September 4. The following books are representative examples :—

1. Léonce DUPONT DE NEMOURS—Tours et Bordeaux, Souvenirs de la Republique à outrance (Paris, 1877), is an example of the work of a monarchist whose aim was to discredit the Republic at the same time as the Government of National Defence.

2. Gustave FLOURENS—Paris livré (Paris, 1871) gives the views of an extreme Republican who condemns the Government of National Defence no less roundly than the monarchists, but for different reasons, for its moderation and neglect of extremist counsels.

3. Alcide DUSOLIER—Ce que j'ai vu du 7 août, 1870 au 1 février, 1871 (Paris, 1874), is an example of the apologetic of the admirers of the men of September 4. The author was one of Gambetta's young followers at Tours.

B. The more critical works of later historians ; especially :—

1. Paul DESCHANEL—Gambetta (Paris, 1919). This appeared on the eve of the author's election to the Presidency of the Republic and he was in a position to have access to all available material. It did not, however, throw much new light upon the first period of Gambetta's career, and though more discriminating than earlier lives by Republican authors, it is not a book of great distinction.

2. Henri DUTRAIT-CROZON—Gambetta et la défense nationale, 1870-71 (Paris, 1914). Dutrait-Crozon is the pen name used by Colonel Larpent and Colonel Frédéric Delebecque. This " great and fine book," as M. Ch. Maurras calls it,[1] is the most thorough attempt that has been made to heap discredit upon Gambetta and upon the national defence as conducted by Republican civilians. Equipped with a great armoury of documentation and detailed appendices and written in a dry economical style, it appears at first sight a most formidable indictment. It is in fact a masterpiece of innuendo with a most skilful juxtaposition of all the evidence unfavourable to Gambetta in such a way that the documents appear to speak for themselves and join in a chorus of utter condemnation. Though its bias renders it valueless as a historical estimate of the national defence, the book raises many questions of interest and contains some important appendices.

In languages other than French there are many books which deal with the war, general military histories or accounts of particular episode but, so far as I am aware, very few special studies of Gambetta. In English there are only two biographies of any importance :—

1. F. T. MARZIALS—Gambetta (London, 1890).

2. H. STANNARD—Gambetta and the foundation of the Third Republic (London, 1921).

[1] *Action Française*, Jan. 1, 1933.

Of the books concerning the war two must be specially mentioned :—

1. Colmar von der GOLTZ—Léon Gambetta und seine Armeen (Berlin, 1877). A critical examination of Gambetta's conduct of the national defence by an able German officer who fought through the war : fair and judicious.

2. Col. Lonsdale HALE—The People's War in France, 1870-71 (London, 1904). A critical examination of German operations against the army of the Loire from the end of September until the recapture of Orléans at the beginning of December, and a clear demonstration of the difficulties which confronted the Germans when they found themselves involved in a " People's War ".

A SELECT BIBLIOGRAPHY OF BOOKS AND ARTICLES NOT ALREADY MENTIONED IN THE NOTE ON THE PRINCIPAL SOURCES

I. GENERAL

BAINVILLE, Jacques. La troisième République, 1870-1935 (Paris, 1935).

HANOTAUX, Gabriel. Le Gouvernement de M. Thiers, 1870-1873, t. 1 (Paris, 1925).

MAURICE, Sir Frederick. Cambridge Modern History, Vol. XI, ch. xxi.

ROUX, Marquis de. Origines et fondation de la troisième République (Paris, 1933).

SEIGNOBOS, Ch. Vol. VIII in E. LAVISSE's Histoire de France contemporaine depuis la Révolution jusqu'à la paix de 1919.

THOMAS, Albert. Cambridge Modern History, Vol. XI, ch. xvii.

II. GAMBETTA AND POLITICAL PARTIES BEFORE THE WAR

CHESNELONG, Ch. Les derniers jours de l'Empire et le gouvernement de M. Thiers (Paris, 1932). The impressions of a Bonapartist but Catholic deputy.

DARIMON, A. Histoire d'un parti. Les irréconciliables sous l'Empire (Paris, 1888). The notes of one of the " Cinq " who rallied to the Empire.

DREYFUS, Robert. Les premières armes de Gambetta. Articles in the *Revue de France*, Dec. 15, 1932, and Jan. 1, 1933.

DREYFUS, Robert. Monsieur Thiers contre l'Empire, la guerre et la Commune (Paris, 1928).

DURIEUX, J. Le ministre Pierre Magne, 1806-1879 ; d'après ses lettres et ses souvenirs, t. 2 (Paris, 1929).

GHEUSI, P. B. La vie et la mort singulières de Gambetta (Paris, 1932). While this book, written by a kinsman of Gambetta, professes to disregard " ses actes et ses discours déjà entrés dans l'Histoire " (*sic*), it throws interesting light upon his relations with his family, his habits and his health.

GOYAU, Georges. Patriotisme et humanitarisme. Articles in the *Revue des deux Mondes*, July 15, Oct. 15, 1900.

LAFAGE, L. Le Pays de Gambetta (Paris, 1933).

LA GORCE, P. De. Histoire du second Empire (Paris, 1894-1905).

LEFRANÇAIS, Gustave. Souvenirs d'un révolutionnaire (Brussels, 1903).

OLLIVIER, E. L'Empire libéral (Paris, 1895-1915). An elaborate apologetic, but contains much valuable material and is important for an understanding of the development of parties under the Empire, their nuances and reactions.

PESSARD, H. Mes petits papiers, 1860-70 (3rd edn., Paris, 1887). Memoirs in which there is a jumble of gossip and direct observation.

REINACH, Joseph. La vie politique de Léon Gambetta, suivre d'autres essais sur Gambetta (Paris, 1918).

SENCOURT, R. E. Life of Empress Eugénie (London, 1931).

TCHERNOFF, I. Le parti républicain au coup d'état et sous le second Empire (Paris, 1906). The best analysis, clear and authoritative.

TOURNIER, A. Gambetta : souvenirs anecdotiques (Paris, 1893). The author was closely associated with the radical Republicans.

WEILL, Georges. Histoire du parti républicain en France de 1814-1870 (Paris, 1900).

III. THE WAR

A. DIPLOMACY

BISMARCK-SCHOENHAUSEN, O.E.L., Prince von. Reflections and reminiscences (Vol. II, tr. A. J. BUTLER, London, 1898).

MORLEY, J. The Life of William Ewart Gladstone (1903).

NEWTON, Lord. Life of Lord Lyons (London, 1913).

REITLINGER, F. Une mission diplomatique en octobre 1870 (Paris, 1899).

SALOMON, H. L'Ambassade de (Prince) Richard de Metternich à Paris (Paris, 1930).

SOREL, Albert. Histoire diplomatique de la guerre franco-allemande (Paris, 1875).

WASHBURNE, E. B. Recollections of a Minister to France, Vol. I (London, 1887).

WELSCHINGER, H. La guerre de 1870. Causes et responsibilités (Paris, 1911).

B. PARIS

CLARETIE, Jules. Histoire de la révolution de 1870-71 (Paris, 1871). The most interesting contemporary history, well documented and illustrated.

FERRY, Jules. Lettres, 1846-93 (Paris, 1914).

D'HÉRISSON (IRISSON), Comte. M. Journal d'un officer d'ordonnance, 1870-71 (57th edn., Paris, 1896).

LAMY, Etienne. Le Gouvernement de la défense nationale. Articles in the *Revue des deux Mondes*, May 15, June 15, 1896.

LEFRANÇAIS, G. Étude sur le mouvement communaliste à Paris en 1871 (Neuchâtel, 1871).

MAILLARD, F. Histoire des journaux publiés à Paris pendant le siège (Paris, 1871).

MARX, K. The Civil War in France preceded by the two manifestoes of the General Council of the International on the Franco-Prussian War, with a historical introduction by R. W. POSTGATE (London, 1921).

RANC, Arthur. Souvenirs et correspondance (Paris, 1913). A posthumous compilation by his widow.

SARCEY, F. Paris during the siege (London, 1871).

THOUMAS, Gen. Paris, Tours, Bordeaux (Paris, 1892). The work of a regular officer who was capable of appreciating Gambetta's achievements.

TROCHU, Gen. Oeuvres posthumes. I. Le siège de Paris (Tours, 1896).

WHITEHURST, F. M. My private diary during the siege of Paris (London, 1875).

C. THE PROVINCES

ANDRIEUX, Louis. La Commune à Lyon en 1870 et 1871 (Paris, 1906). The author was a member of the Lyons Committee of Public Safety of September, 1870, and played an important part in the events of this time.

D'AURELLE DE PALADINES, Gen. La première armée de la Loire (2nd edn., Paris, 1872). In which is to be found the General's not very impressive defence of his conduct and the expression of his bitter resentment at the way in which he was treated by Gambetta and Freycinet.

BAKUNIN, M. A. Lettres à un Français (1870).

BARNI, Jules. Manuel républicain (Paris, 1872). Articles written for the *Bulletin de la République*, an important example of Republican propaganda during the war. The author was a distinguished Kantist.

CASTELLANE, Marquis de. Men and Things of My Time (tr. A. T. DE MATTOS, London, 1911).

CHEVALIER, Mgr. C. Tours capitale (written in 1871, published posthumously at Tours in 1899).

CHUQUET, A. Le Général Chanzy (Paris, 1884).

FALLOUX, Comte de. Mémoires d'un Royaliste (Paris, 1888).

FRANQUET DE FRANQUEVILLE. Souvenirs intimes de la vie de mon père (Paris, 1878).

GALLI, H. Gambetta et l'Alsace-Lorraine (2nd edn., Paris, 1911).

GENEVOIS, H. La défense nationale en 1870-71 (Paris, 1906).

GUIGUE, Lt.-Col. Le gouvernement de la défense nationale. Article in *Revue militaire française*, June, 1932.

GWYNN, S., and TUCKWELL, G. M.   Life of Sir Charles Dilke, Vol. I (London, 1917).

HALÉVY, L.   Récits de guerre. L'Invasion, 1870-71 (Paris, 1891).

KÉRATRY, Comte E. de.   Le 4 septembre et le gouvernement de la défense nationale (Paris, 1872).

LEHAUTCOURT, P.   Histoire de la guerre de 1870-71 (Paris, 1901).

LEROY-BEAULIEU, Paul.   La province pendant la guerre. Articles in *Revue des deux Mondes*, March 1, 15, 1871.

NADAUD, Martin.   Discours et conférences (1870-78). Six mois de préfecture et comment j'ai connu Gambetta, etc., t. 2 (Guéret, 1889).

RIVIÈRE, A.   Trois mois de dictature en province (Paris, 1871).

SCHLUMBERGER, Gustave.   Mes Souvenirs (Paris, 1934).

STEENACKERS, F. F., and LE GOFF, F.   Histoire du gouvernement de la défense nationale en province (Paris, 1884). The authors both held administrative posts under the Government and were warm supporters of Gambetta.

STOSCH, A. von.   Denkwürdigkeiten (3rd edn., Stuttgart and Leipzig, 1904).

VERDY DU VERNOIS, J. V.   Im grossen Hauptquartier, 1870-71 (3rd edn., Berlin, 1896).

VIZETELLY, E. A.   My Days of Adventure : the Fall of France (1870-71), (London, 1914).

––––––––

NEWSPAPERS.   *Le Journal Officiel, Le Petit Journal Lyonnais, Le Progrès (de Lyon.), Le Siécle.*

ARTICLES :—

Army Quarterly : April, 1898, *General Bourbaki.*
    July, 1910, *The Dual Control in Bourbaki's Campaign.*

Edinburgh Review : October, 1911, *Gambetta's War Office.*

Frazer's Magazine : November, 1872, *Six Months of Prefecture under Gambetta.*

Revue des deux Mondes : November 1, 1920, *Gambetta.*

In reference to authorities I have used the following abbreviations :—

B.S.P.—British State Papers.

Dép.—*Dépositions des Témoins* in the *Enquête parlementaire* of the Commission set up by the National Assembly.

D.T.—*Dépêches Télégraphiques* in do.

Dép. circ.—*Gambetta, Dépêches, circulaires,* etc., ed. J. REINACH.

F.O.—Foreign Office Papers at the Public Record Office.

H.H.u.S.A.—Papers in the Haus, Hof und Staats Archivs, Vienna.

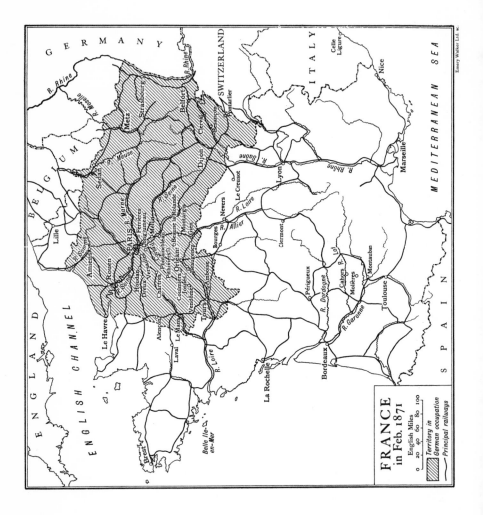

FRANCE
in Feb. 1871

English Miles
0   20 40 60 80 100

▨ Territory in
   German occupation
— Principal railways

Emery Walker Ltd. sc.

I

DEBUT

LÉON MICHEL GAMBETTA was born on April 2, 1838, the son of Joseph Gambetta, an Italian grocer living in Cahors, and of Marie Magdeleine Massabie his wife. It was not until he came of age in 1859 that he acquired French nationality. His political enemies were to take the obvious advantage of this alien descent. They would not admit that a man with so much Italian blood in his veins could have the feelings of a true Frenchman. Still less could they endure that a metic should by vast numbers of Frenchmen be regarded as the very model of a French patriot.[1]

This Italian, however, was only half Italian by race, and by up-bringing hardly at all. The grocery business over which his father, Joseph, presided at Cahors had originated in the enterprise of his grandfather Baptist Gambetta.[2] Two generations of Gambettas were associated with Cahors before Léon Gambetta was born. The Italian father maintained connection with Celle-Ligure, the fishing village between Savona and Genoa from which his family hailed, and was never naturalised a Frenchman ; but he was an Italian living in France ; he had settled at Cahors before the birth of his children, and he had taken a Frenchwoman to wife. The

---

[1] Cp. e.g. H. DUTRAIT-CROZON, *Gambetta et la défense nationale*, 37 ff.

[2] P. B. GHEUSI, *La vie et la mort singulières de Gambetta*, 22 ; P. DESCHANEL, *Gambetta*, 9.

mother of Léon Gambetta was of sound Gascon stock, the daughter of a chemist of Molières in Tarn et Garonne.   Son of a Frenchwoman, the future great man was born, brought up, and schooled in France.   Except through reading and hearsay the land of his father's fathers was unknown to him until he was eighteen.   Then he was taken by Joseph Gambetta to visit his relations in Italy.   He was thrilled ; he could write ecstatic letters about the beauties of the Ligurian coast ; he could feel a much deeper sympathy with Italy than the ordinary Frenchman, and regard it as a second " patrie ".   Nevertheless, France was indubitably the first.   When he came of age and, as the son of a foreigner resident in France, was free to choose his country, the choice was not difficult.   Environment was as compelling as heredity, and it was in France that Léon Gambetta had his roots.   France was the country which for him was home, the centre of all his friendships, ambitions and interests.

It is easy to attribute to the Italian side of Gambetta's ancestry the suppleness, the skill at manœuvring and the diplomatic talent which were his to a marked degree, and which are popularly supposed to be peculiarly Italian qualities ; but those qualities are not necessarily or exclusively Italian, and they were not marked in Gambetta's father.   The dominant traits in the character of Joseph Gambetta were remarkable obstinacy, strong will, and an authoritative disposition, qualities which are still less exclusively Italian.   Yet it was these if any which Léon inherited from his father ; he, too, was to show an authoritative disposition, strong will, and tenacity.   It was here he resembled his Italian father, while in his good nature and vivacity he no less certainly took after his French mother.   Beyond this it is difficult to dissect the Italian from the Gascon, for earlier generations of Gambettas and Massabies are now little more than names ; personalities and family character-istics have been buried by time.[1] But if the Italian is elusive, the southerner is evident. Heredity and environment com-bined to make Léon Gambetta essentially " un homme du Midi ". His manner, his accent, his exuberant conversa-tion betrayed him at once. It was in the south of France that he was born and bred, and spent his life until, great adventure, he set out for Paris to study law. Paris then, as now, was the magnet which attracted all young men of ambition, and the ambition of the eighteen-year-old pro-vincial was as great as his means were small. He quickly succumbed to the fascination of the capital, and found in the Quartier Latin great scope to display his powers. This " energetic determined-looking young southerner with long black hair " [2] was never so happy as when he had an audience to regale with ready talk, vivid recitations from Rabelais, or impassioned declamations from Mirabeau's speeches and Demosthenes' Olynthian orations. The elo-quence and memory of the young law student were indeed astonishing, and won him a wide reputation and a large following of admirers, whose affections he retained all the more readily because of his radiant geniality and unaffected good nature. The ease with which he became a leader in the student world of his time confirmed his self-confidence and stimulated his ambition. In despondent moments he admitted the defects of a southern nature, " a mixture of ferocious energy and of terrible indolence," [3] but the moments of despondency were rare ; at twenty-one he

[1] But cp. L. LAFAGE, Le pays de Gambetta, 35 ff., for a vivid account of the Molières chemist, François Massabie.

[2] Action Française, Aug. 21, 1932, cit. Clemenceau to Ranc, Oct. 5, 1858.

[3] P. B. GHEUSI, La vie et la mort singulières de Gambetta, 64.

believed there was a star awaiting him in " the firmament of fate," [1] and, strong in this belief, he applied himself resolutely to the task of carving a career.

The first important step was in 1861, when, after taking the oath at the bar, he overcame the strong opposition of his father and remained in Paris to plead. Provincial the young Gambetta still was in manner and speech, but, after four years of Paris, he was no longer attracted by life in the provinces ; it seemed too narrow for his vaulting ambitions. The victory he now won with maternal aid over the obstinate grocer in Cahors was decisive for his future.   In Paris there were infinite possibilities of advancement for an able and energetic young barrister, and Gambetta entered upon his profession with great enthusiasm :   " I read, I write, I reflect, I listen to good masters, I work in order to become an orator ; I give you my word of honour if energy and desire to succeed, encouragement from my seniors, and the ambition necessary to the beginning of every career can help me to succeed, you can count upon me, I shall reach the goal." [2]   He retained and extended his influence in the Quartier Latin, and the cafés of the Left bank no less than the law-courts heard him at this work of becoming an orator. The critics who glibly condemn the young Gambetta as a good-for-nothing who frittered away his time bawling and brawling in cafés forget what an important institution the café is in French student life.   And if it is important now, it was no less important under the Second Empire at a time when the press was severely censored and political meetings vigorously controlled.   Then the cafés were among the few public places where speech was tolerably free, and so they became, in the words of Alphonse Daudet, " real schools of

---

[1] P. B. GHEUSI, *Gambetta par Gambetta*, 132.   [2] Ibid. 186.

opposition, or rather of legal resistance. . . . Every one of them had its own regular orator, and a table which at certain moments became almost a tribune." [1] A Café Procope had re-echoed the vigorous loud-voiced speeches of the young lawyer Danton ; a Café Procope now had a regular orator in Gambetta and resounded with the sonorous eloquence of another young lawyer, who, too, was to win fame as the tribune of a revolution. It was the words of Danton that Gambetta quoted on the eve of his first important case : " The bold and the violent shall seize the empire of the world ". [2]

Absorbing as legal work might be, Gambetta's life as a barrister was no less interesting for the opportunities it provided for contact with the world of politics. The bar, then as now, was a regular training ground for politicians, and the seniors of whose encouragement he spoke, Crémieux, Jules Favre, Ernest Picard, Ollivier, were prominent political figures and opponents of the Empire as well as noted lawyers. Under such conditions the attraction of politics, to which he had never been indifferent, vastly increased. He began to attend the sessions of the Legislative Body with such assiduity that he was soon better versed in parliamentary procedure than many of the deputies themselves. [3] He cultivated political acquaintances widely, and boldly forced the doors of M. Thiers to ask what a budget really was. Thiers was impressed by the young man's evident ability, and gave him advice which was as acceptable as it was sound. He urged him not to warp his judgment in frequent private lawsuits, to plead seldom and reserve himself for political cases ; [4] and the advice was justified by Gambetta's striking success

[1] A. Daudet, Souvenirs d'un homme de lettres (Paris, 1889), 17.

[2] P. B. Gheusi, op. cit. 184, Jan. 15, 1861.

[3] I. Tchernoff, Le parti républicain au coup d'état et sous le second Empire, 387.

[4] A. Tournier, Gambetta, Souvenirs anecdotiques, 1.

in his first political trial.[1]   The Duc de Morny was curious
to see the new orator,[2] and the son of the Cahors grocer was
spoken of as a rising man in the ranks of the political opposition as well as in the legal world of the Palais.

Gambetta had professed himself a Republican since the
early days when he had written " Vive Cavagnac ! (*sic*) A bas
Bonaparte ! " in a letter home from his first school at Montfau-
con.   In coming to Paris he had come to the chief stronghold of
Republicanism, but it was to find a party divided and scarcely
yet recovered from the effects of the *coup d'état*.   There
was division between Republican Liberals and Republican
Socialists, and many of the principal leaders of both factions
were in exile.   Socialist opposition had been driven under-
ground ; that of the Liberals was confined to certain salons,
to a few newspapers and to the parliamentary efforts of the
" Cinq ".[3]   But the attitude of the five deputies who had
consented to take the oath of allegiance to the Emperor in
order to be able to voice their criticisms of his government in
the Legislative Body was by no means universally approved.
Those who considered themselves as the most faithful
guardians of the ideals of 1848 could not look upon the oath
as a mere formality to be observed only as a necessary prelude
to effective political action.   They condemned any sort of
recognition of the " man of December " as a moral weakness, and preferred to maintain an attitude of protest by
complete abstention.   Thus there was also a cleavage between
" assermentés " and " insermentés " ; the Republican party
was weak and disunited, a party which tended to live upon
its past and upon the memories of its brief period of power,

---

[1] I. TCHERNOFF, *Le parti républicain au coup d'état et sous le second Empire*, 372.

[2] L. HALÉVY, *Trois diners avec Gambetta* (Paris, 1929), 8.

[3] Jules Favre, Ernest Picard, Emile Ollivier, Hénon, and Darimon, the
members of the Opposition elected in 1857.

to look regretfully backward to the golden age of 1848, instead of forward to a vigorous future.

Despite some reading of Proudhon, the young son of the " petit bourgeois " grocer had little interest in questions of social reform. From the first he was a Liberal democrat, and in the Liberal group a strong supporter of those who, untroubled by scruples of conscience, were prepared to take an active part in parliamentary opposition. Accordingly, he hitched his wagon to the star of the " Cinq ". Assiduously he cultivated their acquaintance, studied their methods, even memorised their speeches. " No pupil of the ' Cinq ' was more diligent than he," said Ollivier.[1] Not only did the policy of the abstentionists appear naïve and absurd to Gambetta and his young Republican contemporaries, but the achievements of the men of 1848 themselves were severely criticised, and the criticisms corresponded to the new outlook of a new generation, sceptical, positivist,[2] and realist. " The young men," said Challemel-Lacour, " have a horror of absolute principles and of the intransigence and integrity which, it must be said, have made us men of character." [3] The difference between the new and the old republicanism was vividly illustrated by Mme Adam's report of a conversation between the veteran Garnier-Pagès and Peyrat (editor of L'Avenir national and author of the phrase which Gambetta was later to borrow and make famous, " Clericalism—there is the enemy "). " The third Republic," said Peyrat, " must be built upon the foundations of the first." The second had been a childish affair ; its rulers had failed to realise that a government must place durability above principles. Garnier-Pagès, himself a man

---

[1] E. OLLIVIER, L'Empire libéral, V, 47.
[2] Cp. I. TCHERNOFF, op. cit. 188, 189.
[3] Mme ADAM, Mes sentiments et nos idées avant 1870, 45.

of 1848, protested vigorously : " Perish the Republic rather
than the principles by which it will always be possible to
give it new birth," and he went on to define the Republic as
" free play for all the liberties which a society can assimilate."
" That Republic," retorted Peyrat, " is a thing of the past,
and is not worth 45 centimes." [1] Gambetta was not,
perhaps, the originator of this revolt of " les jeunes," but he
soon became identified with it, and distinguished himself by
his independent and critical attitude.   While he frequented
the salons of " vieilles barbes " such as Crémieux and
Garnier-Pagès, and while he sought to form connections
with Liberals of all shades, the men whom he flattered least
were the Republicans who had held power and lost it, as he
hinted, through their own incompetence.   Not for him an
attitude of mute protest or a devotion to rigid principles.
His energetic nature demanded an active policy which
would produce visible results.   The Empire should be
fought with its own weapons and principles must be dis-
carded during the battle ; it would be easy to restore them
once the third Republic had emerged triumphant.[2]   Such
was the essence of the views which he developed during the
years before his election as a deputy, and in expounding them
he was one of the most conspicuous representatives of the new
Liberal realism in France.   In his belief in the effectiveness
of a policy of results he went further than many even of his
young associates.   Save for one or two friends like Jules
Ferry and Philis, he was alone in following Ollivier for a
while after that politician was first accused of treachery and
desertion to the Empire.[3]   For Gambetta a liberal reform
was a liberal reform, no matter whence its source ; if it

[1] Mme ADAM, *Mes sentiments et nos idées*, 32 ff. (1864).
[2] Ibid.
[3] OLLIVIER, *L'Empire libéral*, VI, 556 ; Mme ADAM, *Mes premières armes
littéraires et politiques*, 415 ; *Mes sentiments et nos idées*, 47, 20, 21.

came from the Emperor so much the better ; the Emperor was driving nails into his own coffin thereby. But for the majority of Republicans a liberal reform granted by Napoleon was an object of deadly suspicion ; " timeo Danaos et dona ferentes " was the reaction of Favre and of most of his colleagues. The policy of results did not, however, lead Gambetta to the same goal as Ollivier. The opportunist statesman of the Third Republic was opportunist from the very outset of his political career, but not so opportunist as to abandon his Republican creed. Whereas Ollivier, captivated by the charm of Napoleon III, came to believe that all the essentials of democratic liberty could be won without a change of regime, Gambetta always maintained that true democracy and Bonapartist Empire were wholly incompatible.[1]

The elections of 1863 which increased the numbers of the Opposition deputies from five to thirty-five gave Gambetta his first opportunity to play an active part in politics. He revelled in the fray, and distinguished himself as an electioneer of remarkable energy and as a supporter of all those whom he thought likely to be the most effective opponents of the Empire, regardless of whether they were Republicans or no. While the parliamentary opposition was still such a small minority of the whole Chamber it must be composed of the best men available, and common hostility to the Empire should prove capable of being a real bond of union between all opposition groups. Thus it was that he spent his eloquence in favour of Tolain, the proletarian candidate, and of Prévost-Paradol, the brilliant young Orleanist pamphleteer, as well as of Republican Liberals like Favre.[2] Also, determined advocate of a

---

[1] Cp. below, p. 26.

[2] Mme ADAM, *Mes premières armes littéraires et politiques*, 415 ; R. DREYFUS, *Revue de France*, Dec. 15, 1932, *Les premières armes de Gambetta ;* A. TOURNIER, *Gambetta, Souvenirs anecdotiques*, 132 ; M. RECLUS, *Jules Favre* (Paris, 1912), 242.

vigorous policy, he strenuously championed the return of
all the members of the " Cinq," the men who were the
pioneers of active opposition in the Legislative Body.[1] In
his own words, he put himself " into touch with all that is
live, generous, and scientific in the liberal and democratic
movement. Thereby I have won real influence. At the
moment of writing, I am convinced that these three months
of electoral struggle which have just passed have done more
for my future than three years of quiet and peaceful struggle."[2]
He was right ; this election campaign had been a valuable
experience and a great opportunity to attract attention, an
opportunity of which he made the most. Observers were
impressed by his amazing vitality, eloquence, skill in handling
crowds, and by the modernity of his outlook.[3] Henceforth
he felt himself attracted to politics by a " two-fold feeling
of personal passion and of general interest," [4] and while
awaiting the next general elections, the elections of 1869,
a year which he optimistically declared would be as fatal
to the Second Empire as was 1852 to the Second Republic,
he set himself to consolidate the reputation he had won, to
extend his political influence, and to prepare to "take an
active and honourable part in events ".[5] He continued his
policy of maintaining touch with all that was " live " in
the Liberal movement, and even accompanied his friend,
Clément Laurier, on a visit to Twickenham in 1865.
Despite the desirability of effective co-operation between
opposition groups, such fraternising was not always appreciated. The news of a meeting between two Republicans
and an Orleanist prince in his place of exile caused an outcry,

---

[1] OLLIVIER, L'Empire libéral, VI, 230 ; E. SPULLER, Figures disparues (3me
série), (Paris, 1886), 289.

[2] P. B. GHEUSI, Gambetta par Gambetta, 221, June 22, 1863.

[3] Mme ADAM, Mes premières armes littéraires et politiques, 415.

[4] P. B. GHEUSI, op. cit. 252, 253.   [5] Ibid. March, 1866.

and the gesture was construed by purists and gossips alike
as a desertion to Orleanism and a betrayal of Republican
principles.[1] So much was made of the incident and so
persistent were the rumours, that even in September, 1870,
an English resident in Paris could write : " Gambetta is
very Orleanist (that I have long heard)." [2] But for the
tactician Gambetta the use that might be made of any
temporary ally offered by circumstances was more important than any consideration of the ally's principles. " We
are under the Empire ; let us fight the Empire with the
Empire's methods." The man who said this was capable
of joining forces even with Rouher if Rouher was in
opposition.[3]

Nevertheless, despite his scorn for the idealism of 1848
and lack of sympathy with the abstentionist attitude, he
preserved the friendship of many of those whose political
wisdom he criticised, and his enthusiasm and ability raised
high hopes not merely among the enthusiastic young
admirers of the Quartier Latin, who already beheld in him
the Hercules who would slay the Napoleonic Hydra, but
also among staid abstentionists such as the banker Edmond
Adam. This young realist Gambetta, Adam told his wife
in September, 1868, seemed to combine all the qualities of
the great trinity of 1848, the courage of Cavaignac, the
eloquence of Lamartine, and the democratic passion of
Ledru-Rollin.[4] But, though his prestige had steadily increased in Opposition society, Gambetta's reputation was
not yet fame ; to France and to Europe his talents were
still unrevealed. His opportunity came two months after

---

[1] See Appendix I, p. 281.
[2] FELIX WHITEHURST, *My Private Diary During the Siege of Paris*, Sept. 10.
[3] Cp. Mme ADAM, *Mes sentiments et nos idées avant 1870*, 308.
[4] Ibid.

Adam's appreciation ; in November, 1868, official interference precipitated an event in which he could take " an
active and honourable part ".

A new book, Eugène Ténot's *Paris in December 1851*, had
recalled the death of a young Republican deputy on the
barricades, and modern Republicans were quick to seize
an opportunity for propaganda and demonstration.   The
memory of this forgotten martyr of constitutional government was revived.   A pilgrimage was made to Montmartre,
where his obscure tomb was rediscovered, and three
Republican journals[1] opened a list for subscriptions towards
the erection of a memorial to Baudin.   The fund would have
grown slowly but for the ill-judged interference of the
magistrates, who prosecuted the editors of the three papers
on the charge of inciting to hatred and distrust of the
Government.   Subscriptions immediately poured in from
Liberals of all shades.   The Affaire Baudin was one of the
principal events of the close of the year : Gambetta made it
famous, and by a single speech became famous himself.
That speech was no technical legal defence of an individual,
his client Delescluze, one of the accused editors ; it was a
vigorous attack upon the whole system of government, a
thundering denunciation of the *coup d'état* of 1851 and of
the regime which it initiated.   No such public accusations
had been heard in France since the Empire began.   Therein
lay the significance of the speech and in the timeliness of its
delivery.   The voice of the accuser had spoken and it re-
echoed all over the country, an opportune encouragement
to the forces of the Opposition which were preparing for
elections in the spring.   The radical Opposition already
had its pamphleteer in Rochefort, and its philosopher in

---

[1] *L'Avenir national*, ed. PEYRAT ; *Le Réveil*, ed. DELESCLUZE ; *La revue
politique et littéraire*, ed. CHALLEMEL-LACOUR.

Jules Simon ; now it hailed its tribune in the person of
Gambetta. The tribune's speech did not secure the
acquittal of his client, nor did the Empire succumb to his
condemnation of it, but it was the culmination of his legal
career and the real beginning of his career as an active
politician.[1] The offer of a seat to contest in the coming
elections was certain ; equally certain was his intention to
accept. During the next two years he pleaded seldom ;
after 1870 only once.[2] It was in the political firmament that
the star which he believed awaited him was beginning to
dawn.

" M. Gambetta," wrote Thiers in a letter of introduction
not long before the trial, " is what we in France call a
Republican. But he has more wit, good sense, and real
ability than many conservatives and I should be glad if
most party leaders had as much. . . ."[3] A few months
later the Republican emerged as M. Thiers' opponent in
the electoral contest for the seat at Marseilles vacant owing
to the death of Berryer. The " vieux petit bourgeois "
already felt the rivalry of which this election was the
first sign, for he was no longer so sure of Gambetta's good
judgment. The young orator, he told Adam, was an
Italian, and France had never been ruled by an Italian for
her good. Gambetta could not be a Mazarin or a Bonaparte ; he would be a Rienzi. It was a misfortune that
Gambetta and Brisson, whom he coupled as the two ablest
of the young men, were agreed in their hatred of Catholicism.

[1] It also led to two liaisons with feminine admirers, one of which was to
be of enduring importance to Gambetta after 1872 ; cp. EMILE PILLIAS,
Léonie Léon amie de Gambetta (Paris, 1935), 50 ff.

[2] In 1879 in defence of his friend Challemel-Lacour ; cp. A. TOURNIER,
Gambetta, Souvenirs anecdotiques, 82.

[3] Cit. P. DESCHANEL, *Gambetta*, 23. The letter was to Prince Nicholas
Bibesco.

" I am becoming the enemy of your friends, Adam. Your
Gambetta is a political and a social danger. Your Brisson
is a moral and national danger." [1]   Adam smiled at Thiers'
forebodings, for he himself sympathised with Gambetta and
Brisson ; but Thiers had rightly detected the importance of
a social philosophy which was to rend his country many
times during the last quarter of the century.   Much water
had flowed under the bridge since the clergy had hailed the
advent of the Second Republic and planted trees of liberty.
The Church had rallied to the support of the new Bonaparte.
It had welcomed the accession of a pious Empress, and
encouraged Napoleon III in his ill-starred Roman policy,
and Gambetta was the child of a new generation which had
been brought up to believe in a natural and eternal alliance
of altar and throne, of the two despotisms, Catholic and
Bonapartist.   He had attended the lectures of the Comtist,
Pierre Laffitte, and acclaimed the anti-clerical teachings of
Taine.[2]   Anti-clericalism and scientific materialism were a
part of the creed of most Continental Liberals at this time.
In France they were as much a characteristic of the young
Republican group as scorn for the idealism and rigid
principles of the men of 1848, and Gambetta was one of
their most vigorous exponents, so vigorous that even the
radical Jules Simon was alarmed by the violence of his
language.[3]   Accordingly " lay " ideas figured prominently
upon his election programmes of 1869, and in Marseilles
the candidate consented to be enrolled as a member of the
influential masonic lodge " Reform ".[4]   But though the
lodges played an important part in the development and

---

[1] Mme ADAM, *Mes sentiments et nos idées avant 1870*, 320.
[2] Ibid. 47.   [3] Ibid. 376.
[4] A. TOURNIER, *Gambetta, Souvenirs anecdotiques*, 143 ;   I. TCHERNOFF, *Le
parti républicain au coup d'état et sous le second Empire*, 324.

direction of Republican feeling, the new initiate never became an ardent freemason, and despite the force of his language, he was not a fanatical anti-clerical like Challemel-Lacour and others of his contemporaries. Violence of speech was often the effect of calculation, and with Gambetta anti-clericalism, like much else, was subordinated to political expediency.

The Baudin trial had rejoiced the hearts of the elder Republicans, since it led Gambetta to contrast the Republic with the Empire which succeeded it, and to make an eloquent defence of the men of 1848 and their ideals.[1] But their hopes of a permanent reconciliation and of a new attitude of respect in " les jeunes " were to be speedily and cruelly disappointed. Gambetta profited from the authority he had acquired by the trial to exert his influence all the more effectively in favour of the young men's choices of election candidates, and to assert his own independence all the more vigorously.[2] Old and new republicanism were soon to appear in open opposition. Not long after he had accepted candidature at Marseilles Gambetta was invited to contest the first division of Paris as well. The situation was delicate, for there was already a Republican candidate, a stalwart of 1848, in the field. Nevertheless, Gambetta determined to risk the alienation of " les vieux " and to stand in opposition to Hippolyte Carnot, and the reasons he gave in a letter to his friend and doctor, Fieuzal, were very illuminating. The most important were purely personal, purely political and, he admitted, very ambitious : " I want to fight Carnot : (1) because I hope to beat him, (2) because, if I beat him I shall enter the Chamber by the strength of battle and I shall be more than a deputy of the Republican list, I shall

[1] Mme ADAM, op. cit. 317, 318.
[2] Ibid. 355.

be a *force ;* I shall depend only on my electors and myself, whereas if I defeated Darimon [1] the *Siècle* would support me, Favre, Picard, and even M. Sacy, would in the end support me, and I should be the creature of these folk. In such a case I should enter the Chamber as a small boy. I have no desire for this role ; I aim higher and further ; I wish to enter the Chamber by free and direct election of the people, uninfluenced by the patronage of the Bonzes and of the press coalition. . . . If I succeed I shall have an unequalled position in the Chamber, and I shall be master of my own attitude." [2]

Success at Belleville was, therefore, quite as important as success at Marseilles, and in his campaign against " the old Sertorius," as he called Carnot, he was lavish with promises and denunciations calculated to please the most turbulent and radical constituency in Paris. Another reason, he told Fieuzal, which induced him to accept this candidature, was that the electors were willing to accept conditions " of the highest interest " which he had imposed upon them. [3] But, when the Belleville programme appeared, it seemed rather as though it was the electors who had imposed conditions upon Gambetta. " To-day," he said, in his first electoral address, " I shall bring you no programme or profession of faith. The committees of your division are to address me their programme, and I shall reply to it. In this way we shall make a public contract visible to all." [4] Ostensibly this was a revival of the " Mandat impératif " in

---

[1] Darimon, formerly one of the " Cinq " and secretary to Proudhon, had been reconciled to the Empire. Laurier had wished Gambetta to stand against Darimon in the 7th division.

[2] Cit. J. V. LABORDE, *Léon Gambetta, Biographie psychologique*, 30 ff. With this letter cp. that of March 28 to his electoral committee at Belleville, cit. A. TOURNIER, *Gambetta, Souvenirs anecdotiques*, 167.

[3] Ibid. ; cp. P. B. GHEUSI, *Gambetta par Gambetta*, letter to Laurier, April 2.

[4] GAMBETTA, *Discours et plaidoyers politiques* (ed. J. REINACH), I, 420.

its simplest form. In order to escape the patronage of "the Bonzes and the press coalition" he had thrown himself into complete dependence upon his electors. But he knew what he was doing ; a great part of the art of electioneering, he was to tell his friend Laurier, consisted in preliminary management of electoral committees, and this was not neglected at Belleville.[1] The direct mandate was a convenient device to enable him all the more easily to win an independent position in the Chamber, but he had no intention of being the mere tool of his electors or of allowing them to restrict his freedom of action after the manner of the Cordeliers. (Six months later he could gaily put his signature to a manifesto in which his colleagues expressly condemned the " Mandat impératif ".[2]) If the electors later took too literal a view of the contract he had made with them, then, no doubt, his persuasive eloquence and skill in dealing with crowds would be adequate to smooth over any embarrassments. The defeat of Carnot was the immediate and all-important object, and to obtain that he was prepared to pay a high price in promises.

The famous Belleville programme appeared as the " Cahiers " of his electors.[3] In fact, it was merely an elaboration and popular statement of the policy which had already been outlined by Jules Simon in his book, *La politique radicale*, but as such it was to provide the basis of all later French radical programmes. In his work on French parties and politics published so lately as 1921, Mr. Soltau noted a " recent " manifesto of the " Ligue de la République," which declared that it recognised as

[1] P. B. GHEUSI, op. cit., letter to Laurier, April 2, 299-301.

[2] Cp. OLLIVIER, *L'Empire libéral*, XII, 167 ff. ; GAMBETTA, *Discours et plaidoyers politiques*, I, 94 ff.

[3] See Appendix II, p. 285.

Republicans all those who "accept without qualification the Republic as defined by Gambetta in his Belleville programme." [1] But how far the programme represented Gambetta's own views rather than the views he found it convenient to accept at the moment it is difficult to decide. Later he declared that he had never been one of those who denounced standing armies ; [2] but the Belleville programme demanded their suppression as "a cause of ruin to the nation's business and finances and a source of hatred between peoples and of distrust at home " ; and Mme Adam, after a description of his electoral campaign—". . . He wants this. He wants that. He wants everything. He wants too much "—noted, significant note, "in private he says : 'One can always cut down '." [3]   Election campaigns with such mental reservations on the part of the candidate were to be frequent enough under the Third Republic, and the thirst for reform, vigorous reform, but reform to-morrow, not to-day, was to be a feature of "radical mysticism ".[4]   But with some of the Belleville electors' demands, such as those for the disendowment and disestablishment of the Church, for complete freedom of the press and of meeting and association, and for free elementary education, Gambetta was no doubt in complete sympathy, and these were the more practical, less Utopian, part of the programme.   The others were probably all the more easy for the realist to accept because he understood how Utopian they were.   But he advocated them none the less vigorously, and the man who

[1] R. SOLTAU, *French Parties and Politics, 1871-1921* (London, 1921 ; new edn. 1930), 68.

[2] P. DESCHANEL, *Gambetta*, 29.

[3] *Mes sentiments et nos idées avant 1870*, 355, 356.

[4] Cp. A. THIBAUDET, *La République des professeurs* (Paris, 1927), and A. SIEGFRIED, *Tableau des partis en France* (Paris, 1930), passim.

[5] GAMBETTA, *Discours et plaidoyers politiques* (ed. J. REINACH), I, 426.

denounced demagogy at Marseilles [5] seemed to many to act the demagogue at Belleville.

These methods showed clearly enough that if Gambetta was a master of political tactics he was no reformer of political morality. But they were successful, and he was elected at Belleville [1] as well as at Marseilles. His ambition was realised, and realised in the way he desired. He could enter the Chamber as an independent member; he could be a force even though he abandoned Belleville and chose to sit for Marseilles. He had braved charges of treason and ingratitude, he had dared to oppose Hippolyte Carnot, and in defeating him he had won a signal victory for the Republicanism of " les jeunes ".

[1] The figures were : Gambetta, 21,734 ; Carnot, 9142 (P. B. GHEUSI).

II

THE DEPUTY

THE new deputy was thirty-one years of age, but careless living had made him appear older. His thick beard and long dark hair were already streaked with grey, he had a high colour, and already showed a slight tendency to stoutness.[1] His head was fine and massive, but the lips were sensual, the nose was Hebraic in its curve,[2] and the charm of expression was lessened by the glass orb which filled the socket of the right eye.[3] His dress was invariably disordered and generally shabby, for he neither could nor cared to afford much money for clothes.[4] His gestures were uncouth and his movements clumsy. His ordinary conversation abounded with gross images and with vulgar expressions, and respect of place seldom restrained the disagreeable habit of constant spitting. He had yet to be civilised by Juliette Adam. He had yet to learn that in normal times of peace it was necessary to be accepted by the " Tout-Paris " in order to govern France.

Nevertheless, despite this unattractive appearance and

[1] Cp. A. LAVERTUJON, *Gambetta inconnu,* 54 ff. ; *Daily Telegraph,* Jan. 6, 1871 ; P. B. GHEUSI, *Gambetta par Gambetta,* 331.

[2] Which, of course, was no proof of Semitic origin. See Appendix III, p. 288.

[3] As the result of a childhood accident which had been badly treated he was compelled to have his right eye removed in 1867. The eye was preserved and may now be seen in the Gambetta museum at Cahors.

[4] Cp. A. TOURNIER, *Gambetta, Souvenirs anecdotiques,* 99.

despite these repellent habits, Léon Gambetta exercised an extraordinary fascination, and even bitter political opponents admitted his charm.[1] In cold print many of his speeches which won the most frenzied applause seem both banal in content and devoid of any peculiar beauty of language or style.[2] Their success was due as much to the magnetic personality of the orator, to the richness of his voice, to the forcefulness of his gestures, as to the excellence of his matter. Present at one of Gambetta's election meetings, the publicist Jules Claretie had the impression of listening to the tremendous voice of " one of those men of the Convention who have made us what we are," [3] and when they heard him Barbey d'Aurevilly and the song-writer Gustave Mathieu, thrilling with enthusiasm, cried that Mirabeau lived again.[4] The comparison was apter than they knew. Not only was Mirabeau one of the orators whom Gambetta had studied most closely, and whose speeches he most loved to declaim, but he in his day had exercised precisely that peculiar kind of fascination which was Gambetta's strength. " It seems difficult to speak of moral power about Gambetta. His kind of power was almost purely physical : it was a power of courage, energy, and oratory." [5] There was no more illuminating comment upon the nature of Gambetta's influence than this made at the time of his death by Sir Charles Dilke, his most intimate English friend, and it could be applied with still greater force to Mirabeau, the orator whose notorious immorality proved a fatal political handicap in an age by no means strait-laced. It was appropriate that

---

[1] Cp. OLLIVIER, L'Empire libéral, XI, 91.

[2] Cp. E. ZOLA, Une Campagne (Paris, 1882), 98.

[3] J. CLARETIE, La Débâcle (Paris, 1870), 205.

[4] A. TOURNIER, op. cit. 96, and 184, for Castelar's opinion ; MAXIME RUDE, Confidences d'un journaliste (Paris, 1876), 136.

[5] S. L. GWYNN and G. M. TUCKWELL, Life of Sir C. Dilke, I, 513.

a bust of Mirabeau should later have been the only orna-
ment of Gambetta's study.[1]   The descent of the Riquetti-
Mirabeaus from the noble Italian family of Arrighetti is
dubious, but, however much or little Italian blood ran in
his veins, the deputy for Marseilles, Mirabeau, like the deputy
for Marseilles, Gambetta, was typically " homme du Midi ".
Both men exerted great political influence at a comparatively early age, and both won their influence largely by
an eloquence which was spontaneous and compelling and
truly southern in its richness and warmth.   Both were in
a sense revolutionaries, often violent in speech, and yet
essentially men of practical insight, realists, inclined to be
moderate in action.   Gambetta was scarcely handsome ;
he was unkempt, and often repulsive in his personal habits.
Equally unkempt and positively ugly was pock-marked
Mirabeau.   Yet both exercised an extraordinary fascination
and seemed to radiate a magnetic force which captivated
all those who came within the sphere of its influence.   But
it was the son of the Cahors grocer, and not the *déclassé*
aristocrat who left the more lasting impress of his power
upon the history of France.   Gambetta's morals were those
of the students of his time, neither better nor worse, and
they were no hindrance to his political career except in so
far as they caused ill-health.   Mirabeau, on the other hand,
entered politics under a cloud ; the deep shadows of his
past life darkened his whole career as a statesman, and
prevented him from ever winning complete confidence or
forming an effective political party through which to achieve
his aims.

It was the need of making the Left, the Republican Left,
into an effective political party that the new deputy for

[1] E. A. VIZETELLY, *Republican France* (London, 1912), 209 ; cp.
I. TCHERNOFF, *Le parti républicain au coup d'état et sous le second Empire*, 383.
He refers to " une gravure ".

Marseilles now proclaimed in the summer of 1869. In earlier days, when the Opposition was much weaker, Gambetta had worked especially for the co-operation of all its different groups. Lately, in order to win a position of independent authority for himself, he had taken up an attitude of defiance, even towards fellow Republicans, but in doing so he was still a Republican, and had advocated a Republican policy more and not less radical. Now that he had forced an entry into the Chamber by the defeat of opponents such as Carnot and Thiers, he was in a position to propound his own policy for the whole party. The same elections which carried him to the Palais Bourbon had increased the numbers of the Opposition from 35 to 87, and the increase was significant, even though the supporters of the Government still held 205 of the 292 seats. Gambetta, however, always optimistic by temperament, and now perhaps the more so owing to his success, was inclined to exaggerate its importance and the weakness of the Empire. No sooner had he become a deputy than he looked forward to the next step, that of obtaining power. "The most terrible and invincible of our allies, the force of circumstances," he wrote, had already begun the dissolution of " the Imperial organism," [1] and it seems really to have been in the belief that the end was not far off that he now urged the Republicans to close their ranks. The Left was a word with " definite, precise, and restricted meaning ; it denotes and defines a political party composed of homogeneous elements, identical in origin and possessed of common principles. . . . We must organise a Left party exclusively composed of citizens who adhere to the same principles. It is not a question of purification but of uniformity." [2]

[1] J. V. LABORDE, Gambetta, Biographie psychologique, 36.

[2] GAMBETTA, Discours et plaidoyers politiques, I, 428 ff. Letter to his electors of the Seine, July 28, 1869.

The Left as it existed ought to be divided into two. There should be a clear division between those who were true Republicans, believing " that the People is the one lawful sovereign and must really exercise power," and those who were merely Liberals, believing that universal suffrage could be fitted in with the essential liberties granted by limited monarchy. The believers in the full sovereignty of the people recognised the inadequacy of " mere responsibility of ministers to Parliament " and the need of checking all office-holders, particularly the head of the executive. The others, simple Liberals, could join Thiers. This clear division would serve to avoid confusion for the future, but it was not to exclude " good neighbourly relations and momentary co-operation ".[1]

This programme was outlined by Gambetta in July, 1869, from Ems, whither illness had driven him on the morrow of the elections. In October, convalescent at Montreux, he was advocating a vigorous policy of action. The Legislative Body had been prorogued until November 29, but a watchful and impatient Opposition held that the legal term of prorogation expired on October 26, and the Comte de Kératry proposed that they should assemble that day and make their way into the Palais Bourbon, if necessary by force. Gambetta warmly approved : " Ours be the task to defeat the miserable temporisings of a dictatorship which is dying of atrophy. . . . I shall be there," and on the 12th he wrote to Laurier that the country, well aware that the Government was " at its last gasp," was looking for a guide. That guide must be the Left. " The Left must make up its mind between now and October 26 to seize the helm. The Left must appear as our future master, reassuring and

---

[1] Cp. I. TCHERNOFF, *Le parti républicain au coup d'état et sous le second Empire,* 570-1.

ready to cope with the present and the past." [1] Nevertheless, the Left did not seize the helm, nor was Gambetta there on October 26, for Kératry foolishly gave warning to the authorities by publicly announcing his plan. Revolution by violence was not the argument which Gambetta favoured for convincing the public of the fitness of the Left to govern, and the almost certain failure of any attempt to force an entry into the Chamber, now that the authorities were forewarned, would have no other effect than that of familiarising the leaders of the demonstration with the interior of the prison of Mazas and retarding the fruition of their policy. His colleagues for the most part agreed that discretion was the better part of valour : the project of a manifestation to uphold the letter of the law was a fiasco.

It was to the other object mentioned in his letter to Laurier that Gambetta now devoted himself, namely, to the reassurance of the public as to the nature of the Left and its capacity to govern. " France," he had written to his electors of the Seine, " is bound under the pain of humiliation and perhaps of social death to complete the French Revolution. It is the task of the nineteenth century ; it is particularly the task of our generation. The centenary of 1789 must not dawn upon us without the reconquest by the people for itself and for the rest of the world of the political heritage of which it has been dispossessed since the 18th Brumaire." [2] But the word Revolution was associated with other ideas besides those of social and political progress. If the long struggle to complete the Revolution was the key to the history of nineteenth century France, the length of the struggle was largely due to the spectre of Terror by which the Revolution was inevitably haunted, and which Royalists

[1] P. B. GHEUSI, Gambetta par Gambetta, 306, 307.
[2] GAMBETTA, Discours et plaidoyers politiques, I, 435, July 28, 1869.

and Imperialists naturally exploited to the utmost.   It was
this spectre which Gambetta attempted to lay.   The people,
he said, already possessed the weapon by which it could
reconquer its political heritage ; that weapon was universal
suffrage, and by it the Revolution could be completed
peacefully and bloodlessly.   In place of the Empire, he
told a Bonapartist Chamber, " a series of institutions should
be organised in harmony with Universal Suffrage and with
the sovereignty of the nation—(that) we should be given a
Republic peacefully and without any revolution."   Between
the rights and aspirations of Universal Suffrage and the
present form of government there was absolute incompatibility.   " But "—and here was the essence of the speech,
the gilding of the pill for peaceable citizens—" this does not
in any sense mean that, because I am dissatisfied with the
present, I shall endeavour to find a remedy by appealing to
physical force.   No, no ! I believe . . . that the time will
come . . . and is perhaps not far distant, when the majority
which will have taken your places will be led inevitably,
without disturbance, without rebellion, without use of the
sword, without an appeal to subversive forces, and by the
mere logic of events to inaugurate a new order of things,
for you are no more than a bridge between the Republic
of 1848 and the Republic which is to come, and over that
bridge we are now passing." [1]   The majority addressed
grew restless at this description of their role.   Gambetta's
bold words, shrewd as they were bold, showed that the
irreconcilability of which he had boasted at Belleville had
in no wise relaxed because of the new turn to the Left which
the Empire had taken with the formation of Ollivier's
Liberal ministry in January 1870.   For the champion of the
new idea of a " gauche fermée " no compromise of con-

[1] GAMBETTA, *Discours et plaidoyers politiques*, I, 115, 116.

stitutional charter, bourgeois monarchy, or liberal Empire, was admissible ; such expedients had already been weighed and found wanting. But, while as irreconcilable as ever, Gambetta was at pains to give a definition of that epithet which would reassure the pacific bourgeois as much as it disappointed the professional agitator. " The irreconcilable has recourse neither to violence nor to riot nor to conspiracy. The principle on which he leans is not one of those which look to force for their triumph." [1] To the extremist disciples of Blanqui, " the spider of revolution " and terror of Conservatives, this idea of a constructive revolution by constitutional means was either incomprehensible or futile, and they clung to the destructive methods of tradition. Gambetta condemned them : " I believe," he declared at the Banquet de la Jeunesse on April 19, "in order and stability. Be assured that if I desire and do all I can to appeal for the accession of our Republican form of government, it is because it will be a real Government which will be conscious of its duties and know how to make itself respected. . . . I protest most vigorously against those who attack the governmental institutions of the country because they are in the hands of a man who makes bad use of them and forget that in a free society we ourselves should be the Government." [2] These speeches revealed to enemies as well as to friends that Gambetta was something more than a demagogue or turbulent conspirator, and that this " Italian " was nearer to Cavour than to Mazzini. The tribune of Belleville showed not only that he could be moderate, but that he was possessed of real political sagacity. He soon realised his ambition to be a force in the Chamber, and Bonapartist deputies heard him with as much attention as

---

[1] Speech at Belleville, cit. J. CLARETIE, *Histoire de la Révolution de 1870-71*, 91.
[2] GAMBETTA, op. cit. I, 254.

Republican electors. His oratorical powers were no less effective in a new arena, and the speech of April 5, 1870, in which he opposed the new Constitution of the Liberal Empire and denounced the plebiscite, was generally agreed to be a masterpiece. A good judge, Ludovic Halévy, pronounced it " magnificent, politic, and original ".[1] *La France* declared that the " neo-Republican " party had found a statesman and a master, and the *Figaro* hailed in Gambetta a worthy successor of Mirabeau, Royer-Collard, and Berryer.[2] This speech was his greatest oratorical triumph as a deputy in the Legislative Body.

But if journalists and deputies were impressed, the sovereign people (for Gambetta elicited the admission that the sovereignty of the people was the right divine of Bonapartists), beyond the range of his eloquence and fascination, remained deaf to his arguments. The plebiscite upon the new Constitution was duly held and, despite the more personal appeals of Republican propaganda and Gambetta's energy in organising anti-plebiscitary committees, the voting gave the Empire a majority of more than five and a half million. The Opposition might point to the solid Republicanism of Paris and to the increase in the number of noes since the last plebiscite, an increase especially notable in the ranks of the army ; they might claim a " moral victory," but the result was in reality a bitter blow to their hopes. Gambetta was forced to acknowledge that the Empire, of which he had spoken so hopefully as a decaying organism, had been given a new lease of life.[2] The vote of May 6 showed the naivety of his belief in the speedy triumph of the sovereign people, for though the people possessed in universal

---

[1] LUDOVIC HALÉVY, *Carnets*, II, 93 (ed. DANIEL HALÉVY, Paris, 1935).

[2] P. B. GHEUSI, *Gambetta par Gambetta*, 311 ff.

[3] Cp. OLLIVIER, *L'Empire libéral*, XIII, 401 ; ANATOLE CLAVEAU, *Souvenirs politiques et parlementaires d'un témoin* (Paris, 1913), I, 383.

suffrage the means to assert its sovereignty, it still had to be
educated to use it aright.   Now it was evident that patience
and time and assiduous propaganda would be needed if the
irreconcilable was to achieve his Republic and complete the
French Revolution by methods that were not revolutionary.
Would Gambetta be patient ?   Would he persist in the
policy he had outlined so clearly and cogently during the
last year, or would the prospect of a long period of liberal
Empire drive him either to the use of violence or to the
abandonment of irreconcilability ?   His immediate reaction
to the plebiscite was noted by Juliette Adam.   As usual, the
optimistic trend in his temperament prevailed.   At least, he
said, it would now rain liberties, and so the Empire would
gradually drown ; and he repeated his conviction that the
Republicans had no interest in seeing the Revolution triumph
by revolutionary means when the heroes of the revolutionary
party were men such as Flourens, Rochefort, and Delescluze.[1]
His political sense, not lack of courage, made him eschew
violence, but would he, the energetic advocate of a policy
of results, be content to remain indefinitely in opposition,
indefinitely excluded from power?   Able, intelligent, good-
humoured, devoid of personal rancour, realistic in outlook,
not over scrupulous, eager to exercise authority, the man
who had opposed Carnot, championed Prévost-Paradol, and
once sympathised with Ollivier, seemed to some even of his
friends quite capable of rallying to a liberal Empire and
emerging one day as a Bonapartist minister.[2]   But before
he had given any hint of such an evolution, there occurred
an incident which suddenly provoked the Empire to throw
its new-found security to the winds, and to rush headlong to

---

[1] *Mes sentiments et nos idées avant 1870*, 442 ; cp. speech at Belleville, cit.
CLARETIE, 91, where he reaffirmed his irreconcilability but denounced violence,
[2] Mme ADAM, op. cit. 372, 425 ; cp. OLLIVIER, op. cit. 283, 284.

disaster.   The " force of circumstances " which had done
the Republicans little service at the time of the plebiscite
was unexpectedly and dramatically to prove a grim and
terrible ally, and after Reichshoffen and Forbach there could
be no question of Gambetta rallying to the support of a
Bonapartist regime.   What he would have done had there
been no Franco-Prussian war or had the Empire been
victorious must remain matter merely for pleasant, idle
speculation.[1]

[1] Cp. Appendix IV, p. 290.

III

FROM THE OUTBREAK OF WAR TO SEDAN

On April 5, 1870, in his greatest speech as a deputy in the Legislative Body, Gambetta had ruthlessly dissected the Empire's new Liberal Constitution, urged the necessity of making the Emperor directly responsible, and criticised his powers of war and peace. On May 8 the full results of the plebiscite had shown that an overwhelming majority of the electorate accepted this new Constitution. Less than two months later, on July 3, Paris was startled by the news of Prince Leopold of Hohenzollern's candidature for the crown of Spain, and on July 19 France and Prussia were at war. " Post hoc propter hoc " : later it was easy for the Republican politician, Gambetta, wise after the event, to make a facile demonstration of cause and effect and to declare that he had foreseen the war as an inevitable consequence of the plebiscite : " The whole trouble came from the plebiscite. To give the executive the right of war and peace is to head straight for war." [1] But this explanation, invented to discredit an Imperial instrument of government, was much too simple. The inevitability of hostilities, if hostilities could be said to be inevitable at that particular moment, was the result of Bismarck's well-timed provocations and of the folly of a particular French ministry, and the

[1] *Dép.* I, 546 ; cp. his interpretation of the plebiscite in Oct. 1877, and OLLIVIER's properly severe criticisms, *L'Empire libéral*, XIII, 344.

attitude of the majority in the Legislative Body was on this occasion at one with that of the executive. The most that can be ascribed to the plebiscite as a contributory cause of the war is that it tended to increase the confidence of those Bonapartists who regarded it as a triumph for the Empire, while those who regarded it as a reverse were more than ever anxious to retrieve the position by means of a successful campaign.

It needed no great prescience to foresee that a Franco-Prussian war must come some day, and there were many Frenchmen who had regarded it as possible, probable, and even necessary, ever since Sadowa. What were wholly unexpected and unpredictable were the actual moment and circumstances of the outbreak. The train so silently laid by Bismarck exploded in Paris according to plan, and there everything conspired to bring about the result he deemed necessary for the consummation of German unity. The Gallic bull saw red : popular indignation was roused by visions of a revival of a German hegemony like that of Charles V and kept aflame by anti-democratic Bonapartists, by a military party strongly in favour of war, and by those who believed that the day to avenge Sadowa had come at last ; and an ambitious Foreign Minister, overreaching himself in his desire to win a striking diplomatic victory, played directly into the war party's hands. Success was considered as certain, for Marshal Le Boeuf declared the army to be ready, equipped " down to the last gaiter button," and if Sadowa had been a blow to French political prestige, there were few clear-sighted enough to see that the victors in that battle might prove a match for the legions of a Napoleon. Much-needed military reforms had been shelved, partly owing to considerations of internal politics, and, despite the warnings of Italy and Mexico, generals remained blindly confident in the perfection of the

Imperial war machine.   Their awakening was to be swift
and rude.

Gambetta's attitude in this sudden crisis was markedly
different from that of the majority of his Republican colleagues.   In matters of foreign policy, as in many other
questions, his realist outlook was in sharp contrast with
their doctrinaire idealism.   The Jacobin doctrine that the
disappearance of kings would ensure peace to the peoples
had led to the lasting association of a vague and optimistic
pacifism and humanitarianism with the cause of the Republic.
And it was this strain which had re-emerged conspicuously
at the time of the Revolution of 1848-9 when men listened
to Hugo describing the blissful day on which the United States
of America would stretch out the arm of friendship across
the ocean to a United States of Europe.   This humanitarian,
pacifist strain had particularly influenced the thought and
conduct of the men of 1848 and made them singularly
blind to the realities of foreign politics.[1]   Both Gambetta and
his colleagues had ardently supported the Italian war,
Gambetta from natural sympathy with the aspirations of
his father's compatriots, Liberals and " vieux " from their
belief not only in the idea of nationality, but also in the more
truly Republican notions of the liberation of oppressed
peoples which should in turn lead to fraternity between the
nations and to universal peace.   But this belief had also led
the elders to favour Prussia in 1866, and, even after Sadowa,
there were still many Republicans who regarded Prussia's
victory as the triumph, not merely of the ideas of nationality, but also of liberal Protestantism over the hated ultra-
montane Catholicism.   Here Gambetta parted company ;
his anti-clericalism was not so rabid as to lead him to share

[1] *Vide* Georges Goyau, *Patriotisme et humanitarisme* in *Revue des deux Mondes*,
July 15, 1900.

these sympathies and illusions. He perceived the danger to France of a strong neighbour on the east and the hegemony in Germany of the most undemocratic Prussian monarchy had no attraction for him. At Ems in July, 1869, he had noted with surprise (not perhaps unmixed with pleasure at the tribute to his reputation) : " Even the King of Prussia, who is now in Ems, asks after my health, and yet he is not in ignorance of my hatred for the victors of Sadowa." [1] That hatred was reflected in his attitude in July, 1870, when the King of Prussia was again at Ems. He regretted that the Government had not shown itself more vigorous in 1866 ; the foreign policy of Napoleon, which since the affair of the Duchies had contributed to the rise of Prussia, was a policy which " I deplore, which I detest, and which I should repair if it were in my power," [2] and there is no reason to doubt that, as he said later, he was as anxious as anyone could be to see France recapture her leading position in Europe, [3] and so as anxious as anyone to settle accounts with Prussia. Ollivier relates that when it was known that a peaceful settlement seemed probable, and that it had been decided not to call up the reserves, Gambetta went up to the journalist Mitchell, who was rejoicing, took him by the coat, and exclaimed angrily : " Your satisfaction is infamous ! " [4] Whatever the truth of the story, it truly illustrated the force of Gambetta's anti-Prussian feelings. From the Republican point of view, however, the desirability of war was much less obvious, and Gambetta at one moment appears to have had doubts ; he was reported to have said on the 13th that it was not yet time to undertake a war which would have

---

[1] P. B. GHEUSI, *Gambetta par Gambetta*, 293, 294.

[2] GAMBETTA, *Discours et plaidoyers politiques*, I, 281 ff.

[3] *Dép.* I, 546.

[4] *L'Empire libéral*, XIV, 293. OLLIVIER is not the most reliable of authorities ; cp. LUDOVIC HALÉVY, *Carnets*, II, 175, 176.

inconveniences from the democratic standpoint, and that
" in spite of the urgent need there is in my opinion to make
it ".[1]   But such doubts might be set at rest by the argument
with which he parried the congratulations of a Bonapartist
deputy upon his patriotism : " So much the better for your
Emperor if he washes away the stain of December 2nd in
the waters of the Rhine and if he profits by the victory for
which I long.   The Republic will profit by it later." [2]

But, whereas Gambetta showed himself capable of
thinking nationally upon a vital issue of foreign policy, the
majority of his colleagues could think only in terms of opposition to the Empire, and this preoccupation strangely blurred
their vision of realities abroad.   In the Chamber of August,
1914, Sembat and his Socialist followers thundered against
the folly of armaments, and refused to vote the military
credits demanded ;   in the Legislative Body of June 30,
1870, four days before news of the Hohenzollern candidature reached Paris, Garnier-Pagès expressed the belief that
powerful influences would soon lead to the reduction of
military forces in Germany, and proposed a complete reorganisation of the existing system of recruitment as a
prelude to progressive disarmament ; [3] and, while Thiers
urged the now classic French thesis that a strong army is the
best guarantee of peace, and once more drew attention to
the danger of a united Germany, Jules Favre inquired what
interest 40,000,000 Germans could have in throwing themselves upon France.   The answer was to come soon, and
to be disastrously clear.   But for Favre and his colleagues
the German danger was a myth, the Napoleonic peril an
ever-present reality.   The *coups d'état* of the 18th Brumaire

---

[1] *Le Progrès* (Lyon), July 16.   [2] Cit. P. DESCHANEL, *Gambetta*, 47.
[3] The occasion was the debate upon the Government's proposal to reduce
the 1871 contingent by 10,000 men.

and the 2nd December had been achieved with the aid of
the army ; hence the army was an instrument of Cæsarism
which the Opposition must endeavour to weaken as much
as possible.   Motives such as these were a powerful reinforcement of the pacifist argument among freemasons and
Republicans, but when that argument was still used after
the Spanish question had become acute, Gambetta was
prompt to dissociate himself from his colleagues : " I am
sorry," he declared to the *Figaro*, " to see that our Republican traditions are being weakened and effaced by the
influence of humanitarian doctrines.   We who are Republicans should no more than other Frenchmen be patient in
tolerating the claim of a military and reactionary power to
impose its will and preponderance upon our country and
upon the rest of Europe.   Danton did not refuse his aid." [1]
Nor did Gambetta.   The tribune of Belleville, who had
subscribed to a programme which demanded the abolition
of standing armies, was certain that in case of war the
Chamber would incur a criminal responsibility if it refused
to vote ways and means adequate for the defence of the
country.   He did not abstain as did seven members of the
Opposition, or vote against the grant of credits, as did ten
of them, including Jules Favre and Jules Grévy.

Later, however, wise again after the event, he represented
his attitude in this month of July in a very different light :
" When war was declared, I was convinced that it would
end in disaster, and I said ' we are rolling blindly towards
the abyss and France does not suspect it '." [2]   But if Thiers'

---

[1] Cit. R. DREYFUS, *M. Thiers contre l'Empire, la Guerre et la Commune*, 96.

[2] *Dép.* I, 546.   At the end of Lavertujon's book, *Gambetta inconnu*, there is a
photographic reproduction of a sheet of paper covered with notes for a speech in
Gambetta's handwriting.   The substance of these notes and Lavertujon's comments (pp. 99, 100) indicate that they must have been written down some time
between August 18-23.   One of the more legible phrases is as follows : " Le pays

claim to prescience was doubly justified Gambetta's was not. In the frenzied debate of July 15, he spoke as an irreconcilable Republican, not as a prophet of ruin, and the reason with which he appealed for a hearing was promptly interpreted by the Right as a condemnation of the gloomy pessimism of M. Thiers.[1]   The reasons he gave for demanding communication of the despatches upon which the Government based their case for war were excellent, and there was much wisdom in his technical criticisms and in his plea for a dispassionate review of the situation, but their motive was distrust of the dynasty.   If the communication of despatches were refused, he must conclude that "your war is only a pretext (i.e. for strengthening the dynasty) and will not be national."   Gambetta was thinking of the plebiscite and of the doctrine of responsibility, not of the possibility of defeat, and there was nothing in his speech, or in any other of his sayings recorded at this time, to suggest that he was not as wholly confident of victory as any member of the Bonapartist majority.

But Gambetta's appeal for calm deliberation fell upon deaf ears, and the voice of Thiers was the voice of Cassandra in that tumultuous session of July 15.   It was, in fact, already too late.   The French Ministers, missing a brilliant

roule vers l'abîme sans en avoir conscience ". Presumably this is what Gambetta had in mind when he made his deposition. He evidently did fashion and probably use the phrase in the latter part of August, but I can find no evidence to suggest that he could have said such a thing at the time of the declaration of war in July.   Had he shown pessimism so early, admirers would surely have observed it and recalled it later as a tribute to his clear-sightedness. But Lavertujon who was his close companion from July 24 to August 7, gives no hint of pessimism. This, I think, is an instance in which negative evidence, so often deceptive, must carry weight, for the point at issue is a man's whole attitude to the dominant question of the day.   Moreover, the conclusion which it indicates is reinforced by the positive evidence as to Gambetta's attitude on and before July 15.

[1] R. Dreyfus, op. cit. 97 ; Gambetta, Discours et plaidoyers politiques, I, 285.

diplomatic victory, had now by their tactless arrogance
precipitated a new conflict from which it would have been
impossible to withdraw without the appearance of a second
humiliation. The insistence of the Empress, of Gramont,
and of the generals, won the day, and the hesitating Emperor
was allowed to hesitate no longer. At 9 that morning the
Council had voted for war, and the support of a Chamber
in which the Bonapartists had a majority of 118 was certain.
The formal declaration of war was made on July 19, and
five days later the session of the Legislative Body came to an
end. Gambetta at once left for Switzerland to nurse his
health and to enjoy a holiday in the company of Lavertujon.[1]
His friend's memoirs give no hint that it began under the
cloud of anticipated disaster, or that either he or Gambetta
were in the least prepared for the series of defeats which soon
followed one another with shattering rapidity. But when
the news of Forbach succeeded that of Reichshoffen, and
there were rumours of a special session of the two Chambers,
Gambetta hastened back to Paris.

The rumours proved true. As a result of the emergency,
the Empress-Regent summoned the deputies to assemble on
August 9, and a state of siege was proclaimed in the capital.
It was to a much altered city that Gambetta now returned.
The laconic telegrams by which the tidings of defeat were
communicated to the Parisians had caused the greatest
excitement and dismay. It seemed incredible that they
could refer to the glorious armies of France, the men who
had marched forth so short a time before, whom in vision
they had seen easy conquerors, travelling the old Napoleonic
road to Berlin. The Boulevards were thronged with anxious
uneasy crowds ; the " Marseillaise " and cries of " Vive la
République " could be heard. Journalists and deputies of

[1] A. LAVERTUJON, *Gambetta inconnu*, 54, 62.

the Left, with new prospects opening up before them, met in the Rue de la Sourdière and the representatives of six newspapers published a manifesto in the *Siècle* demanding " the immediate arming of all citizens and the institution of a committee of defence composed in the first place of the deputies of Paris. Let all patriots rise and join us ! The country is in danger." [1] The Ministry feared revolution, and Chevandier de Valdrôme urged strong preventive measures. He proposed to arrest twenty-two deputies of the Left and to deport them to Belle Ile for a compulsory rest cure. His list included Gambetta, Jules Favre, Ernest Picard, Jules Ferry, Eugène Pelletan, Ordinaire, Kératry and Dorian. The idea was approved by Ollivier, the apostle of the new Imperial Liberalism, but it was not put into execution. Ollivier has explained that he dared not risk such a *coup d'état* while the Empress was still Regent ; her unpopularity was too great, and so the measure, approved in principle, was to be deferred until the Emperor's return. [2] But the Empress has declared that the proposal was submitted to her by Ollivier, and that she emphatically rejected it as certain to provoke the evil it was intended to avert. [3] In any case, the Emperor did not return, and two days later the Ollivier ministry was no more. The deputies of the Left, unmolested and ignorant of the fate which it had proposed for them, assisted at its overthrow.

August 9 was in some sort a rehearsal of September 4, with the difference that the forces of order, less unnerved, knew their part and did not fail to act it. Crowds of workmen descended from Belleville. All the curious, the idle, and the agitators of Paris made their way to the Place

---

[1] OLLIVIER, *L'Empire libéral*, XVI, 337.   [2] Ibid. 376.

[3] R. E. SENCOURT, *Life of the Empress Eugénie*, 254 ; M. PALÉOLOGUE, *Les Entretiens de l'impératrice Eugénie* (Paris, 1928), 203, 204.

de la Concorde and other places in the vicinity of the Palais Bourbon, to see the reassembling of the Legislative Body. The Emperor was with the army and defeated, the Empress was unpopular and distrusted ; for the moment the hopes of the people centred upon their representatives, despite their signal lack of any glorious tradition. But the cheers were reserved for the deputies of the Left as they arrived. The moment desired by Gambetta a year before, the moment when the Left might " seize the helm of public opinion and keep it," seemed to have come. The current was running clearly and strongly against the Empire. On this day Ludovic Halévy wrote in his notebook that the Empire's hours were numbered, and that a Republic alone seemed possible. " But," he added significantly, " what a mediocre thing is the Republican party except for Gambetta." [1] Pacifism forgotten, parliamentary Republicans of all shades were now united in demanding national measures to meet a national emergency, and when Gambetta demanded the re-establishment of the National Guard, and declared that " in presence of a nation in arms we too must raise up a nation in arms," [2] he was voicing not merely his own personal views, but the programme of the Republican party. The policy outlined by the Republican journalists in the *Siècle* was reproduced in the Chamber, with but slight modification, as the policy of the Republican deputies, and to its cardinal points, the arming of the nation and the assumption by the Legislative Body of special powers for the national defence, they adhered throughout.

There was no interruption of the deliberations of the Legislature on August 9, for the Palais Bourbon was well guarded. But there was already a breath of revolution in

[1] *Carnets*, II, 217, 218.
[2] GAMBETTA, *Discours et plaidoyers politiques*, I, 311.

"The Parliamentary Empire."

OLLIVIER

(Vanity Fair, Jan. 15, 1870)

the air, and to members of the Bonapartist majority the " national " programme of the Republicans was more than suspect. Granier de Cassagnac denounced the motion in which it was embodied by Jules Favre as the beginning of a revolution timed to coincide with the beginning of an invasion, and the new Palikao ministry no less clearly believed that the proposals of the Left were mere attempts to achieve revolution under the guise of constitutionality and on the pretext of national danger. A part of the Republican programme did, however, secure speedy adoption ; the majority of the deputies was impressed by the gravity of the situation, and saw the need for a closer association of the nation with the war, and for the removal of the taunt about a purely dynastic adventure : the motion for the re-establishment of the National Guard was carried, and a law of reorganisation was passed next day. On the 14th, however, there occurred an incident which seemed to justify ministerial suspicions. A band of extremists led by the veteran conspirator, Blanqui, attacked the firemen's barracks at La Villette, and attempted to seize their arms and to begin a popular rising. The attempt was a complete fiasco, for the populace, more intent on spy hunting than on revolution, mistook the rebels for Prussian agents, and helped to suppress the movement which depended upon their active support for its success. In itself the incident was slight, but it served to increase the mutual distrust of parties, and, despite a public and unequivocal condemnation of the rising by Gambetta, the proposals of the Left were more than ever suspect. An " Union Sacrée " was out of the question in August, 1870, when Bonapartists feared that Republicans were plotting revolution and when Republicans dreaded that they might at any moment be the victims of a *coup d'état*, a last desperate and typically

Bonapartist measure to save a tottering dynasty.[1] And yet each feared the others excessively : despite the rumours, there is no proof that the Palikao ministry ever thought of executing Chevandier de Valdrôme's plan, and despite the talk of revolution, none but the most extreme Republicans were willing unnecessarily to incur the charge of provoking civil war in face of the enemy. The war was in a sense, as the affair of La Villette had shown, an obstacle rather than an encouragement to revolution by violence, and those who had most to gain by the fall of the Empire were wisest in biding their time.

For, if revolution was in the air, it was because it was felt that the Empire was about to seal its own doom.[2] There was no popular frenzy. Paris had recovered from its first panic at the news of defeat. The Emperor's abandonment of his command, the fall of the Ollivier ministry, and the appointment of the popular General Trochu to be Governor of the city, had restored some measure of calm. The capital was still remote from the battlefield, and despite the drilling of National Guards, and the construction of defence works, its gay life continued almost as gay as ever. Always a centre of opposition, it regarded the successive disasters of the Imperial armies with peculiar indifference, if not with hopefulness. There was an atmosphere of suspense indeed, but it was not charged with the dread of an impending terror of bloodshed and barricades. Dazed rather than maddened by the sudden reversal of French fortune, Paris awaited the final catastrophe. And as August drew on to its close, nothing showed more vividly than the attitude of the Bonapartists themselves that the end was felt to be near.

---

[1] E. A. Vizetelly, *My Days of Adventure*, 59.

[2] Cp. Ch. Chesnelong, *Les derniers jours de l'Empire et le gouvernement de M. Thiers*, 58.

What a contrast between the majority in the Chamber of July 15, and that same majority five weeks later ![1] It no longer had the confidence of a majority. The proposals of the Opposition no longer raised storms of protest. Cowed and passive, the majority no longer had the courage to defend its Imperial patrons : it betrayed the ineffective hesitations of despondency, and aided neither one side nor the other. This attitude was typical : as early as August 16 Lord Lyons could write that the Foreign Minister, La Tour d'Auvergne, was the only person he knew who spoke like a loyal subject.[2]

With Bazaine blockaded at Metz, the fate of the Second Empire depended upon the movements of the Emperor, and of the army of Châlons. It was on Prince Napoleon's advice that the Emperor had appointed Trochu to be Governor of Paris, and Trochu had accepted on condition that the Emperor followed him to the capital.[3] But all three had reckoned without the Empress. She feared that the return of Napoleon would be the signal for revolution, and that his life would be in danger. She was indignant that the Emperor should seem to desert his post ; and perhaps she clung to her Regency. She was furious at the nomination of Trochu, and when she heard of Napoleon's intention she wired imperiously forbidding his return. Weakly he obeyed : the unwanted sovereign remained with his army, and the Liberal general, Trochu, deprived of the support which was essential to make his position tolerable, was left to face a hostile ministry and a hostile Empress. He was deliberately ignored, and thus a man, whose great popularity might have been used to save the Empire, confined

[1] Cp. CHESNELONG, op. cit. 58, 59, 220.

[2] NEWTON, *Life of Lord Lyons*, I, 308.

[3] P. DE LA GORCE, *Histoire du second Empire*, VII, 165 ff.

himself to supervision of the defence works and the performance of routine duties. The Left's attempts to strengthen his position had no success, but it seems clear that they understood and hoped to reap advantage from his false situation. Some of them certainly visited the Governor of Paris,[1] but the purpose of these visits has remained shrouded in obscurity. If definite overtures were made to him, it is unlikely that Trochu, whose chief characteristic was a fatalistic devotion to duty, consented to compromise himself in any way so long as the Empire existed. But its existence was a matter of days when, despite his protests and the protests of Thiers, the army of MacMahon was despatched on the mad attempt to make a junction with Bazaine in order that the Emperor might be kept away from Paris. " You have one Marshal blockaded," said Thiers on September 1, " now you will have two." [2] But the Government was deaf, and it was then too late. " We must know whether we have chosen between the safety of the dynasty and that of the nation," Gambetta had cried on August 13 [3] : the Government had now made its choice, and thereby imperilled the safety of both. To extract news from the War Minister, Palikao, was like squeezing water from a stone, but at the end of August it was generally known that the decisive struggle was about to take place. The army of MacMahon had indeed manœuvred its way to destruction, and there was about to occur one of those events " which," as Thiers said, " put an end to all false situations ".[4] The great battle near the Belgian frontier raged throughout August 31 and September 1. On the 2nd the doom

---

[1] I find no record that Gambetta was one of them ; cp. TROCHU, *Le Siège de Paris*, 166.

[2] Cit. R. DREYFUS, *M. Thiers contre l'Empire, la Guerre et la Commune*, 117.

[3] Cit. P. DESCHANEL, *Gambetta*, 49.

[4] OLLIVIER, *L'Empire libéral*, XVII, 402.

of the Empire was sealed. At 11.30 that morning was signed the capitulation of Sedan. It left the whole army, with all its material, 84,000 men, 2700 officers, and 39 generals, prisoners in Prussian hands, and among the captives were Napoleon III, Emperor of the French, and his Marshal, MacMahon. There had been no disaster in French history more complete or more humiliating.

IV

THE REVOLUTION OF SEPTEMBER 4

THE news of Sedan reached Palikao the same day. Jerome
David heard it at 6 p.m. and whispered it to M. Thiers
after the meeting of the Committee of Defence that evening.
But the public as yet knew nothing ; the reports received
by Ministers were conflicting, and the details uncertain.
Palikao preferred to delay any announcement of disaster
until it was confirmed officially, and beyond a doubt. On
the morning of the 3rd rumours began to circulate ; telegrams arrived from Brussels and passengers from Belgium
spread the news of a great defeat. At the session of the
Legislative Body in the afternoon Palikao made a statement : the attempted junction with Bazaine had failed ;
MacMahon's men had been forced to retreat to Mézières
and Sedan, and " perhaps even in small numbers on to
Belgian territory ".[1] This cautious admission prepared his
audience for the worst. Such a statement from the reticent
Palikao had an ominous significance, and when the Minister
further confessed that no news or instructions had been
received from the Emperor, Jules Favre declared that, since
the Government had in fact ceased to exist, all parties should,
in order to avoid confusion, give place to a soldier who
would undertake the defence of the nation. Every one
understood who was the soldier thus referred to by a

[1] *Journal Officiel.*

member of the Left. It was clear that, once the news of complete disaster was officially confirmed, deposition would be demanded in the streets and formally proposed in the Chamber. That confirmation arrived shortly after the close of the afternoon sitting, and news of the Emperor did reach his capital. The Empress, who as yet knew nothing, received the laconic telegram : " The army is defeated and captive ; I myself am prisoner. Napoleon." [1]

On the boulevards and in streets and cafés rumour was now busier than ever, and drew large crowds in its wake. Catastrophe seemed certain, and its details related by a thousand tongues with a thousand variations were stupefying, for rumour seldom belittles reality. " We have touched the bottom of the abyss," exclaimed Lavertujon, when he heard the news, but Gambetta silenced him. [2] His optimism did not fail, and grief at the disaster was probably not unmixed with joy at the Empire's doom. Now, indeed, the " Imperial organism " was on the point of dissolution. It remained for the Republicans to make the most of their opportunity, but the war which had produced the opportunity also greatly complicated its use ; it was an unenviable legacy the Empire was about to bequeath to its successor.

Once again, as after the first great reverses a month ago, the Palais Bourbon became the centre of interest. The people turned again to its deputies, and the deputies prepared to assume the mantle of authority which was fast slipping from the Empire. " We shall witness and help on the exact counterpart of December 2," wrote Gambetta in 1869,— " a Chamber dispossessing the monarch." [3] The prophecy was now to be strikingly fulfilled. As the shadows of

---

[1] J. SIMON, *Souvenirs du 4 septembre*, I, 357.

[2] A. LAVERTUJON, *Gambetta inconnu*, 100.

[3] P. B. GHEUSI, *Gambetta par Gambetta*, 288.

invasion lengthened upon France the deputies of the Left had been almost alone to increase their reputation and popularity. Now the Empire was at their mercy, but much might depend upon the way in which they used their advantage. In the negotiations of the next twenty-four hours they showed that they intended to use it moderately, and that they adhered to the belief so often expressed by Gambetta in a peaceful transference of powers. A full meeting of the Left at 9 p.m. on September 3, the first attended by Picard and his followers of the "gauche ouverte" since April,[1] approved the policy already foreshadowed in the Chamber—namely, the deposition of the Emperor and the transference of authority to a Committee of Defence chosen from among the deputies of the Opposition—and five prominent members of the party hastened to seek the adherence of M. Thiers.[2] Nothing, urged Favre, could inspire the country with greater confidence in the new Government than the name of Thiers. Of this M. Thiers was perfectly aware ; but he had no wish to impair his great prestige by membership of a Government which would have the ungrateful task of liquidating the affairs of the Empire, and the unpleasant responsibility for the conclusion of a humiliating peace. His hour had not yet come. Others might serve the provisional needs of the moment ; it would be for him to follow after and achieve the durable. Despite the most urgent entreaties, he was adamant in his refusal to serve on Favre's proposed governmental committee. The Republican leader accordingly sought another combination. He now suggested the establishment of a triumvirate : Palikao,

---

[1] GUYOT-MONTPAYROUX, *Dép.* II, 197.

[2] FERRY (*Dép.* I, 379) places this meeting on "Aug. 31 or Sept. 1," but from Thiers' account it is quite clear that it must have been after the news of Sedan had reached, and was generally known, in Paris ; cp. Comte O. B. P. E. D'HAUSSONVILLE, *Mon Journal pendant la guerre*, 89 ; J. FAVRE, *Dép.* I, 320.

Trochu, and Schneider, the President of the Chamber. This M. Thiers felt able to accept, and the little group broke up and hastened to canvass colleagues on both sides of the house for support of this suggestion. It was a curious solution for a Republican to propose,[1] and it was almost certain to be impracticable; not only was the enmity between Trochu and Palikao a matter of common knowledge, but it would be very difficult to persuade the other deputies of the Left to accept Palikao. Their opposition was, in fact, the rock on which the suggested combination was wrecked. But these negotiations with Thiers clearly indicated that on the evening of September 3 the Republican leaders were almost as reluctant as Thiers himself to assume the reins of government at such a moment. Not only did they wish to preserve the appearance of constitutionality in their method of proceeding, but they were anxious at least to share the great responsibilities of office with the other parties of the Opposition. This was one of the moments when co-operation with mere Liberals must be desirable, even for Gambetta's radical Left; and Gambetta presumably thought so, for he was one of the five Republicans who vainly tried to win Thiers. The Republic, no doubt, was within grasp; Kératry had already proposed its proclamation.[2] But was it expedient for the Third French Republic first to see light when the heavens were black with catastrophe?

Meanwhile a council had been summoned in haste at the Tuileries. Yet, though many of the Ministers had now been acquainted with the news of Sedan for twenty-four hours, they

---

[1] Palikao and Schneider were Bonapartists; Trochu was reputed to be an Orleanist.

[2] At the full meeting at 9 p.m., Sept. 3. Comte E. DE KÉRATRY, *Le 4 septembre*, 28.

could agree on no vigorous action to meet the situation, and would not even admit that the official confirmation of the disaster necessitated a special sitting of the Legislative Body. This inactivity was typical of the paralysis with which Bonapartists were seized. The council broke up at 8 with the intention of meeting again in the morning before the session of the Chamber which had been announced for midday. But, while Ministers showed inertia and sought counsel in delay, there were many deputies who were eager for action, and the President of the Chamber, Schneider, was allowed no rest until he consented to call a special session on his own responsibility. Hurriedly summonses were despatched to bid the national representatives attend at the Palais Bourbon for a midnight deliberation, and surprised and angry Ministers were aroused from their beds.

The news of the great defeat was now generally known in the city. It was a Saturday, and fine, and all Paris was in the streets, eager to learn details, and demanding what would happen next. Between 10 and 11 p.m. the deputy Dréolle came out of the Palais Bourbon into the small courtyard on the side facing the river, and found the Quai d'Orsay thronged with a vast crowd. In the courtyard, too, several deputies had gathered, including many members of the Right, and conspicuous among them was Gambetta, mounted on a chair and haranguing the multitude outside from behind the locked grille. His speech seemed to meet with approval, for it was punctuated by cries of " Vive Gambetta " and " Vive la République ". But, to one of these interruptions he answered, " Citizens, the Government whose name you have just pronounced is one I should most gladly welcome, but we must show ourselves worthy of it ! It must neither be responsible for, nor inherit the misfortunes which have befallen the country. Count on me, count on yourselves, and we promise that in these grave circumstances none of us will fail in his duty." [1] Then he urged them to return peacefully to their homes, and descended from his chair. But the crowd did not at once disperse, and at the instance of several deputies Gambetta remounted and made a fresh appeal. At this moment Dréolle approached, and told him of the special session of the Legislative Body. Gambetta at once announced the news to the crowd as proof that their representatives were not being inactive. They received it well with cheers for Gambetta and for the Legislative Body, yet they did not disperse, and Gambetta called for the concierge, and asked him to unlock the gate so that he might go out and try the force of individual persuasions. But the Quæstor, General Lebreton, had now come into the courtyard and hastened to intervene. He forbade the concierge absolutely to open the gate for anyone, and declared later that, had Gambetta's order been obeyed and the gate opened for one moment, no matter how little, the crowd would have pressed forward and made it impossible to close it again. [2] The Chamber would have been invaded that night, and the Revolution anticipated by fifteen hours. Meanwhile Dréolle, close to the grille, had been accosted by one of the crowd outside, who asked to speak to Gambetta, and whispered : " I have come from the Rue de la Sourdière ; there are ten thousand of us there who are going to come here ; we thought we should find the Left assembled. Warn the Left ; we must

---

[1] E. DRÉOLLE, *La journée du 4 septembre au Corps Législatif*, 32 ff. ; cp. LEBRETON, *Dép*. II, 148. Dréolle's account, written shortly after the events, is likely to be the more accurate. No doubt Gambetta said as much as both Lebreton and Dréolle report and more besides : but the interesting point is that neither of those witnesses was Republican, and that both testify to the " sagesse " of Gambetta's words.

[2] LEBRETON, *Dép*. II, 148.

prevent anyone from coming here at all costs." Dréolle turned to look for Gambetta, but he had already left the courtyard. The strange, significant, message remained undelivered, for Dréolle did not think it so important as to justify a search for the deputy of the Left.[1]

No less animated than the Quai d'Orsay was the interior of the Palais Bourbon ; everywhere groups of deputies were hurrying to and fro, weaving plans, hatching governments, and speculating on the issue of the coming debate. A Council of Government was generally expected by members of the Right, and Dréolle declared that there was already a plan afoot for forming one of five deputies of all shades of opinion—from the Left Picard and Gambetta, from the Left Centre Thiers, and then two members from the Right Centre and Right.[2] The rumour was interesting ; while Favre, the acknowledged leader of the Republicans, was omitted, Gambetta and Picard were named as the leaders of two distinct groups within the Republican party ; the plan was a tribute to the parliamentary reputation won by Gambetta as chief of the irreconcilables. But Dréolle was ill-acquainted with the intentions of M. Thiers. The news of a midnight session had brought that experienced veteran back to the Chamber. Soon after his arrival the little group of Republicans, accompanied this time by Ernest Picard, met him with fresh proposals. Jules Favre now suggested a governmental committee of nine deputies : " We shall take four members from the majority, four from our own people, and you, for we count you as one of us. In this way we shall have the majority, and that suffices us." [3] M. Thiers, however, was not to be tempted ; even the prescient

---

[1] Cp. J. SIMON, Souvenirs du 4 septembre, I, 361, 362.

[2] DRÉOLLE, La journée du 4 septembre, 34, 35.

[3] Comte D'HAUSSONVILLE, Mon journal pendant la guerre, 92.

flattery of being counted among the Republicans could
not lure him from his prudent reserve. "Very well," said
Favre, " we will proceed differently. I am going to propose
an act of deposition, the nomination by the Chamber of a
Committee of Government, and the maintenance of Trochu
as Governor of Paris."

Soon after, the deputies began to assemble for the sitting,
but many had only just received the summons, Ministers
were late, and the session announced for midnight did not
begin till one o'clock. Palikao, irritated at the convocation
without his consent, was still without any plan, and refused
to be persuaded of the need to act quickly. He contented
himself with an official declaration of the capitulation, but
said that its consequences could not be discussed at the
moment. He complained that he had been dragged from
his bed, and he proposed adjournment until midday. But
the Left was not so lacking in policy, nor was it willing to
lose its opportunity. Jules Favre rose to fulfil the intentions
he had outlined to Thiers, to move the deposition of Louis
Napoleon Bonaparte and of his dynasty, the naming of a
commission, "which will be invested with all the powers
of government, and will have as its express mission to
resist the invasion to the utmost (à outrance) and to drive
the enemy out of the country," and the maintenance of
Trochu. " At this moment," said Dréolle, " I expected to
see one of the Ministers jump from his seat and leap to the
tribune." [1] But they remained seated and silent. Of all
the Bonapartist deputies present, only one raised his voice
in protest. The diminutive M. Pinard, deputy of the Nord,
was the solitary champion of the House of Bonaparte and of
the Second French Empire. Members of the Left, amazed
at such inertia, believed that it must be deceptive ; more

[1] Dréolle, op. cit. 42.

than ever they dreaded the *coup d'état* of despair. But their fears were groundless; they over-estimated the strength and underrated the patriotism of their old opponents; the Empire at that moment was as feeble as it seemed.

The sitting came to an end. It had lasted only twenty minutes, but in that nocturnal atmosphere charged with depression and doom twenty minutes seemed an eternity. In the corridors, however, tongues were unloosed, and there was a fresh orgy of speculation and of intrigue. Jules Favre and Thiers did not leave the Palais Bourbon until two o'clock. Even then they were held up by a large crowd, still massed upon the Place de la Concorde, and shouting for the deposition of the Emperor.[1]

The crowds of the night had barely dispersed before those of the morning began to gather, for Paris was early astir in the brilliant sun of September 4. It was a Sunday too; everything conspired to lure the citizens out of doors, the day, the weather, and curiosity above all. Every one was athirst for news, and the fall of the Empire was generally taken for granted. The *Siècle* once again gave a lead; in small print, but on its front page, appeared a short but significant paragraph: "We learn that some National Guards are to go to the Place de la Concorde to-morrow to greet the deputies favourable to the national cause as they pass by. We are asked to announce that they should be unarmed." [2] Further on it reprinted the National Assembly's decree of August 10, 1792, and the second clause was conspicuous in italics: "The chief of the executive power is provisionally suspended from his functions." All the papers announced the session of the Legislative Body for midday, and at an early hour crowds began to form near the centre

---

[1] *Le Siècle*, Sept. 4.   [2] Ibid.

of interest. People flocked from all quarters ; workmen
came down from Belleville, and the defence works of the
city were abandoned. In accordance with the " mot
d'ordre " given by the *Siècle*, National Guards proceeded to
the Place de la Concorde " to greet the deputies," but the
question of arms gave rise to a controversy. Their officers
wished to march upon the Chamber with their battalions
but unarmed. The Revolution, they said, must be accomplished without the shedding of a drop of blood. " If we
have our rifles clumsiness may lead to a struggle." But they
were met by three prominent Republicans, and close friends
of Gambetta, Ranc, Spuller, and Challemel-Lacour. " You
are wrong ! " said Ranc. " Come armed if you wish to
make sure that blood will not flow. There is nothing to
fear from the troops ; the soldiers will not stir. But the
police may stand firm ; the central brigades, if they are
well commanded, will offer resistance to the crowd and to
National Guards who come unarmed." [1] This passage of
Ranc's *Souvenirs et Correspondance* throws a clear light on the
attitude of many members of the Left outside the Chamber.
They had little care for avoiding the appearances of a revolution or scruple about violating the sanctity of the Legislative Body ; their chief concern was to seize control, or at
least to ensure that the Empire should last no more.

   While a last Council held by the Empress Regent at the
Tuileries was tardily determining a programme of action
and the formation of a new " Council of the Government,"
in which Palikao was to have the strange title and unusual
office of " Lieutenant-General of the Council," the deputies
in the Chamber were busy preparing for the momentous
midday session. The Empress with dignity rejected the
advice of those who urged her to act herself and of her own

---

[1] A. RANC, *Souvenirs et Correspondance*, 156.

initiative to cede her authority to the Legislative Body : she
would accept deposition with thankfulness, if it was for the
country's good, but she would not abdicate ; at such a
moment that would be to desert her post in the presence of
the enemy.[1] But nearly all the deputies, friends as well as
foes of the Empire, were by now agreed that it was they, the
elected representatives of the nation, who must assume
power in this crisis, and that the present regime was no
longer viable. The question was how best to disguise the
change as a regular and constitutional proceeding, for tender
consciences feared to violate their oath of allegiance or to
risk incurring the charge of violation at some later date.
Thus the great game of formula hunting began. M. Thiers
also had a motion to propose, and his phrasing was to be the
happy mean between the formulæ of Favre and Palikao :
designing to win the support of as many of his colleagues as
possible, he modified the introductory consideration " in
view of the abeyance of the sovereign power " to " in view
of the circumstances ". This was very colourless and very
safe. The deputies of the Left agreed that if there was no
chance of the adoption of Favre's motion they would rally
in support of Thiers' ; this would not be difficult, for,
apart from certain niceties of phrasing, in substance they
were almost identical.

All these negotiations took time. The midnight session
had not begun till 1 a.m. ; the midday session did not begin
until 1.15 p.m. The delay of over an hour was fatal when
the population of Paris was waiting at the gates. Shortly
before the session began Dréolle was again discussing the
composition of the Council of Government. The name of
Gambetta was generally approved, and Dréolle, perceiving
the deputy of the Left not far away, went to sound him :

[1] R. E. SENCOURT, *Life of the Empress Eugénie*, 267.

" On my side we are choosing you and Picard for the Left,
Thiers for the Left Centre, and two members of the majority,
of whom one will be M. Schneider." " So be it," replied
Gambetta, " but first we must settle the question of deposition. . . . Pronounce deposition and then I will do anything
you wish." [1] On a sheet of rough notes made by Gambetta
a fortnight before there was written : " Proclaim simultaneously and in the same act *La Patrie* in danger and the
deposition of all the Bonapartes." [2] The irreconcilable was
as irreconcilable as ever ; the experience of the last month
could only have strengthened his conviction that riddance
of the Empire was the necessary preliminary to regeneration
of the country whatever its form. Thus, when the session
began and priority was asked for Thiers' motion, Gambetta
protested vigorously, and reminded his colleagues that the
Left demanded " deposition pure and simple ". The protest
was effective ; the deputies retired to their bureaux to
discuss all three motions together, and to name the commission charged with presentation of the report.

At 1.40 the Salle des Pas Perdus, " the ordinary meeting
place of petitioners and discontented people," presented a
scene of unusual animation, crowded with excited groups of
spectators, journalists, Republicans, Orleanists, and National
Guards, who freely left their posts to revel in political
argument.[3] Several deputies of the Left and journalists
for whom they had gained admittance, went out on to the
steps of the main façade overlooking the Seine and the Place
de la Concorde beyond. The vast crowd was now still
vaster, more unwieldy, and more restive. The news that
the Republic had already been proclaimed at Lyons was

---

[1] DRÉOLLE, *La journée du 4 septembre,* 64, 65.
[2] LAVERTUJON, *Gambetta inconnu,* Facsimile II.
[3] DRÉOLLE, op. cit. 67.

known to the soldiers on guard near the Rue de Bourgogne as early as 12.15.[1] Such tidings has wings, and must have whetted the impatience of militant Republicans to act, while it provided an example and a rallying cry for the hesitant. The appearance of the deputies on the steps was as a signal to the National Guards outside. The first battalion forced its way to the bridge ; others followed, and for the moment there was danger of a collision, since the police threatened to resist—Ranc had been well informed—but at the critical moment they were ordered to give way. A wave of humanity surged up to the railings of the Palais Bourbon. Small groups of National Guards and others gained admittance with the aid of friendly deputies. Among the newcomers was Ranc, who " mounted the steps and joined those who with hands and voices were giving the signal to those outside ".[2] The thin end of the wedge of invasion had been inserted, and deputies themselves, deputies of the Left, among whom Kératry, Glais-Bizoin, Steenackers, and Jules Ferry were the most notable,[3] were doing their utmost to widen the breach. It widened speedily. The crowd burst in and thronged the vast building, pouring like a torrent through courtyard and through corridor, prying into every hall and office, imprisoning or carrying with it the deputies who tried to leave their bureaux. National Guards and street urchins, workmen and bourgeois families in their Sunday best,[4] a motley audience, found their way to the Salle des Séances. It was empty save for a dozen deputies ; the majority were still in their bureaux or attempting to force their way back. Eight of the nine commissioners had been chosen and all, including the Republican Simon,

---

[1] J. DAVID, Dép. I, 155.   [2] RANC, Souvenirs et Correspondance, 158.
[3] Rapport DARU, 31.
[4] THIERS, Dép. I, 17 ; L. HALÉVY, Le 4 septembre, 12.

favoured the adoption of Thiers' motion.   It remained only
for Martel to draft his report, and at 2.15 he prepared to do
so ; but at 2.15 it was already too late ; the invasion of the
Chamber had begun.   The deputies of the Legislative Body
saw authority slipping from their grasp just at the moment
when they were preparing to seize it more firmly and fully
than ever before.

But all was not yet lost, for no irrevocable decision
had yet been made.   The "constitutional" transference of
powers now depended upon the ability of the deputies in
the Salle des Séances to control the crowd, and the crowd
was noisy, but not yet disorderly.   It had no plan, organisation, or acknowledged chief, and clearly awaited a lead
from the deputies of the Left ; but it had a cry which
indicated what the lead should be ; the cry was "Vive la
République !"   At this moment Republic was the only
conceivable alternative to Empire.   Of the few deputies in
the Salle when the first wave of invasion poured in Gambetta
was one.   After addressing the invaders, and bidding them
be orderly spectators of the coming deliberations, he had
withdrawn to a neighbouring room with some of his
colleagues.   At 2.30 the President, Schneider, appeared to
reopen the session, and Palikao took his seat on the Government bench ; but the din made it impossible to begin the
proceedings.   The veteran Crémieux attempted to procure
silence : "My dear good friends . . . I hope you all know
me.   I am the citizen Crémieux . . ."   But his voice was
powerless to carry ; the uninvited public was unimpressed,
and M. Crémieux's appeal for respect of the freedom of
debate was drowned by a confusion of interruptions and
cries of "Vive la République".   More stentorian tones were
needed to dominate the Babel, and Gambetta reappeared.
His "Citizens!" immediately attracted attention, and there

were cries for silence. He proceeded : " In the course of
the speech I made to you just now, while the sitting was
suspended, we agreed that one of the first conditions of the
emancipation of a people is order and regularity. Do you
wish to keep the contract ? (Yes ! Yes !) Do you wish us
to do things regularly ? (Yes ! Yes !) Since this is your
will, and since this must be the will of France (Yes ! Yes !)
you must make us a solemn engagement, and promise not
to violate it straight away : to allow the debate which is
about to take place to proceed with full liberty." [1]   (Yes !
Yes !) The public was attentive and approving, but at
this moment there was a fresh disturbance. New parties of
invaders forced their way into the front rows of the tribunes,
and began to shout for the Republic. Gambetta continued
his efforts to procure order and silence, but the applause
which greeted much of his advice did not signify obedience.
"A citizen " drew attention to the President, and Schneider
seized the opportunity to reinforce the appeal of Gambetta,
prudently paying tribute to him as " one of the most patriotic men of our time ". But he, Glais-Bizoin, and Girault
alike, were ineffective, and powerless to prevent fresh tumult.
Gambetta alone could make himself heard : " The deputies
are coming back. . . . It goes without saying that we shall
not leave here without having obtained a result in the
affirmative." This remark, which each member of the
public could interpret according to his own wishes, drew
immense applause ; from advice Gambetta was veering to
concession. But another wave of invasion now broke in
by a door hitherto closed, and the disorder increased. In
despair Schneider declared the session at an end, and left
the hall. His seat was promptly seized by two young men,
who amused themselves by vigorously ringing the presi-

---

[1] L. HALÉVY, *Le 4 septembre ; Le Siècle*, Jan. 12, 1871 ; *Journal Officiel.*

dential bell. It was ten minutes past three, and a rumour spread that a provisional Government had been proclaimed outside. Groups of deputies of the Left were to be seen in anxious consultation, and after a few hasty words with Jules Favre, who had now joined them, Gambetta reappeared in the tribune. He was greeted by cries of " Vive Gambetta!" and his utterance was followed by a tumult of applause. Now that Schneider had gone, the Legislative Body could have no hope of retaining or regaining authority. If the deputies of the Left did not give the lead that was expected of them, they risked losing all, for they were not the only aspirants after power. So Gambetta came forward to give that lead, and he himself had the pleasure of pronouncing the " deposition pure and simple " which he had so emphatically demanded : " Citizens, considering that the country is in danger ; that all the time that was needful has been given the representatives of the nation to pronounce the deposition ; that we are, and we constitute, the regular power issuing from free universal suffrage—We declare that Louis Napoleon Bonaparte and his dynasty have for ever ceased to reign over France."

The frantic cheers were followed by a fresh clamour for the Republic, and Jules Favre took up the cry : " The Republic ? Yes ; but it is not here but at the Hôtel de Ville we must proclaim it ! " In France revolution has its own traditions, and it was at the Hôtel de Ville that provisional Governments had been set up both in 1830 and in 1848. To Favre, himself " a man of 1848 " and of a sentimental disposition, the parallel between 1870 and 1848 must have been as appealing as it was obvious, and so he followed in the footsteps of Lamartine. Gambetta echoed the cry " to the Hôtel de Ville ! " and the crowd, glad to have leaders at last, took it up with enthusiasm.

In these events Gambetta had played a leading part. He had apparently done his utmost to restrain the impatience of the crowd, to restore order, and to secure the regular transition of powers to a Government regularly chosen by the Legislative Body. But he also was a leader of the movement to the Hôtel de Ville, and had been responsible for the deposition of the Emperor without any other sanction than the applause of the public ; and these acts caused doubt to be cast upon the sincerity of the others. " Many persons," remarked Napoleon III, " have believed that the future dictator simply wished to put himself in a good light by giving excellent advice which he knew could not be followed ; " [1] and those who believed this of Gambetta on September 4 could also believe it of him on September 3, when he spoke wise exhortations to the crowds on the Quai d'Orsay.[2] They could suggest that he had gone to the little courtyard of the Palais Bourbon with the intention of letting the people in, but that his plan was defeated because the concierge had strict orders to keep the gate locked, and because the courtyard was already occupied by other deputies, by no means all of the Left ; that Gambetta thereupon promptly attuned his words to suit his unlooked-for audience, and his speech to the people outside was a model of " sagesse " ; that nevertheless, he attempted, apparently in all innocence, to obtain the opening of the gate, but when the ruse was prevented by the intervention of Lebreton, there was nothing more for him to do in the courtyard ; he returned to the Palais to discuss the new situation arising from the midnight session.

The theory is ingenious, but the evidence [3] is much

[1] Count MAURICE FLEURY, *Memoirs of the Empress Eugénie* (New York, 1920), II, 438.

[2] See above, pp. 50, 51.   [3] I.e. DRÉOLLE's story.

too slight to convict him of such duplicity. Gambetta, unfortunately, unlike Thiers, had no d'Haussonville to chronicle his hopes and impressions, and the details of the negotiations in which he was concerned during the last days of the Empire : but it is difficult to see what could have been his object in encouraging an invasion of the Chamber at that hour of night when there was no session. The case against him on September 4 is stronger. The Left met at 11 a.m. that morning to reconsider its policy and at this meeting, according to Kératry, Gambetta, who held back the evening before, was " for action "[1] The words are tantalisingly vague, but they suggest the desire for the Left to take a bold initiative, and perhaps to proclaim the Republic whatever happened in the Legislative Body. There is no doubt at all that some of the deputies of the Left connived at and encouraged the invasion of the Chamber ; it seems improbable that Gambetta was ignorant of their intentions, or unacquainted with the paragraph in the *Siècle*, and with the conduct of Ranc, Spuller, and Challemel-Lacour, who were three of his most intimate friends. If he approved, it was because he surmised that the invasion would assure the Republic.[2] The presence of the people would intimidate the majority of the deputies into the adoption of more revolutionary measures, while the semblance of legality was still maintained. It would seem that Gambetta was not at this moment as reluctant for the Republic to shoulder the responsibilities of government as he later wished to make out.[3] Nevertheless, approval of the invasion need not have meant insincerity in attempting to restrain the invaders :

[1] Comte E. DE KÉRATRY, *Le 4 septembre*, 28.

[2] Cp. GAMBETTA, *Dép.* I, 547.

[3] E.g. letter to Mme ADAM, cit. Marquis de ROUX, *Les Origines et fondation la 3me République*, 63.

and there is every reason to suppose that he was as much averse from a mob revolution as he had always professed to be, and that he genuinely wished to make debate possible. Thus, the transition to the Republic would have the appearance of regularity, because effected by the Legislative Body, while at the same time it would be complete, because effected under the eyes of the people. His error was that he over-estimated his capacity to direct a crowd. The wisest refutation of the charge that Gambetta was merely playing in his own interests when he tried to restore order came from the man who, though not an eye-witness, was most closely affected by these events, and afterwards closely studied their details : " It is more probable," said the ex-Emperor Napoleon, " that he really meant what he said, for it was to his own friends' interest to check the insurrectionary movement, which had gone as far as they wanted . . . it was their intention to coerce the members of the majority by means of violent threats, though it was not probably their intention to break up the assembly as was finally done ; in a word, they wished to accomplish their own ends by means of the mob, but they did not all wish to accomplish the ends of the mob." [1]

[1] FLEURY, *Memoirs of the Empress Eugénie*, II, 437.

V

THE GOVERNMENT OF NATIONAL DEFENCE

ONCE again Paris saw vast crowds sweep through her streets
revolution-making, and at the head of the multitudes marching towards the Hôtel de Ville on either side of the Seine
were Favre and Gambetta, the men who had been most averse
from revolution by other than parliamentary means. But
parliamentary means had proved too slow, and now they
found themselves true revolutionaries of necessity. Did they
not proclaim the Republic others would, and those others
were the extremists whose violent doctrines Gambetta had
consistently opposed. The Republic of men such as Flourens
and Delescluze might fatally prejudice the Republic of Gambetta, and by its excesses make the name Republic anathema
in France for years to come. Now or never was the
moderates' chance. Extremist leaders had been prominent
among the invaders of the Chamber, their activities were
still more noticeable after the invasion of the Hôtel de Ville.[1]

Though guarded by troops of the line, the traditional
seat of revolutionary government opened its gates to the
invaders still more easily than the Palais Bourbon. It was
not the resistance of Bonapartists and soldiery which was
the chief danger to the leaders of the Left at this moment,
but the rivalry of Republicans. It was an easy task to

[1] OLLIVIER, *L'Empire libéral*, XVII, 469 ; J. FERRY, *Dép.* I, 382 ;
R. DREYFUS, *M. Thiers, contre l'Empire*, 130, 311.

proclaim the Republic, much more difficult to decide who should compose the new Republican Government, and, while deputies were conferring, extremist agitators who had found their way into the great hall of the building were busy crying the names of their own candidates, men like the journalists and future Communards, Félix Pyat and Delescluze, Gambetta's former client. Some of them compiled lists which they threw from the windows, and a rain of suggested governments descended upon the throngs which filled the square below. But Gambetta was at hand, and loudly and energetically denounced these proposals. He had no wish to share power with the extremists, and with them in the Government the Republic could inspire no confidence either at home or abroad. Yet time pressed ; once again the deputies of the Left risked losing their influence if they did not act promptly. A solution which would be generally accepted by the populace and would exclude the dangerous extremists before they could gain the upper hand was urgent. Gambetta's great voice and great influence were again exercised in the interests of moderation, and this time with more effect. The solution adopted had its disadvantages, but it had both the merits required at the moment. It was decided that the Government should be composed of the deputies of Paris, including those who had been elected at Paris, but had chosen to represent another constituency.[1] In this way Gambetta, deputy for Marseilles, and Jules Simon, deputy for Bordeaux, both became members of the new Government. The people of Paris was won by the choice of its own deputies, and with one exception they had not the reputation of being extreme. The exception was

---

[1] PICARD, *Dép.* I, 476 ; OLLIVIER, *L'Empire libéral*, XVII, 513, attributes the solution to Ledru-Rollin : but it was foreshadowed by the *Siècle* in August when it proposed a Committee of Defence to be composed in the first instance of the deputies of Paris.

Rochefort, for the formula meant his inclusion, and the name of the editor of *La Lanterne* did not suggest moderation. But his inclusion was a timely sop to the extremists, and Jules Favre's hope that he would prove less dangerous within the Government than outside it was to be perfectly justified.[1] The aristocratic demagogue was drawn to the Hôtel de Ville in triumph by an enthusiastic crowd, which escorted him from the prison of Ste. Pélagie and on his arrival there were loud cries of " Rochefort Mayor of Paris ! " But the hero showed his prudence, and declined to deprive Etienne Arago of a post of which he had already been acclaimed the holder.

" Once again Paris gives the law to France," said M. Peyrusse.[2] But it was still more remarkable that she had done so peacefully, and for the first time in her history achieved a revolution without bloodshed. Ranc's advice to the National Guards had not been rash, and they had attained their object without the use of their arms. The Empire had been as anxious as the Opposition to avoid incurring responsibility for civil strife at such a moment. Tocqueville's prediction made to a Tours librarian in 1856 had come true : " Alas ! it will fall only through war, but most certainly it will fall through war," [3] and the Bonapartists had the wisdom not to question the verdict of Sedan by an appeal from war to civil war. Europe, which regarded violence and terrorism as essential ingredients of revolution in France, was amazed.

The troops had made no attempt to oppose the revolution, but the new Government of the Hôtel de Ville could not yet be certain of their support. Civilians themselves, they required the co-operation of the military, both for the

[1] Cp. NEWTON, *Life of Lord Lyons*, I, 313 ; TROCHU, *Dép.* I, 278.

[2] DRÉOLLE, *La journée du 4 septembre*, 113.

[3] Cit. STEENACKERS and LE GOFF, *Histoire du Gouvernement de la défense nationale en province*, I, 86.

maintenance of their own position and for the continuation of the war. There was one man whose aid was indispensable, and one of their first acts was to despatch a deputation to entreat the support of General Trochu. The Governor of Paris had been singularly inconspicuous during the last twenty-four hours. Inactivity had been forced upon him by Palikao's assumption of entire responsibility for the military defence of the Palais Bourbon,[1] and in a difficult position, bound by oath to serve a regime for which he had little sympathy, and to which he himself was suspect, he thought it prudent to adopt a policy of " wait and see ". Nevertheless, in answer to an urgent appeal from one of the Quæstors, he had made a fruitless attempt to reach the Palais Bourbon in order to prevent the invasion. So dense were the crowds that he had made his way no further than the Pont de Solférino when Favre passed by and urged him to accompany them to the Hôtel de Ville.[2] But the situation at that moment was too obscure, and the General had refused. Now, however, on the arrival of a formal deputation from a provisional Government, the position was clearer : the Empress had fled from the Tuileries, the revolution had evidently triumphed, and Trochu was appealed to as a saviour by the Republican deputies. The role was flattering, and the call seemed a call of duty. The parallel with 1848 occurred to him too : " I am going to act the Lamartine over there," he said to his wife, as he prepared to follow his petitioners, and the claim he made later was scarcely exaggerated : " The provisional government was for the country on September 4 what Lamartine's government was on February 25, 1848. It saved a situation which was lost.

---

[1] Cp. OLLIVIER, *L'Empire libéral*, XVII, 494.

[2] TROCHU, *Une page d'histoire contemporaine devant l'Assemblée nationale* (Paris, 1871).

It prevented the demagogues from undertaking the defence of Paris and from causing a vast social upheaval throughout France." [1]

Knowing that the new Government was dependent upon his support, Trochu was able to make his own terms. No Republican himself, he first required assurance that it would indulge in no extreme anti-clerical measures or socialistic reforms, that it would respect God, the family, and property, and then demanded the presidency of the Government council : " If we are to have any chance of success it can only be by concentrating all powers in the hands of one man. As military commander my authority must be limitless." The demand was conceded, and Jules Favre, who otherwise would have been President, contented himself with the Vice-Presidency. In the irony of circumstances, the first act of the Republicans who in opposition had strenuously upheld the superiority of the civil authorities, was to give themselves a military chief, and one who was not a Republican. But this was not to imply that their doctrine was abandoned.

When Trochu reached the Hôtel de Ville, only six members of the new Government were there to receive him.[2] Though the distribution of ministries was reserved for a council to be held later in the evening, three of the future ministers had made their choice and hastened to stake their claims. One, Crémieux, was to be seen in the Place Vendôme, making an inglorious advance upon the Ministry of Justice, surrounded by a troop of ragamuffins.[3] The other two, Gambetta and Picard, both coveted the same office, the Ministry of the Interior, and the situation was piquant

---

[1] *Dép.* I, 281.

[2] Favre, Ferry, Rochefort, Etienne Arago, Glais-Bizoin and Pelletan.

[3] D'HAUSSONVILLE, *Mon journal pendant la guerre,* 105.

when both drove there together.[1] A leader of the parliamentary Republicans, Gambetta had succeeded in excluding the extremist rivals from the Government, a leader of the radical " gauche fermée " among parliamentary Republicans, he now found himself confronted by a rival for control of the Government's policy in the departments in the person of Picard, the leader of the Liberal " gauche ouverte ". The Ministry of the Interior was the seat of control of the provinces, and, war or no war, it was a key position immediately after a change of regime ; upon it more than upon any other ministry the permanence of the Republic might depend.   In the hands of Picard, the man who had wished to continue close co-operation with other Liberal groups as before 1869, who had objected to the " Mandat impératif," and refused to sign the same anti-plebiscitary manifesto as ultra-radical journalists like Delescluze, it would mean the conduct of the defence upon liberal lines, renewed co-operation with other Liberals, and the submergence of party politics as far as possible.[2]   But for Gambetta, more Republican than Liberal, the Liberal policy was futile, if not fatal, and he desired the ministry for himself.   It was largely his action which had given direction to the Revolution once it had become inevitable, his action which had maintained the authority of the deputies of Paris, determined the composition of the Government and the acceptance of the decision by the populace, and he was eager to consolidate the regime he had thus helped to create. He held that the defence could only be effective if the country was under the undisputed control of a well-disciplined party. Now was the time for the Left to secure its position and

[1] PICARD, Dép. I, 476 ; E. LAMY, Revue des deux Mondes, May 15, 1896 ; OLLIVIER, L'Empire libéral, XVII, 537.

[2] PICARD, op. cit. 476, 477 ; H. PESSARD, Mes petits papiers, I, 327 ; OLLIVIER, op. cit. XIII, 463.

"The hope of France."

TROCHU

(Vanity Fair, Sep. 17, 1870)

show its capacity for government. Hence all governmental posts should be given to Republicans and to Republicans only. His criticism of the weaknesses of coalitions had lost none of its force since 1869, and for him the phrase " concours de tous " must have definite limits, and not imply any sharing of authority. Invincibly optimistic, he believed in a success which would achieve both the aims of the defence and the definite establishment of the Republic ; but he was certain that the Liberal policy of conciliation would fail to achieve either, and he was determined to prevent Picard from obtaining the post in which he would have the greatest opportunity to ruin Republican prospects by the practice of an unpractical Liberalism. Thus it was Gambetta who, on this afternoon of September 4, took more complete possession of the Ministry of the Interior, and Picard, probably trusting that the decision of the Government Council in the evening would unseat his rival, went on to the Ministry of Finance. But he under-estimated the rival's cleverness and tenacity. The young leader of the irreconcilables would leave nothing to chance, and did not scruple to play the Minister in advance. It was important that the departments should learn the news of the change of Government as soon as possible from an authoritative source, and Gambetta served the interests of the Republic in telegraphing an announcement of its pro-clamation : but he also served his own interests at the same time, for he signed that telegram " the Minister of the Interior, Léon Gambetta ".[1]

A few hours later the Council of the Government of National Defence held its first meeting, and the allocation of ministries was its first and most important business. There was agreement upon all except the Ministry of the Interior, disputed by Gambetta and Picard, and here, at

[1] Cp. Appendix V, p. 293.

the very outset of its career, the Government found that it must choose between a radical and a liberal policy. But it is very possible that this question of policy was not the only factor which decided its vote, and that Gambetta had shrewdly judged that in this instance possession would count as nine-tenths of the law. The provinces now knew him as Minister of the Interior ; if he was not confirmed in this post, what confidence would they have in a government which changed its ministers within the first twelve hours of its existence ? By his signature to that first " ministerial " telegram he had introduced a powerful argument in his own favour, one which was irrelevant to any merits of policy, and it may well have helped to carry the day. A majority of two confirmed him in his occupation of the Place Beauvau ; [1] the Radicals had won the first round in the struggle for control of Republican policy, and if any one man was to be responsible for the moulding of the Third French Republic it would be not Picard but Gambetta.

The Revolution of September 4 was thus complete. The Second Empire fell ignominiously at Paris, as it had fallen disastrously at Sedan, and Léon Gambetta, son of an Italian grocer in the provincial town of Cahors, at the age of 32, became one of the principal ministers of a provisional Republican government. Opposition from legally constituted authorities was no longer to be feared. The Empress had found brief refuge with her American dentist, the first stage of flight to England. The Senate had adjourned— for ever—after vainly waiting for invasion by crowds which never came ; and deputies who had rallied to fresh debate at the Presidency after the wave of invasion had receded were forced to recognise that their authority was gone and

[1] Cp. Appendix VI, p. 295.

their chance of power irretrievably lost. The Legislative Body was a thing of the past, the Revolution an accomplished fact, and under the circumstances protests and threats of opposition, if they satisfied tender consciences, could be of no benefit to an invaded country. There was nothing for deputies to do but follow M. Thiers' advice : " Let us return honourably to our homes, for it is not right for us either to recognise or to oppose those who are about to struggle with the enemy ".

Paris, on the evening of September 4, was a city transformed. Gone was the atmosphere of depression and suspense which had hung about the capital like a pall during the last days of August. Nervous despondency had yielded to extravagant optimism, and the Parisians' reputation for volatility was seldom better justified. Good-humoured crowds had carried through a revolution which no ugly incident had marred. Now they openly rejoiced. Two days after Sedan, one of the greatest disasters which had ever befallen French arms, they were as gay as at the celebration of a glorious victory. All work was at a standstill. Imperial Ns and crowns and bees were joyfully demolished. The cafés were full, and the boulevards thronged with light-hearted crowds. The mere proclamation of the Republic was as good as a rout of the enemy, and the Revolution alone seemed to be the solvent of every trouble.[1] The Parisians fêted it, and forgot the advance of the German legions, forgot that the German press was howling for the destruction of their city, " the modern Babylon," that one French army was on its way to internment in the land it had expected to invade, and the other immured far away in Metz, forgot that their country was without an ally in the world, and had only a poor remnant

[1] Cp. F. Sarcey, *The Siege of Paris*, 21.

of regular troops to oppose to the most powerful and efficient army in Europe.

Of all this the new Government could not be forgetful. Throughout August the Left had clamoured for a Committee of Defence ; after Sedan they had moved the election of a governmental commission of National Defence ; now that they were themselves the Government it was natural as well as politic that they should take the title of Government of National Defence. Their first proclamation had declared that the people placed its representatives " not in power, but in peril " in order that they might save the country. An address to the army explained : " We are not the Government of a party ; we are the Government of National Defence. . . . Now as then (1792) the name of Republic means close union of army and people for the defence of the country," and Gambetta's announcement of the composition of the Government had been accompanied by the assurance that it was merely a provisional authority, set up with but one object—the defence of the country.

One object, but an object beset with formidable obstacles. The task assumed by the deputies of Paris was enough to tax the most skilful statesmen and generals ; and they were neither. With the exception of a few " vieux " who had had a brief experience of Government in 1848 [1]—a dubious training-school whether for diplomats or administrators— they had never held office before. Their political experience had been confined to electioneering, to assiduous opposition to the Empire in the Legislative Body, and to the organisation of propaganda for the Republic of their dreams. Six of them were lawyers, and five were publicists ; that is to say, that they belonged to two of the callings which

---

[1] Crémieux had been Minister of Justice, Emmanuel Arago Minister to Berlin, and Jules Favre Under-Secretary for Foreign Affairs.

most encourage the fatal delusion that speech is action.[1]
Criticism was their sword and eloquence their shield ;
the forum and the debating hall were their accustomed
arenas. Such equipment seemed scarcely adequate to
achieve the salvation of France and to oppose to the cool
diplomacy of Bismarck and to the mailed fist of Prussia.
As a Swiss colonel wittily remarked, the Government of
National Defence was better suited to adorn the French
Academy than to " fill the breach ".[2] Moreover, from the
outset there was a tendency to division in their ranks.
Although they declared that they were not the Government
of a party, they were, and none the less remained, Republicans. It was the Republic which had been proclaimed at
the Hôtel de Ville ; it was the Republic which they desired
to see established as the permanent form of government in
France. Only upon the manner and degree of Republicanism which it was expedient to practise at an hour so critical
they were not unanimously agreed. To the natural difference
in outlook between men of different generations, between
"jeunes" like Gambetta, Ferry, and Rochefort and "vieilles
barbes" like Crémieux and Glais-Bizoin, there was added
the difference between the views of Radicals and Liberals
which had emerged at the outset in the contest for the
Ministry of the Interior, and the difference was to persist
throughout the rule of the Government of National Defence.
Thus, not wholly at unity in itself, beset by extremists at
home, inexperienced and ill-prepared, this Government
did, indeed, seem but little fitted to carry through its " one
object " with any hope of success. But the vote upon the
Ministry of the Interior which had revealed its divisions
had also placed its youngest, most energetic, and most

[1] Cp. E. LAMY, *Revue des deux mondes*, May 15, June 15, 1896.
[2] Cit. E. A. VIZETELLY, *Republican France*, 9.

eloquent member in possession of one of its most important offices. There at least policy was likely to be directed with vigour, if not with discretion. The Revolution of February, 1848, was the nearest parallel to the Revolution of September, 1870, but the parallel to the situation inherited by the men of 1870 was the situation which confronted the men of 1792—the might of Germany marching through French provinces, the forces of resistance feeble and disorganised, and Paris itself in danger of attack. In those dark days of August and September, 1792, France had found the tremendous energy and the indomitable spirit of a Danton to give fresh hope and courage to the defenders of the soil. Who could be the Danton of the national defence of 1870 ? Surely not the sentimental Favre, despite his eloquence, nor the irresponsible Rochefort, despite his lashing satire, still less the witty, sceptical, Picard, the antique " revenants " like Crémieux and Arago, or the elderly, routine-loving Orleanists, General Le Flô and Admiral Fourichon, who, in default of Republican warriors, had been called to take charge of the Ministries of War and Marine. In this Government of journalists and lawyers there was only one man who might seem to possess something of those qualities which had made the lawyer Danton the personification of the national spirit and will to resist ; the lawyer Gambetta, Minister of the Interior, alone might be capable of kindling such a flame of enthusiasm as had been kindled by the Minister of Justice of 1792. 1870 demanded a Danton no less imperiously than 1792. The opportunity was there for the man who was capable of playing the role ; the question was whether there was such a man in existence and, if Gambetta was that man, whether he would seize his opportunity.

VI

GAMBETTA, MINISTER OF THE INTERIOR

WAR was the heritage of the Government of National
Defence, war the duty imposed upon it by its name. Yet
striking as was the parallel between 1870 and 1792, the
diplomatic situation seemed wholly different. Whereas in
1792 the King of Prussia had shown himself an open enemy
to the revolutionary disturbers of a throne, had not his
descendant in 1870 declared that he was making war not
on the French nation, but only against its ruling dynasty ? [1]
And now that dynasty lay in the dust, and many members
of the revolutionary Government of September 4 were men
who had been known both for their pacifist opinions and
for their friendliness to the rising German nation. What
need, then, to prolong the war ? There were still optimists
who hoped for the speedy conclusion of peace ; but their
hopes were soon to be disappointed.

The new Government was dependent upon the support
of Parisian opinion, and in Paris the spirit of defeatism and
indifference had yielded to a frenzy of patriotic excitement
and desire to wipe out the stain of invasion and military
disaster. By proclamations invoking the memory of the
glorious days of 1792 the men of September 4 had themselves swelled the wave of militant Republican enthusiasm,

[1] L. ANDRIEUX, *La Commune à Lyon en 1870-71*, 23 ; cp. M. BUSCH, *Count
Bismarck, Some Secret Pages of his History* (London, 1898), I, 407.

77

and now they were borne along on the crest of the wave. "Jules is dying to make peace," reported Prince Metternich on September 8 [1] (referring to the new "bourgeois" Minister for Foreign Affairs with amused familiarity), but it was to be a peace on French conditions, and a Parisian Government which at this moment consented to accept any other could not have lived for a day. The proud French nation had no mind to submit to upstart Prussia as meekly as had Austria in 1866, and France's conditions were proclaimed with proud, uncompromising language in Favre's first diplomatic circular of September 6 : " We shall yield neither an inch of our territory nor a stone of our fortresses. . . . Paris can hold out three months and conquer. If it fell France, ready at its call, would avenge it ; she would continue the struggle and the aggressor would perish." [2] Thus, when the Third French Republic was no more than two days old, its Foreign Minister committed it to achieve the seemingly impossible. The whole of Europe knew, and

---

[1] *H.H.u.S.A.*, METTERNICH to BEUST.

[2] In insisting on territorial integrity, Favre was merely adhering to the policy of his predecessor. The only two possible bases for the coming peace, said La Tour d'Auvergne, were the integrity of French territory and the maintenance of the dynasty (*H.H.u.S.A.*, METTERNICH to BEUST, Aug. 19). M. BAINVILLE (*La Troisième République, 1870-1935*, 36) writes : " But for the disturbances of September 4 there would have been no Republic. Had the Legislative Body retained the direction of affairs it would at once have concluded peace without prolonging a useless struggle." I am not clear about this. It is to be remembered that preparations, however unimportant, had already begun for the transference of Government departments to the Loire, and for facing a siege of Paris. Moreover, disturbances or not on September 4, the Bonapartist majority must have been greatly discredited after Sedan, and the stock of the Republicans correspondingly raised, especially in a city which was the chief Republican stronghold. The Legislative Body might have concluded peace had it left Paris at once. But I doubt whether it would have ventured to do so while it remained in the capital. It was not Republicans alone who were eager for continued resistance. Cp. L. HALÉVY, *Carnets*, II, 213, 214.

was disposed to ridicule such vainglory. But the high-flown phrases were the reflection of a will and determination which was suspected by none, least of all by the German enemy. German armies and people alike had confidently expected that Sedan would mean peace, and that peace would mean a cession of territory by France : opinions differed only about the extent of the provinces she must be forced to yield. " They think," wrote Lord Lyons of Favre and Thiers, " they can bring public opinion to accept a peace with a large pecuniary indemnity." [1] But what French public opinion could accept would be no satisfaction to the public opinion of Prussia, and Bismarck, two days earlier, had declared : " It is the fortresses of Metz and of Strasbourg that we need, and we shall take them ".[2] French pride and Prussian greed were irreconcilable, and their irreconcilability was to demand a new period of war more bitter than the first. Gambetta's hour was to come : in continued conflict lay his opportunity.

But he did not at once emerge as the dominant member of the Government of September 4 in the way that Danton had revealed himself the ubiquitous, all-powerful personage of the Ministry of August 10. In this new war of national defence which loomed ahead, the Government of National Defence was confronted by three obvious problems : the immediate defence of Paris, which required the co-operation of all, but was naturally directed by Trochu ; the quest for foreign aid, which was the business of Jules Favre ; and the awakening of the provinces to support of the Government in Paris, and to active participation in the defence, which was the task of Gambetta. Of the three, however, the defence of the capital appeared by far the most important. With

---

[1] NEWTON, *Life of Lord Lyons*, I, 312, Sept. 6, 1870.
[2] M. BUSCH, *Graf Bismarck und seine Leute*, I, 135.

Bazaine immobilised in Metz, there was no obstacle to hinder the enemy's march upon Paris. The peril of the city was far greater than in 1792, the enemy far more formidable, Moltke no Brunswick to be turned back by a mere Valmy cannonade from the defenders. But to the men of September 4 no less than to Danton in 1792 Paris was France in this hour of danger. The heart of the country and its most vulnerable point, the city which had made the Revolution was also its last bulwark of defence. In Paris were concentrated the bulk of the remaining active regular troops and the best of the Gardes Mobiles. Paris alone seemed capable of offering any organised resistance, and through her resistance, the Government hoped that the Republic would at least have the glory of saving the honour of France which Bonapartist surrender had sullied at Sedan. Paris, then, would resist ; but her resistance seemed a gesture of despair, and there were few responsible men— in the Government itself perhaps none except the optimist Gambetta—who believed that she could fulfil either of Favre's audacious boasts—hold out three months or conquer.[1] It was feared that the fortifications constructed in Louis Philippe's day under the auspices of Thiers would now prove inadequate to withstand modern artillery, and sieges themselves were regarded as relics of an age to which the perfection of long-range guns was unknown.[2] Apart from the difficulties of feeding a population which refugees from the environs had increased by 40,000, apart from the known shortage of munitions and the questionable efficiency of so many raw recruits among the defenders, even Parisians themselves doubted whether their fellow-citizens had the moral courage and powers of endurance to undergo the ordeal of a lengthy siege. Unstable and volatile by

[1] J. SIMON, *Souvenirs du 4 septembre*, II, 38, 52.   [2] *Rapport* CHAPER, 26.

reputation, they might now seem demoralised too.   Abroad
it was predicted that Fashion's capital would quickly fall ;
the victors of Sedan were sure of it, and Moltke wrote on
September 22, just after the investment had been completed,
that before the end of October he hoped to be back in Creisau
shooting hares.[1]   The capitulation of Sedan had not brought
France to her knees, but the capitulation of Paris would do
so without fail, for to the Germans, too, it seemed that Paris
was France.   The Government of National Defence did not
speak of capitulation, but they well knew that all depended
upon the resistance of the capital.   If it resisted three months
then, indeed, there might be time to raise new armies in the
provinces ; but if it withstood no more than a week or ten
days, surrender and a humiliating peace must be inevitable.
The departments had no forces already organised that were
capable of carrying on the war ; they would be powerless
to stave off the final recognition of defeat.

Thus, from the outset, this new period in the Franco-
Prussian war was dominated by the problem of Parisian
resistance.   Preparation for the siege was the most urgent
task of the Government of National Defence, the prospects
of the siege were the universal preoccupation, and when all
eyes were fixed on Paris the role played by the Minister of
the Interior in the capital could seem (though it was not) as
important as his activities in the provinces, the more so
because his connection with Belleville and his part in the
Revolution gave him special prestige with many Paris
Republicans.   But connections with extremists were now to
prove an embarrassment rather than an advantage ; they
may have diminished his influence with his colleagues in
the Government—his advice was by no means always

[1] *Letters of Field-Marshal von Moltke* (tr. C. BELL and H. W. FISCHER, London,
1891), II, 51.

accepted ; [1] they almost certainly confused his attitude in Parisian affairs, for the realist politician who knew the value of moderation was not allowed to forget his former ties. The Minister of the Interior was also the man who had sworn his acceptance of the programme of Belleville ; and one of his first duties was to receive a deputation from the International and the Syndicalist Chambers of Workers which demanded a programme of reforms very similar to that he himself had so vigorously advocated in the elections of 1869.[2] Gambetta was able to satisfy the more moderate requests of these petitioners : full liberties, he explained, were a " necessary consequence " of the proclamation of a Republic, and an amnesty for political prisoners, he declared, was already at the printer's. He promised further consideration for their other demands, but only one of these was to be the subject of prolonged debates in the Government Council, and that was the request for immediate municipal elections.[3] It was significant, because it was through control of the municipalities that the extremists now hoped to exert pressure upon the Government from which they had been excluded. For the moment, however, the request was ignored, and the new mayor of Paris chose to act upon his own authority. His colleagues were surprised and indignant to read in the *Journal Officiel* of the 6th a list of persons appointed mayors of the twenty Paris *arrondissements*, and signed by the name of Arago alone. Only one Minister appeared to have been consulted, and he was Gambetta.

[1] Cp. A. Dréo, *Procès-verbaux des séances du conseil du gouvernement de la défense nationale*, passim.

[2] G. Lefrancais, *Étude sur le mouvement communaliste à Paris, 1871.* The suppression of the prefecture of police and the election of magistrates were demands which did not appear specifically in the Belleville programme.

[3] There was, however, some discussion about the suppression of the prefecture of police which the Prefect Kératry himself proposed ; cp. Dréo, op. cit. Sept. 23.

The choice of persons gave offence no less than the arbitrary and secretive procedure, and one of the names most criticised was that of Ranc, a close friend of Gambetta, but a man suspect to the moderates as a former associate and admirer of the terrible Blanqui.[1] Not the least offended was the military President, Trochu, who severely rebuked Arago and Gambetta, and recorded that the young Minister of the Interior was profuse with apologies for his conduct.[2] He could afford to be ; for the second time in two days he had confronted his colleagues with a *fait accompli*, and here, too, it was successful ; despite much show of indignation and talk of immediate municipal elections, the nominations were allowed to stand. But Gambetta's victory was of doubtful advantage to himself ; an act of this kind must have helped to sow the seeds of suspicion and jealousy which were to grow so rapidly after his departure from Paris.

The municipal election question, however, was not to lie dormant for long, and ten days later, when it was suggested that elections should be held throughout the provinces, it was none other than Gambetta who proposed that they should be held in Paris too.[3] Although the situation of Paris was exceptional, Paris should not be excluded if elections were to be held generally. Trochu and Rochefort agreed that principles should overrule expediency ; but such was not ordinarily Gambetta's reasoning, and it was curious that he should have clung to the universal application of a principle when the argument of expediency against it was so weighty as that put forward by Ferry. The actual mayors, who had been the objects of criticism on September 6, now seemed preferable to those who would be likely to come into power through election ; they were often surrounded

---

[1] Dréo, op. cit. 78, Sept. 23.   [2] Trochu, *Dép*. I, 285, 286.
[3] Dréo, op. cit. 125, Sept. 15.

and sometimes dominated by extremist committees, but
new mayors were only too likely to be the willing creatures
and nominees of these committees, and Ferry feared that,
once elected, they would attempt to substitute their authority
for that of the Government.[1]   His colleagues preferred to
hope for the best, but were soon led to reconsider their
decision.   Still more curious was it that Gambetta should
so stubbornly have clung to the decree ordering municipal
elections in Paris when after Favre's return from Ferrières
the Government determined to cancel elections of every
kind.   At first he even refused his signature to the new
decree of cancellation, and, when at length he yielded, it
was with evident reluctance.[2]   On the 22nd a troop of
National Guards and others had manifested against the
holding of municipal elections ; on the 26th there was
another demonstration and its leaders were received by
Gambetta, but not by Gambetta alone.   That evening at
the Government council Dréo noted a strange conflict of
opinion :   " M. Gambetta reports the wishes expressed by
the deputation of battalion commanders.   They now ask
for municipal elections.   MM. Ferry and Dréo declare that
in their presence these same battalion commanders asked
through their spokesman, M. Lermina, that there should be
no elections at present because an electoral contest would
distract attention from the defence." [3]   What was the
reason for Gambetta's insistence ?   Did the Republican
realist think municipal elections really necessary to the
defence ?   Were the mayors he himself had helped to choose
not Republican enough ?   Or was this the voice of the
mandatory of Belleville trying to give satisfaction to his
radical associates, demanding " the most radical application

---

[1] DRÉO, Procès-verbaux, 133, Sept. 18.
   Ibid. 151 ff., Sept. 22 and 23.   [3] Ibid. 161, Sept. 26.

of universal suffrage "—in Paris at least. This seems much the more likely explanation of his conduct, for it is difficult to believe that he could free himself entirely from the influence of the radical extremists whose aid had contributed to the foundation of his political career.

If the question of Paris municipal elections showed the weakness of Gambetta's own personal position as Minister in a besieged city where he had won an election, the organisation of the National Guard, for which he was responsible, showed the weakness of the position of the Government as a whole and the dangers which might arise from naïve, undisciplined Republican enthusiasm. The National Guard was now an essentially democratic and Republican institution. Its re-establishment in August at the instance of the deputies of the Left had been applauded by Gambetta as a " very politic and patriotic measure " ; [1] and the policy of the measure was manifest soon after when, true to its traditions, the Guard took a leading part in the events of September 4. The new Government had been prompt to express gratitude for its assistance by a special proclamation : " It is to your resolution that the civic victory which has restored liberty to France is due. Thanks to you this victory has not cost one drop of blood . . . in rivalry with our noble army and together with it you will point the way of victory." [2]

According to the law of August 12 the duty of organising the National Guard fell to the Minister of the Interior. This did not satisfy the Left when the Minister was a Bonapartist, and they had unsuccessfully tried to obtain the transference of control at least of the Guards of Paris to Trochu, the Governor of the city.[3] Now, however, that they were

[1] GAMBETTA, *Discours et plaidoyers politiques*, I, 316.
[2] Cit. J. CLARETIE, *Histoire de la Révolution de 1870-71*, 247.
[3] Cp. GAMBETTA, *Dép. circ.*, I, 374, Aug. 27.

themselves the Government, such a measure seemed unnecessary, and Trochu himself formally proposed that the
Minister of the Interior should be recognised as " master of
the National Guard of Paris and of France," and that he
need not refer his actions to any other authority.[1] Thus
Gambetta inherited the full powers of his predecessor,
Chevreau.

" Gambetta," wrote Félix Pyat soon after, " eats, drinks,
and sleeps with his compatriot Machiavelli. . . . He knows
him by heart."[2] But there was one wise passage in the
Discorsi which he seemed to have forgotten : " No one
endowed with wisdom," wrote Machiavelli, " will ever
allow a multitude to take up arms without a certain order
and a certain method. He who commands the defence of
a town will shun arming the citizens tumultuously as he
would shun a reef."[3] The counsel was never more needed
than in Paris in 1870. But Gambetta, if he had not such a
naïve belief in the military excellence of the armed citizen
as Picard, who had declared that the revival of the National
Guard would give France 500,000 trained soldiers in a week,[4]
was eager to furnish the threatened capital with the largest
number of armed defenders in the shortest time possible.
Palikao's Government had decreed the organisation of 60
battalions of National Guards in Paris ; Gambetta, by
decree of September 6, ordered the formation of 60 more,
each to be composed of 1500 men and divided into eight
companies.[5] This meant the arming of 90,000 Parisians on
the morrow of a revolution, and the execution of the decree

---

[1] DRÉO, *Procès-verbaux*, Sept. 9.

[2] Cit. F. MAILLARD, *Histoire des journaux publiés à Paris pendant le siège*, 31.

[3] Cit. OLLIVIER, *L'Empire libéral*, XVI, 349.

[4] *Journal Officiel*, Aug. 10 ; cit. H. DUTRAIT-CROZON, *Gambetta et la défense nationale*, 1870-71, 502.

[5] *Rapport* DARU, 113.

was entrusted to the municipalities, many of which were soon to be subject to the control or pressure of revolutionary clubs and committees ; some no doubt were genuinely obsessed with the idea of a glorious *levée en masse*, but others saw in the control of the National Guard a fortunate opportunity to arm the type of men who would further their own political designs. Furthermore, the battalion lists were to be drawn up by local commissioners who were expressly exempted from " binding themselves to any particular formality," and the battalions once formed were to elect their own officers.[1] The system may have been democratic, but at such a time it could lead only to confusion, confusion which was increased by the rapid approach of the enemy, by the belief that an attack was imminent and that the fate of Paris might be settled by the first encounter, and above all, according to Jules Favre, by " the enthusiasm of the citizens ".[2] This was such that, so far from there being any adherence to any " particular formality," " it was impossible to demand any qualification either of residence or even of nationality. . . . Foreigners, children, old men, vagabonds, and ex-criminals received arms and figured on the rolls ". The " enthusiasm " of such citizens was not unnaturally increased by the system of payment which the Government applied to the National Guards. Gambetta and his colleagues confounded the right of the State to demand unpaid service in the National Guard for the defence of the country with the duty of the State to relieve the poor and needy. They offered 1.50 fr. relief a day to each Guard who should ask for it, as well as a supplementary allowance of 0.75 cm. for his wife and 0.25 cm. for each child.[3] Nor was the payment limited to the days on which

---

[1] *Rapport* CHAPER, 65.

[2] J. FAVRE, *Gouvernement de la défense nationale*, I, 212.

[3] *Rapport* CHAPER, 95 ; *Rapport* DARU, 113.

the Guard did service ; it was to be daily, irrespective of service.[1] The result was that the poor and needy flocked into the National Guard in order to be qualified to obtain relief. The numbers of this citizen army swelled monstrously, and the decree of September 6 was soon a dead letter, because of the freedom with which it had been interpreted. By the 30th the National Guard of Paris contained 360,000 men, instead of the prescribed 180,000 ; there were 134 battalions instead of 60, and they varied in size from 360 men in one to 2600 in another, instead of being composed each of 1500 men.[2]   Of these 134 battalions, 24 were totally unarmed. They were useless as active defenders, and unwilling to labour at the defence works. Gambetta wisely proposed a limitation of the military dole ; it should be paid to unarmed Guards only if they consented to do the work that was required of them.   This was the sole means of pressure the Government possessed, and it had to be used with caution ; any attempt at more forcible coercion might lead to an attack on the Hôtel de Ville.

In the National Guard of Paris the Government of National Defence had raised up a Hydra which was to be cut down only after the long horror of the Commune of 1871. Their intentions had been patriotic and praiseworthy, but, owing to their democratic ideas and connections, they had not the wisdom or the power to execute them efficiently, nor the foresight to subordinate the National Guard to the military authorities from the first.   The political danger of a mass of hastily armed citizens was soon as apparent as their military uselessness.   The system of electing officers not only ensured that the battalions most in need of discipline would be those in which there was least attempt at discipline, but it made the Guards a centre of political

---

[1] DRÉO, Procès-verbaux, 119.   [2] Rapport CHAPER, 66.

intrigue and discussion, and paved the way for the ascendancy of ambitious revolutionaries such as Gustave Flourens, who was elected commander by three battalions of Belleville, and at once attempted to abuse his command by coercing the Government.[1] From September 22 onwards, the manifestations of the National Guards were a frequent threat to the Government, and an unhappy feature of life in the besieged city. On that day there was a general meeting of the " Delegates " of the different *arrondissements*, mostly self-appointed extremists who assumed a general control over the affairs of their municipalities, and exerted constant pressure upon the mayors. They named a commission of 20 members, who were to join 107 officers of the National Guard, and demand the immediate election of the Commune. It was a significant coalition. The demonstrators, led by Jules Vallès, Blanqui, and Millière, marched to the Hôtel de Ville, where Gambetta received them in the great hall. But all his eloquence was unavailing. The extremists persisted in their demands, and the Government would have been at their mercy but for the stratagem of Picard, who announced that the Prussians had suddenly launched an attack.[2] The Communards, however revolutionary, were Parisians and Frenchmen ; they at once dispersed. There were many other demonstrations during the following three weeks ; Gambetta was not in Paris to witness the events of October 31, but before his departure for the provinces he had ample opportunity to discover the dangers and inconveniences of a force which neither he, nor Trochu, nor Tamisier, its commandant, was able fully to control.

No less important and much more clearly marked with the impress of his own policy and personality was Gambetta's

---

[1] Dréo, op. cit. 184.
[2] Ibid. 149 ; cp. G. Lefrancais, *Souvenirs d'un révolutionnaire*, 407.

administrative action in the provinces.   The docile obedience
of the departments had been legendary.   Paris had been
the supreme and acknowledged arbiter ; it had decreed the
changes of fashion and of taste ; it had dispensed ideas, and
in politics its fiat had been law.   " The opinion of the
provinces is of as much value as the opinion of my leg," said
Heine.   In his centralised prefectorial system Napoleon I
had bequeathed to his successors a formidable instrument of
government.   Wisely they had recognised its power, accepted
the legacy, and made no attempt to disrupt it, despite its
Napoleonic origin.   There were changes at the centre :
Paris periodically achieved a revolution ; to the provinces
fell the duty of applauding the result and, as each new
regime maintained the existing system of provincial government, the applause had generally come with alacrity.
Though an independent spirit had grown since Heine wrote,
and the reaction of the provinces to the June Days of 1848
and to the *coup d'état* of 1851 was indeed striking evidence
that there were limits to their docility, yet the tradition of
their subservience endured.[1]

Nevertheless, the Government of National Defence was
by no means confident as to its reception in the departments ;
for it was they which, as recently as May, had furnished the
great majority of the seven and a half million " Oui " of the
plebiscite, and Bonapartist sympathies were still supposed to
be very strong among the peasantry.   Jules Favre told Lord
Lyons on September 5 that one of his reasons for regretting
" the immediate Proclamation of a Republic, which the
impetuosity of the Parisian population had made inevitable,"
was that " it would irritate and alarm a great part of the
population of the French provinces ".[2]   But there had been

---

[1] In some 15 departments, chiefly in the Centre and South, there was
resistance to the Government of Louis Napoleon after the *coup d'état* of 1851.

[2] *F.O.* 146, 1479, LYONS to GRANVILLE.

impetuosity in the provinces no less regrettable. For once Paris had been forestalled. It was now only a very " rough truth " to speak of the provinces as a homogeneous entity in contrast with the capital. There was a marked division between the country and the large towns, particularly in the south, and the development of manufactures and the spread of socialistic ideas had emphasised the differences. The industrial workers despised the peasantry as ignorant upholders of Bonapartist despotism, while the peasantry distrusted the workers with their airs of conscious superiority and their strange social theories.[1] The elections of 1869 had shown that Lyons and Marseilles were strongholds of Republicanism. In August, 1870, they had had their own " affairs," [2] counterparts of the rising at La Villette in Paris, and on September 4 the Republic was proclaimed in Lyons at 9 a.m. The capital of France was anticipated in its revolutionary action by the second city, and the Republicanism which triumphed at Lyons was much redder than the Republicanism of the new Government at Paris. Gambetta had just cause for anxiety in the news that Committees of Public Safety had been formed at Lyons and at Marseilles ; by ill-considered violence there was danger that they would bring the Republic into disrepute, and one of his first cares on his first night as Minister was to seek capable administrators for the departments of Rhône and of Bouches du Rhône.

But, if the doings of Republicans were disquieting, all reports seemed to show that little opposition was to be feared from Bonapartists. Some of the Imperial prefects sent in their resignations. Others offered to remain at their posts until they were replaced, and a large number prudently and

---

[1] Cp. M. BAKUNIN, *Lettres à un Français.*
[2] P. DE LA GORCE, *Histoire du Second Empire*, VII, 198.

patriotically expressed their good wishes for the national defence, which, they affirmed, was their sole preoccupation. M. Demanche, the prefect of Cher, even ventured to send good advice to the new Minister : " No politics—that is the way to rally everybody." [1] But Gambetta thought otherwise. The ready submission and apparent goodwill of the Bonapartist prefects were only one side of the picture ; on the other was the legacy of mutual suspicion, the enthusiasm, expectations, and fervid congratulations of Republicans, accompanied by countless denunciations of Bonapartists and " reactionaries " generally. In some departments ardent democrats announced that they themselves had ejected the Imperial administrators, and they asked to be confirmed in the posts they had usurped.

To one who had grown up in opposition, who had felt the pressure of Imperial administration, and knew the watchful efficiency of Imperial police, it was still scarcely credible that the Second Empire was completely extinct. Republicans had been anxious to avoid all risk of civil war, but they did not credit their old enemies with the same patriotic anxiety. The unusual silence and resignation of the Regency Government in its last days had led them to fear a *coup d'état* all the more, and now the prompt acceptance of the Revolution by the provincial authorities did not entirely reassure them. If the general situation certainly demanded that the central government should exercise an immediate and firm control over the departments, one, and not the least of the arguments in favour of action which would be speedy as well as Republican, was that it would deprive the Bonapartists of time to organise resistance. Loss of authority would also entail a loss of prestige in the

[1] STEENACKERS and LE GOFF, *Histoire du gouvernement de la défense nationale en province*, I, 74.

eyes of countryfolk,[1] and Gambetta replaced prefects and sub-prefects as quickly as he could find men of Republican principles at all fit to replace them. " Mobility of persons and perpetuity of functions " was the formula he had adopted from Chaudey.[2] The personnel was to be changed as completely as possible, and the change would kill three birds with one stone : purge the provinces of the Bonapartist plague, found the Republic, and forward the work of national defence.

" The very essence of Democracy," said Faguet, " is to make centralisation necessary." [3] Certainly the new democratic Government of National Defence felt no difficulty in preserving the centralised prefectorial system bequeathed to it by the Empire, and, so far from diminishing the very extensive powers of its provincial representatives,[4] it was led by the exigencies of the war as well as by its Republican theories, to increase them still further by the addition of a wide military authority. Much, therefore, depended upon the choice of persons to whom these powers were to be entrusted. " When there is a Republic," Gambetta later explained, " the principal agent of the administration ought to be a Republican. But it is to be observed that if you choose prefects of one nuance only you obtain bad results ; they should be taken from all nuances of the party. That is what I did, and so in the prefects of September 4 you have had all varieties of Republicans ".[5] This variety, however, was the result of necessity rather than of design.

[1] D.T. Pref. Loire to Interior, Sept. 16.

[2] GAMBETTA, Discours et plaidoyers politiques, I, 220.

[3] E. FAGUET, Politicians and Moralists of the Nineteenth Century (tr. DOROTHY GALTON, London, 1928), 101.

[4] Cp. Frazer's Magazine, Nov. 1872—Six Months of Prefecture under Gambetta.

[5] GAMBETTA, Dép. I, 560 ; TROCHU, Dép. I, 287.

The need for prompt action allowed little time to prove the new administrators and, provided they were Republicans, Gambetta took them where he could find them. They could not all be men of whose capacities or "nuances" he had personal knowledge, and the recommendations of provincial Republicans were no guarantee of administrative ability. While some of these new officials were Gambetta's personal choice, others were selected by his subordinates, with the result that more than once confusion followed, and there were two candidates for the same prefecture, each claiming to hold authority from the Minister himself; [1] while some were appointed in consideration of past services to the Republican cause, others were men who had installed themselves in the prefecture in the name of the Republic, and had demanded to be confirmed in their possession.[2] These appointments, it is true, were all submitted to the Government Council for ratification—on September 6 " this operation lasted several hours and much bored General Trochu " [3] —but, though each name was discussed, the great majority of Gambetta's nominations was maintained.[4] It was easier to criticise them than to find an adequate substitute in the Republican ranks. The lesser lights of the party were mostly as deficient in administrative experience as their leaders, and the ablest organisers among them, as Gambetta complained,[5] preferred to remain in Paris where, so it seemed in September, there would be more scope for the exercise of their talents.

By September 14 Gambetta had appointed new prefects to eighty-five departments, and the list of appointments was an illuminating comment upon the make up of the Republi-

---

[1] Cp. C. DE FREYCINET's vivid account of his experience, *Souvenirs*, I, 111 ff.
[2] E.g. Esménard du Mazet in Lot.   [3] DRÉO, *Procès-verbaux*, 72.
[4] Ibid. ; CRÉMIEUX, *Dép.* I, 86.   [5] FREYCINET, op. cit. 113.

can party. Like master, like man : as the majority of the
Government of National Defence were either journalists or
lawyers, so no less than forty-four of the new administrators
were, or had been, lawyers, while fourteen were primarily
journalists.[1] These men, who were to be the keystone of
administration in the provinces, were appointed as Republicans, and they seldom failed to show strong party spirit.
What was lacking rather was a sense of party discipline, and
some of the democrats now elevated for the first time to a
place of power and responsibility were to imagine themselves
omnicompetent, and seek to impose their own policies upon
the Government. The centralised prefectorial system remained, but it was in the hands of a party which lacked an
administrative tradition or hierarchy, and the system was
strangely perverted when a Minister had to capitulate before
the independent obstinacy of a prefect who refused to obey
his instructions. Few Ministers since the establishment
of the Constitution of 1875 can have been addressed as
frankly or defiantly by their subordinates as was Gambetta
in 1870. The insubordinate were, however, a small though
conspicuous minority ; the greater number of Gambetta's
prefects did honestly attempt to carry out their instructions,
and to perform their duties creditably in circumstances of
peculiar difficulty which their inexperience did not lighten.
They seldom achieved brilliant success, but to the best of
their ability they worked in what they conceived to be the
interests of the national defence, as well as of the Republic.

[1] Cp. H. DUTRAIT-CROZON, *Gambetta et la défense nationale, 1870-71*, Appendix
D, 537 ff.

VII

THE DELEGATION AND THE ELECTION QUESTION

THE Paris that was France and had just acclaimed a new Government in the persons of its deputies, men of the Left and champions of universal suffrage, was threatened with siege. What was to become of the departments, and what of the sovereignty of the nation in this hour of peril ? Here two tremendous problems confronted the new rulers at the outset of their reign, and upon their ineffective solution of one and the consequent confusion of the other depended, perhaps, the future of the nation, and certainly the glory of Gambetta.

When the news of the fall of Longwy reached Paris in August, 1792, there was panic ; the city seemed in danger and Ministers were for removing the Government at once to the banks of the Loire. But Danton would not hear of it, thundered against such cowardice and declared that Paris was France (as, indeed, it was for revolutionaries of Danton's sort) and could not be abandoned. He carried the day, and the Government remained. But in 1792 there was no siege of Paris ; the precedent was misleading. Now in 1870 the problem recurred—Paris was threatened once more, but this time siege was inevitable ; nothing could avert it save a humiliating surrender, to which the Government was inflexibly opposed ; and this time there were no dangers of

Vendean revolt to make the Loire a perilous refuge. What then would Government do in 1870 ? The question had already been considered by the Palikao ministry, and the lines of its solution had been indicated when the Foreign Minister and the Minister of Justice had been instructed to set up branches of each department and assembly at Tours.[1] But Revolution had intervened before these plans could be executed, and the problem was bequeathed to the Government of National Defence. The new rulers apparently saw no objections to the choice of Tours as a seat of provincial government, and hastened on the preparations for the departure of ministerial delegations to the pleasant city on the Loire.[2] The centre of the stage for the national defence in the provinces had thus been set by the Empire ; but it was for the Republic to arrange the details and to distribute the caste and upon this depended the whole course of the action. Civil servants might go to the provinces to carry on administration, but who were to be the chief actors on the stage ? The main problem—what was the Government itself to do ?—was still unsolved.

To remain or not to remain ? Two notions misled the men of September 4 when they came to consider this question : for all German strength and efficiency they thought it incredible that a city of two million inhabitants could be completely blockaded, impossible that its ordinary means of communication with the provinces and with the outside world should be entirely cut off ;[3] and secondly they too, like Danton, were obsessed with the idea that Paris was France. They could not forget that if they were the Government, it was because they had been the deputies of Paris. It was Paris which had given them their mandate,

[1] JULES BRAME, *Dép.* I, 188 ; cp. also CLÉMENT DUVERNOIS, *Dép.* I, 266.
[2] DRÉO, *Procès-verbaux*, 75, 82.   [3] *Rapport* DARU, 156.

Paris, the capital and historic seat of government, which had made the Revolution of September 4 and acclaimed their Republic.   If the fate of France now depended upon the fate of Paris, how should they abandon the post of danger and desert the city to which they owed their power ? Thus they reasoned, and by their Parisian origin were blinded to the best interests of Parisian defence, for it made them unable to consider the city merely as a fortress and the siege as a purely military problem.[1]   The inability led to fundamental error : what use was it for the Government to remain where it was least able to perform its essential function of government ?

A discussion on the 9th induced the first stage of error when it was decided that any Minister who went to Tours should do so only as a delegate of the main body of the Government which would remain in Paris.[2]   However incomplete the blockade, communications were unlikely to be reliable ; a delegation would be hampered by the necessity for constant reference to Paris.   Once the principle of a division of the Government was accepted, the head should have migrated and the tail remained behind ; the Government in the provinces would thus have been free as well as authoritative.   However, Trochu and his colleagues determined otherwise.   A delegation was to be formed, but it was less easy to decide its composition.   After much discussion, the Council, on the morning of the 11th, agreed that Crémieux should be a delegate,[3] and in the evening that he should be sole delegate.[4]   The departure of Jules Favre was voted by Gambetta and Glais-Bizoin alone, although it should have been obvious that the Minister

---

[1] Cp. the arguments of J. SIMON, *Souvenirs du 4 septembre*, II, 33 ff.

[2] DRÉO, *Procès-verbaux*, 93.   [3] Ibid. 104.

[4] Ibid. 108.   Apparently Pelletan at one time expected to accompany Crémieux, *D.T.* II, 230.

for Foreign Affairs ought to be in a place which was accessible Less obvious was the choice of the Minister of Justice, who was 74, and little known outside Paris. Favre himself was apparently disposed to leave, and requested that Picard should accompany him—a proposal which was unlikely to please Gambetta,—but second counsels more timid and sentimental prevailed : " It was necessary to assemble in Paris all that could make our efforts effectual, and I was under the delusion that in separating myself from it I should have weakened it." [1] The delusion was shared by the majority of Favre's colleagues, and the sentence was a clue to the real reason determining the choice of Crémieux—a reason of chivalry. If Paris was the post of honour, it was also the post of danger, and the venerable lawyer who was the oldest member of the Government should be spared the hardships of a siege. It was precisely M. Crémieux's age which qualified him to be sent to Tours, precisely M. Glais-Bizoin's age which qualified him to be sent after M. Crémieux.[2]

" From the outset," said Gambetta later in his deposition, " I demanded that the whole Government should leave Paris." [3] Once again he desired to establish a reputation for prescience ; but while there is no doubt that he was more clear-sighted than many of his colleagues, there is no evidence that he was as conspicuously clear-sighted as he afterwards declared, or that he, more than anyone else, anticipated the completeness of the impending blockade of Paris. On the other hand, he had a higher opinion than most of the Government of the part which the provinces might play in the national defence, and as Minister of the

---

[1] J. FAVRE, *Gouvernement de la défense nationale*, I, 154.

[2] TROCHU, *Dép.* I, 182. For a lively sketch of Glais-Bizoin as a deputy in the Legislative Body, cp. L. HALÉVY, *Carnets*, I, 78, 147.

[3] *Dép.* I, 548.

Interior he was the person most interested in the composition of the Delegation, for the presence in the departments of other members of the Government would react upon his own administration. He would naturally desire that the chosen delegates should be men who understood him, and were in sympathy with his policy of republicanisation. But, although Crémieux was one of the colleagues with whom his relations had been most intimate, it is doubtful whether Gambetta approved the choice or the reasoning which determined it. After Crémieux had reigned three days at Tours, Gambetta was convinced of his inadequacy. The news from the departments was disquieting ; in the south and south-west the extreme Republicans showed federalist tendencies which seemed likely to be a menace to the unity of the country if they were allowed to develop. On the 15th Gambetta gave a serious account of the situation, and urged that " a real and strong Government should be set up at Tours " [1] (which was by no means the same thing as advocating the departure of the whole Government). He would hear nothing of Picard's remedy, which was to provide Crémieux with " a consultative committee composed of former deputies of the Opposition ".[2] Such a plan would open the door of power to Monarchists, and be the reversal of his own exclusive Republican policy. The Council decided that the delegate at Tours must be reinforced by more of its own members but, while Garnier-Pagès suggested that there ought to be four of them, Gambetta agreed with Favre and Glais-Bizoin that a delegation need not consist of more than three Ministers " provided that they were influential ".[3] This might have been true if the men of influence chosen to compensate the deficiencies in influence of Crémieux had

---

[1] Dréo, *Procès-verbaux*, 120 ; cp. also notes on Councils of Sept. 11.
[2] Ibid. 113.   [3] Sept. 19.

not been Glais-Bizoin and Admiral Fourichon, the Minister of Marine, who was also to act as delegate of the Minister of War. Gambetta's vote and reaction to the votes which produced this "real and strong Government" are unfortunately not recorded.

The new delegates left Paris only just in time. Two days after their departure the investment of the city was complete, and the blockade was to prove more thorough than had been thought possible. The whole circuit of 11 miles was enclosed, the city was cut off from its environs, and the principal members of the Government were imprisoned in their capital. On September 25 their last certain means of communication with the outside world disappeared when the enemy discovered and cut the telegraphic cable in the bed of the Seine. Henceforth there remained only the uncertain ways of the air.[1] Paris was now literally France for these Parisian rulers, and their error in refusing to leave the city was obvious only when it was irreparable. Nine months later Trochu could describe it as "elementary"[2] and Gambetta declare that it was "capital" and that he could not understand that "a town which was going to be besieged and blockaded and consequently reduced to a purely military and strategic role should retain the Government within it ".[3] But this, once again, was wisdom after the event, a lesson learnt by bitter experience. Its warning, however, was not lost upon a later generation, and in 1914 when von Kluck advanced to Compiègne the military authorities insisted that there should be no repetition of the error of 1870. Obedient to the High Command, the Government braved criticism and ridicule[4] and withdrew

---

[1] i.e. the use of pigeons and balloons.   [2] *Dép.* I, 283.   [3] Ibid. 548.
[4] Cp. L. MARCELLIN, *Politique et politiciens pendant la guerre* (Paris, 1922), I, 39 ; " On les a surnommé les francs-fileurs ".

to Bordeaux. As M. Doumergue said to M. Poincaré :
" One's duty is sometimes to allow oneself to be accused
of cowardice ; it may require more courage to confront
popular reproach than to run the risk of being killed ".[1]

The Government of National Defence had at length
settled one of its great problems, while the other was anxiously
discussed and discussed again. It was the problem of elections. " A constituent assembly shall be summoned as soon
as circumstances permit " ; this was not the least important
clause in Favre's motion in the Chamber on the 4th ; he
had proposed the formation of a Government of National
Defence, and the implication was that the defence would be
conducted all the more nationally with the support of a
National Assembly. But revolution had intervened and,
instead of sanctioning an anonymous coalition Government
chosen from representatives of different parties in the Legislative Body, and acting as a provisional directory until a
Constituent Assembly should determine the form of the new
regime, it had prejudged the decision of the electorate and
proclaimed the Republic. Nevertheless, the revolutionaries
were the same men who had supported Favre's motion, and
who so often and emphatically had declared their belief in
the effective sovereignty of the whole nation. The acclama-
tions of some thousands of Parisian citizens were neither an
expression of universal suffrage nor an adequate substitute
for it, and this the men of September 4 well knew. But
they were by no means agreed as to the immediate application of their dearest, fundamental, principle ; by no means
clear that circumstances permitted the summoning of a
Constituent Assembly at this moment. They hesitated, and
their hesitation has been much criticised. Later experience [2]

---

[1] *The Memoirs of Raymond Poincaré*, 1914 (tr. Sir G. ARTHUR, London,
1926 ff.), 122.
[2] Of Feb. 1871.

showed that in emergency an Assembly could be obtained within eight days, and M. Lamy pointed out that if elections had been decreed on September 4 they could have provided the country with a "legal Government" by Sunday 11th.[1] But such inhuman enthusiasm for legality was impossible, and the reasons for hesitation were natural and weighty. Seven departments were already invaded, the enemy threatened Paris, and the whole situation confronting the new rulers was menacing and obscure. While the Liberal Picard would have the immediate application of the principle, the realist Gambetta maintained that such elections would be " an abdication of the Government of National Defence and dangerous under the present circumstances ".[2] It was evident that, apart from the practical difficulties in the way of a free and universal exercise of universal suffrage in an invaded country, the holding of elections so important as constituent elections at such a moment would be far more likely to hinder than to help the preparations for military defence. But besides this, there was another reason for hesitation still more powerful. Would the elections give Republican results ? If they could be certain of this, said Garnier-Pagès, they would hesitate no longer. But there was no such certainty. Whereas Crémieux believed that the Assembly would be " detestable " and Simon thought that all the profit of elections would go to the Orleanists, Favre was confident that they would strengthen the Government and prove the salvation of the Republic ; and he reminded Gambetta that he, too, had desired the continuance of the Legislative Body ; he should, therefore, be all the more desirous of a National Assembly.[3] But Gambetta

[1] *Revue des deux Mondes*, June, 1896.
[2] PICARD, *Dép.* I, 479 ; DRÉO, *Procès-verbaux*, 91.
[3] Ibid. 91.

had adopted the standpoint of one of the Government's first proclamations, in which it declared that it was only a temporary power : " It has only one object—to defend the nation against the invasion of the foreigner. After that we make a solemn engagement that it will disappear." [1] This was a declaration in favour of universal suffrage, yes, but not until the object had been achieved ; and so now " M. Gambetta observes that the Government is not a political Government but a power charged with the defence. It is not a Republican Government; it is entrusted with a mandate for a defence which cannot be deserted." The argument did not remove the objection that this mandate had been entrusted to the Government merely by the plaudits of a Parisian crowd, and therefore required wider and more constitutional ratification, and the declaration that the Government was not a Republican Government came strangely from the lips of Picard's rival. But it was the argument of a realist, and of an optimist who did not fear responsibility and had the courage to accept a revolutionary situation. Patriot as well as partisan, Gambetta thought elections inexpedient from either point of view, and his attitude also suggests that already he saw much greater possibilities in the defence than did the majority of his colleagues.

The decision arrived at appears to have been a compromise. Elections were to be held, but the date fixed for them by decree of September 9 was remote at a time when events had been marching with dramatic swiftness. Sunday, October 16, was nearly six weeks ahead and, despite the official motive of the election decree, which was : " to oppose to the invader a whole people, ready, organised and represented, an Assembly which will carry the living soul of

[1] Cp. J. CLARETIE, *Histoire de la Révolution de 1870-71*, 244.

the *patrie* to all parts and in spite of all disasters," [1] more than one member of the Government expected that the fate of Paris and of France would by then have been decided, and that the Assembly would be concerned with the organisation not of war but of peace.[2] By its decision the Council virtually adjourned the settlement of a difficult question in order that time might clear away some of its uncertainties. Probably, too, the remoteness of the date had its reasons of Republican expediency; it would give Republican candidates the opportunity to nurse their constituencies and the new Republican authorities time in which to propagate Republican ideas and to extend Republican influence.

Nevertheless, there were doubts whether time and propaganda alone would be adequate to counter the forces of reaction. Under the Empire the mayors had played an important part in determining the elections to the Legislative Body. The mayors now in office had been elected early in August.[3] The great majority of them was supposed to be Bonapartist in sympathy, and the Government feared that, as in the past, they would continue to use their influence in favour of Bonapartist candidates. The resurrection of the old Legislative Body in the guise of the new Constituent Assembly would be calamitous. Republican municipalities thus seemed necessary for the production of an Assembly. Were not municipal elections an essential preliminary to constituent elections?

So Gambetta came to think. Already he had been prompt to outline a Republican policy by which his prefects were to be guided in their dealings with municipalities. The initiative of local democrats was to be encouraged, but

[1] Cit. *Rapport* DARU, 533.

[2] Cp. J. FAVRE, *Gouvernement de la défense nationale*, I, 227.

[3] Municipal elections had been held on Aug. 6 and 7 in all towns of more than 2500 inhabitants except Paris and Lyons.

reactionary mayors were to be revoked, " as a means of
influencing " the municipal councils, and, if councils refused
to be thus influenced, they were to be suspended and replaced by "provisional" committees.[1]   At first he had suggested that the existing municipalities should be tolerated
as far as possible ; but soon he gave rein to the reforming
zeal of his administrators and, eager for the process of purification to be complete, stimulated the less zealous among
them to activity himself.[2]   This vigorous Republican policy
was enthusiastically approved by Crémieux, who telegraphed
from Tours on the 14th, that the municipal administrations
were " disastrous," and that the country had " absolute
need of regeneration ".[3]   Gambetta agreed, and while he
welcomed Simon's proposal of the 15th that municipal
elections should be held as soon as possible " in order to
avert the hostile pressure of the municipal councils elected
by the care of the fallen Government," [4] he urged the
prefects to hurry on the formation of provisional councils
so as to be " ready to proceed to the enfranchisement of
universal suffrage in the double elections which are preparing ".[5]   He was determined to be thorough, and to take
no risks : if Republican municipalities were a necessary
preliminary to a Republican Assembly provisional municipal councils were a necessary preliminary to Republican
municipalities.   But what was remarkable was that on the
16th he, Gambetta, proposed not only that municipal
elections should precede the others, but also that the date of
the constituent elections should be advanced by a fortnight
to October 2.[6]

Such a proposal coming from Gambetta seemed to mark

[1] *D.T.* II, 319.
[2] Cp. e.g. *D.T.* II, 234 ; II, 233, to pref. Finistère ; 240, to pref. Cher.
[3] *D.T.* II, 234.   [4] Dréo, *Procès-verbaux*, 124.
[5] *D.T.* II, 238 ; Sept. 16.   [6] Dréo, op. cit. 128.

a complete change in his attitude. Rather it was another instance of his realist outlook and of the readiness with which he adapted himself to circumstances. The Government had decided to hold elections despite Gambetta's opposition, and the decision of the majority was binding upon all.[1] It only remained, then, to execute the decision in the way which would be most advantageous, and advantage might be had abroad as well as at home. Gambetta appears to have been impressed by an official Prussian *communiqué* to an Amiens paper which declared that the Prussian Government would refuse to treat with the Government of National Defence, because it represented nothing more than a fraction of the former Opposition in the Legislative Body. He read it to his colleagues in the Council, and Picard at once seized upon it as a new argument for advancing the date of the constituent elections. For once the two rivals were in agreement ; it was Gambetta who thereupon proposed the earlier date, and the proposal was adopted.[2] There were other reasons of foreign policy, too, which, he must have known,[3] made early elections strongly desirable. The Great Powers of Europe still held aloof, and made it clear that they would give the Government of National Defence no recognition until it had received the sanction of a popular vote.[4] M. Thiers, despite his advice to fellow-deputies to remain in dignified retirement, had consented to emerge himself, and to plead the cause of his unhappy country at the Courts of

---

[1] FOURICHON, *Dép*. I, 639.

[2] DRÉO, op. cit. 128 ; cp. BUSCH, *Count Bismarck, Some Secret Pages of his History*, I, 172, for a similar *communiqué* in a Reims paper.

[3] Cp. *D.T.* II, 242, to pref. of Saône et Loire.

[4] The U.S.A., Spain, Switzerland, and Italy had been the only countries to recognise the new Republic, three of them actuated chiefly by the fraternal feeling of Republicans for Republicans in a world in which Republics were still a minority.

these same Great Powers, but the success of his mission was likely to depend quite as much upon the moderation of the Government of Paris and the good impression made by its conduct, as upon his own considerable eloquence and diplomatic skill ; and the best proof the Government could give of its good intentions would be to hasten the elections for a regular Constituent Assembly. Favre was not slow to point out the significance of the new electoral decree, which was published on the 17th : " It is objected that the Government she (France) has given herself is without regular powers to represent her. We recognise this loyally ; that is why we are summoning a freely elected Assembly at once," —and then followed the inevitable flight of rhetoric—" We assume no other privilege than that of giving our hearts and blood to our country and of surrendering ourselves to its sovereign judgment."

This was all very well, but in deciding that municipal elections should precede the elections for a Constituent Gambetta and his colleagues had reckoned without the prefects and without the newly created Delegation at Tours. Crémieux's appeal for regeneration was not an appeal for regeneration by constitutional means. Republican prefects preferred the surer and simpler methods of abolition or renewal at their own discretion. Gambetta had encouraged them ; his instructions for the creation of provisional municipalities had been repeated and unmistakable, and they had been, for the most part, diligently executed. Now the provisional was to be so provisional that the work had scarcely been completed before it was to be undone. Whereas the change in the date of the constituent elections caused little criticism, the decree fixing municipal elections for September 25 raised a veritable outcry : " What ? " exclaimed Bertholon, prefect of the Loire, " The elections are to be sooner. . . . That means compromising the Republic. You will have Bonapartist municipalities, a Bonapartist Constituent, and finally civil war," [1] and from the Nord Testelin telegraphed despairingly : " Your decree concerning municipal elections is our ruin ! You will see all the former Ministers and members of the majority return at the head of the list." [2] These are but specimen bars of a whole chorus of prefectorial protest (ample confirmation of the opinion expressed by Metternich on September 26, and by George Sand shortly afterwards : " The great mass of the people is not Republican " [3]), which spread perturbation and dismay at Tours. The Delegation sent urgent appeals to Gambetta to cancel this decree. " My friend," cried Crémieux, " the elections of September 25 are exciting an inexpressible stupor and desolation in the majority of the departments. Materially impossible and dangerous—that is the cry which is almost universal ; perilous, and destructive of our situation—that is in all my despatches. Reflect, my dear friend, that through lack of preparation our dear country ever since this odious war began has been cast into the abyss. Since we are unprepared, why deliver this terrible battle in the interior ? I can understand October 2, but do not let it be preceded by municipal elections." [4] But Gambetta heard his former patron's pathetic plea unmoved, and his brief reply admitted no further argument : " The measure taken by the Government in council is irrevocable." [5]

The Delegation was thus compelled to obedience, but it found a solution which had the advantage of being both simple and Republican. On the 20th, after the investment

[1] *D.T.* I, 378.   [2] *D.T.* I, 490.
[3] *H.H.u.S.A.* ; G. SAND, *Journal d'un voyageur pendant la guerre*, 97.
[4] *D.T.* II, 245 ; cp. *D.T.* II, 243, appeals from other members of the Delegation.
[5] *D.T.* II, 245.

of Paris had been completed, it issued a decree dissolving
the existing municipal councils and authorising prefects to
appoint the members of the electoral bureaux. Thus the
elections would be held under the best auspices. The decree
met with general approval, although there were still many
prefects who would have preferred the postponement of
the municipal elections until after the elections to the
Assembly. The Delegation would have been only too glad
to gratify them could it have found an adequate pretext.
Unexpectedly, the pretext was to be provided by Bismarck,
and by the very Government of Paris whose decision
Gambetta had so confidently declared to be irrevocable.

" Every consideration seemed to me to be inferior to the
duty of risking all in order to spare Paris the horrors of a
siege," [1] wrote Jules Favre, in explanation of his interviews
with Bismarck at Ferrières on September 19-20, when he
attempted to negotiate an armistice which would facilitate
the elections. His opinion was shared neither by his
colleagues nor by the general public, who held that Paris
was now bound in honour to resist, and that a French
initiative in negotiation would be interpreted as a sign of
weakness. Nevertheless, though his mission met with little
sympathy and ended in failure, it was of the greatest
importance, for its effect was to clear the air, to stiffen
French resistance, and radically to alter internal policy.
The immediate reaction of the Government in Paris to
Bismarck's harsh terms was to adjourn the constituent
elections indefinitely. The armistice terms were impossible,
while elections without an armistice, if not impossible, would
be unsatisfactory, and perhaps merely an embarrassment
when the Government itself was impotent in a besieged city.
The " socialistic crowd," as Bismarck had contemptuously

[1] J. FAVRE, *Gouvernement de la défense nationale*, I, 131.

called that Government,[1] accepted his challenge. Now there was to be no doubt that it intended to make the defence its one preoccupation, and as fresh evidence of its determination, municipal elections in Paris were also indefinitely adjourned. War was the only alternative to humiliation. Paris must steel itself to siege and hardship, and struggle its utmost to fulfil Favre's rash boast.

The Delegation rejoiced at this resolution. It hailed the postponement of constituent elections as " excellent," and in the adjournment of municipal elections in Paris found its pretext, promptly seized, to adjourn them in the provinces.[2] Prefects were to provide for the situation by " the maintenance of the existing municipalities or by the nomination of provisional municipalities," and reports which reached the Ministry of the Interior from nearly every department on the 29th showed that in spite of great variety of method and procedure, a large number of the municipal councils of France had already been purged of reactionaries according to Gambetta's desire, and brought into harmony of spirit with their patriotic Republican rulers.[3] A first important stage in the foundation of Gambetta's Republic was nearly complete.

The Delegation had seized its opportunity, and acted with impunity, but its rejoicing was short-lived. Any pleasure its members had felt at their unexpected power and independence soon gave way to depression and the consciousness of their own inadequacy to meet a situation

---

[1] BISMARCK, *Briefe an seine Gattin aus dem Kriege 1870/71* (Stuttgart, 1903). Letter to Herbert Bismarck, Sept. 7.

[2] Cp. J. SIMON, *Souvenirs du 4 septembre*, II, 50-53.

[3] Cp. *D.T.* II, 147, statistics for Var, and *Rapport* BOREAU-LAJANADIE, 285-291 (*Actes de la Délégation*). The extent of the purge seems to have varied very considerably. In some departments, e.g. Rhône, Var, Vaucluse, all or most of the mayors were changed ; in others, e.g. Ille et Vilaine, Basses-Pyrénées, Sarthe, none or very few were displaced.

which seemed desperate. The old Jewish lawyer Crémieux, the old parliamentary wit Glais-Bizoin, and the elderly, obscure, routine-loving admiral Fourichon, were no men to stir a country to enthusiasm ; the high-sounding proclamations in which they sought to echo the fiery calls to action of the great Revolutionaries were merely ludicrous.[1] While the Council at Tours was itself in confusion and divided by " stupid intestine quarrels," [2] ill news succeeded ill news ; the fall of Strasbourg followed the fall of Toul ; the Bavarians advanced towards the Loire ; Orléans was evacuated, and Tours itself seemed to be in danger ; conflicts between prefects and generals multiplied and grew more acute ; southern cities were in disorder and the organisation of the Ligue du Midi seemed to be a real menace to the authority of the Central Government.   If the severance of cable communication with Paris increased the independence of the Delegates, it also added to the burden of their responsibilities, and this became greater than they could bear. Overwhelmed by the accumulation of difficulties, the men who had greeted the Parisian decree of September 4 as " excellent " reversed it no more than a week later, and on October 1 themselves decreed constituent elections on the grounds of " a general demand of the departments " and of " unavoidable necessity ".   Their authority must be reinforced, and a National Assembly now seemed to be the only possible source of fresh strength.   " Elections," Laurier frankly explained to Delpech, the prefect at Marseilles, " are for us the principal element of national defence.   Through

---

[1] Cp. letter of Duc d'Audiffret-Pasquier written early in October and quoted by G. Hanotaux (*Le Gouvernement de M. Thiers*, I, 30, n.) in which he refers to " this grotesque duet of old women, Crémieux and Glais-Bizoin . . . old Republican ' babys ' (*sic*) in their second childhood opposing the Prussian hordes ".

[2] *D.T.* II, 257.

them we shall acquire the authority we lack and we shall be able to say that we represent something sacred. . . . Without a Constituent we shall never be able to inspire France with the energy she needs. Remember that the greatest national effort in our history was made by the Convention." Dufraisse, another of Gambetta's friends, was of the same opinion, and the aloof Jules Grévy gave his benediction to the new policy of Tours.[1] It seemed that there was nothing to prevent the execution of the Delegation's wisest decision, and that universal suffrage was to be allowed to exercise its sovereignty at last.

But the wise decision was unwisely announced before Paris was consulted. The Delegates forgot that they were only Delegates, or perhaps, feeling certain of Parisian condemnation, they relied on the success of a *fait accompli*, since the isolation of Paris was so complete. But Gambetta, used to manœuvre thus himself, would not consent that others should manœuvre thus in his despite. He brought the news to the Council that same evening of October 1, and found it easy to rouse the indignation of his colleagues in Paris at the insubordination of their colleagues at Tours. The " general demand " of the provinces for elections was suspect as a pacifist conspiracy, and he had no difficulty in persuading the Government to approve a decree vetoing these elections and declaring that any which were held should be null and void. They must be prevented at all costs ; a man of energy, he urged, should be sent to Tours. Thereupon Arago suggested that Gambetta himself should be the man ; but Ferry proposed Kératry. The only decision taken that evening was negative ; if anyone went it should not be Kératry.[2] However, Gambetta's

[1] Al. GLAIS-BIZOIN, *Dictature de cinq mois*, 250.
[2] DRÉO, *Procès-verbaux*, 172 ; J. SIMON, *Souvenirs du 4 septembre*, II, 58, says that Gambetta peremptorily refused.

suggestion had fallen upon fruitful soil. It would not be enough to send the decree of veto to Tours like any ordinary official despatch : it was necessary not only to ensure its enforcement but to strengthen the Delegation and to guard against any future backsliding, and on the 3rd Favre proposed that a member of the Government should proceed to Tours by the next big balloon in order to put an end to the "mysterious conduct of the Delegation".[1] This time, Trochu and Simon urged that Favre himself should be the envoy. But, noted Dréo in his corner, "M. J. Favre declines this mission, which he judges to be little in harmony with his character or his aptitudes". In other words, he thought Gambetta much more suitable ; as Minister of the Interior he was far better acquainted with the prefects ; moreover, "his youth, his popularity, and his enthusiasm were also precious elements for the success of his mission".[2] Of these last reasons which pointed to the choice of Gambetta, the first and least political was not the least cogent.[3] Flying was not yet a commonplace of ministerial travel, and the necessity of passing over country in enemy occupation made the proposed journey an adventure all the more perilous. It was felt that a young man of 32 would be better able to support its dangers than a veteran of 61. Crémieux and Glais-Bizoin had been sent to Tours on account of their age ; now the extremes were about to join hands, for Gambetta's qualification was youth.

His opportunity had come and, though Favre stated that it was only with the greatest difficulty that he could be persuaded to undertake the mission,[4] it is hard to believe

---

[1] DRÉO, *Procès-verbaux*, 180. "What are the youngest members of the Government of National Defence doing at Paris ?" asked *Le Siècle* on this day, Oct. 3. "Why do they not cross the German lines by balloon ?"

[2] J. FAVRE, *Gouvernement de la défense nationale*, I, 260.

[3] TROCHU, *Dép.* I, 284.   [4] J. FAVRE, *Dép.* I, 336.

that he did not realise it and rejoice, and that his reluctance was not more formal than profound.   For it was Gambetta who, on September 15, had urged the formation of a strong Government at Tours, Gambetta who, on October 1, had proposed that a " man of energy " should be sent to join the Delegation.   Did he not feel himself to be that man ?   Was not his ambition stirred by the prospect of a much wider scope for his great activity and had he no pleasure at the idea of escaping the immediate control of jealous colleagues and the inconvenient pressure of former constituents ?   A letter to Magnin, quoted by Deschanel, shows that he had seriously considered departure for the provinces even before the investment of Paris had begun.[1]   There were many reasons why he as Minister of the Interior should desire it, and his experience of the siege and of the difficulties of communicating with the departments can only have served to strengthen them.   For once one of his own later statements : " I took up my original idea which had been to go to the provinces to try and organise the national defence " [2]—was not an entire misrepresentation.   A show of resistance to the entreaties of his colleagues was doubtless all the easier when there were no other candidates eager to undertake a journey so hazardous.   But once he had accepted, he was full of optimism, and already saw himself triumphant at the head of a nation in arms.   " I shall return with an army," he told Favre, " and if I have the glory of delivering Paris I shall ask nothing more of destiny." [3]   1870 was to have its Danton. The Delegation had called the representatives of the whole nation to their aid : the call was stifled, and there came instead a single man to be their master.

---

[1] P. Deschanel, Gambetta, 58.
[2] Dép. I, 548 ; Picard, Dép. I, 488.   [3] J. Favre, Dép. I, 336.

VIII

GAMBETTA AT TOURS

WIND and weather were belligerents of high importance during the siege of Paris, for not only did they seriously affect the course of operations on more than one occasion, but they also exercised a constant and vital control upon the communications between the besieged city and the outside world. The decision to send Gambetta to Tours had been reached on October 3, and the powers with which he was to be invested determined on the 4th, but it was not until the 7th that a favourable wind and the disappearance of fog allowed him to depart in company with his friend, Eugène Spuller, who was to be his personal secretary and constant companion at Tours and Bordeaux.

Although it was more than eighty years since de Rozier had made the first ascent in a balloon,[1] no Minister of any state had ever been known to entrust himself to the trackless paths of the air, not even for a brief trial flight. Now, in dramatic circumstances, it was Gambetta's lot to be the pioneer. Upon his aerial voyage, upon his successfnl passage of the German lines, upon his braving the risks of forced descent and capture, depended the policy of a government and the fate of a nation. He flew of necessity, not of choice; but there could have been no more fitting or spectacular introduction to the most spectacular period of a

[1] In 1783.

remarkable career than this flight from Paris on October 7. The journey was adventurous and full of incident—Gambetta's hand was grazed by a bullet—and it well illustrated the uncertainty of such means of travel; Tours was Gambetta's destination, but the balloon came down in the Forest of Epineuse, not far from Amiens.

It was with mixed feelings, however, that the news of Gambetta's arrival at Amiens was received by the official world at Tours. " It is my deposition ! " Crémieux had exclaimed when he learnt that Glais-Bizoin and Fourichon were to join him as delegates of the Government at Paris.[1] Now he and they together might have cried, " It is our deposition ! " when a telegram brought the news that the Minister of the Interior was on his way to Tours. " Fatal balloon ! " thought Glais-Bizoin, when he heard that it carried the decree cancelling the elections,[2] and Lord Lyons regretted that it had not capsized on the way, not because of any personal antipathy to Gambetta, but because he rightly saw that his coming must mean the prolongation of the war.[3] The first instinct of the Delegation was to resist, and to uphold the authority of their own decree, but second thoughts made them less bold to oppose the Government from which they had received their powers, and the appearance of Gambetta himself soon put an end to doubts and hesitations and ideas of rebellion.[4] He was inflexible, and the arguments of his old friend Laurier and of others best acquainted with opinion in the provinces were of no avail. Once again Paris that was France asserted its will ; the Delegation bowed before it, withdrew their decree of October 1, and elections everywhere were now indefinitely

---

[1] Al. GLAIS-BIZOIN, *Dictature de cinq mois*, 31.   [2] Ibid. 84.
[3] NEWTON, *Life of Lord Lyons*, I, 325.
[4] Cp. Appendix VII, p. 297.

postponed. Gambetta had come to cancel the elections, and by his coming was himself one of the arguments in favour of cancellation. Ten days before, Crémieux had declared that the demand for elections was general, but now their cancellation was not followed by any general protest. For the Republicans, who had been most conscious of the Delegation's sad inadequacy, and therefore most anxious for an Assembly, now saw that the situation was wholly changed. " The general desire is for something more," Metternich had reported on September 26, " people would like to see one man of energy and talent take the destinies of the country into his own hand." [1] Gambetta came, and the man of energy was recognised at once. The department of Var realised that " a Constituent is useless since the young men are in power," [2] and in the neighbouring Gard " this virile resolution was welcomed with real enthusiasm ".[3] Only from Dordogne came a protest against the spirit of irresolution revealed by a second change of policy.[4] The prefect had not immediately understood that the change was now a resolution to end irresolution, and that the Paris decree meant the close of a period of doubt and vacillation. But Republicans in general took heart again, felt that Gambetta was as good as or better than an Assembly could be, and believed that he could not have too much power if he showed himself capable of wielding it with energy and effect.[5] He himself reported confidently to Favre that the departments were unanimous in their condemnation of elections ; the war was now their one sole preoccupation.[6]

The revocation of the Tours decree of October 1, however, was the least of Gambetta's tasks, though it was the

---

[1] *H.H.u.S.A.*   [2] *D.T.* II, 133.
[3] *D.T.* II, 188.   [4] *D.T.* I, 246.
[5] Cp. *D.T.*, from the departments, Oct. 9 and following days.
[6] J. FAVRE, *Gouvernement de la défense nationale*, I, 284.

" The Cactus "

CREMIEUX

Alfred Le Petit: *Fleurs, fruits et légumes du jour, 1871)*

most immediate and the primary occasion of his coming. That decree had roused the Paris Government to a tardy realisation of the need for " a real and strong " Government in the provinces. They had refused to allow Crémieux to enlist new members in the Delegation in the persons of Steenackers and Laurier.[1] They refused to allow the Delegates to derive new strength from the support of an Assembly. Paris decreed that the Government of France must remain as Parisian as on September 4, even when Paris itself was besieged and isolated from the rest of France. So now when at last they understood that it was necessary to strengthen the Government of the France outside Paris, Gambetta was their obvious and their only possible instrument. Not only would he himself as a " man of energy " be a powerful reinforcement, but he was given the express mission to secure the vigorous maintenance of Parisian policy ; and, to guard against the risk of any further insubordination on the part of the Delegation, it was agreed that he should have the casting vote if there was division in its Council. He was, in fact, properly invested with the authority, which, being what he was, he could not fail to exercise, whatever his official powers. The terms of his mission virtually made him supreme in the Delegation, as Admiral Fourichon at once saw.[2] The first meeting of Gambetta with his fellow-delegates required the use of tact as well as of authority. No sooner had he communicated the wider object of his mission and the special powers which had been given him, than the Admiral rose and announced his resignation.[3] " I saw the dawn of dictatorship," he later explained ; but the whole Council, including Gambetta, was urgent in dissuading

---

[1] Cp. *D.T.* II, 257, tel. of Sept. 25 ff. Laurier was head of the Ministry of the Interior at Tours, Steenackers director of telegraphic services.

[2] For the text see Appendix VIII, p. 299.

[3] FOURICHON, *Dép.* I, 636.

him from this resolution.[1] He reflected, and yielded to
their entreaties, and the solidarity of the Delegation remained
apparently intact.   There is no reason to doubt that
Gambetta was as sincere as his colleagues in wishing
Fourichon to continue in the Delegation.   He intended his
arrival at Tours to create a wave of confidence throughout
the country, and a resignation so obviously the consequence
of his coming would certainly deprive it of half its force.
To provoke the retirement of a fellow-delegate was no way
to " maintain unity of action ".

The incident showed, however, the impression made by
the terms of his mission.   The possession of a casting vote
gave him a dominant position in the Council of Government
at Tours.   His ascendancy was soon to become still greater.
A few days before his arrival, Fourichon had, for the second
time, resigned the Ministry of War (October 3), and this
time the resignation was final.   His tenure of the office had
been marked by a constant struggle against the Republican
pretensions to subordinate the military to the civil authorities,
a struggle in which his efforts had often been frustrated
by his colleagues themselves.   The most pressing entreaties
could not induce him to resume the post, and Crémieux
had temporarily added it to his many other interim Ministries.
Crémieux was the titular, but the duties had mostly been
performed by Glais-Bizoin, who for three days had had
the doubtful aid of an ephemeral War Committee.   The
obvious successor to Fourichon, General Lefort, the principal
delegate from the Ministry of War in Paris, had resolutely
declined the office.   The situation was clearly unsatisfactory,
as the septuagenarian Ministers themselves admitted.[2]   Still

---

[1] Gambetta had brought with him a letter of introduction to the Admiral,
the only one of his colleagues with whom he was not previously acquainted.
[2] FREYCINET, Souvenirs, I, 120 ff.

more clearly did Gambetta perceive its disadvantages, and at the same time his own opportunity. His mission as interpreter of the policy of the Government at Paris was to unite and invigorate the elements of national defence by every means in his power.[1]   He, as Minister of the Interior, with control over National Guards and Gardes Mobiles, as well as over all the prefects and departmental administration, was the most powerful civil authority, and believed as strongly as any of his colleagues in the subordination of military to civilian authority.   The efficiency of the defence had been impaired because of rivalry between the two, and as a result of that rivalry, the Ministry of War was now vacant.   It was essential, both that the rivalry should cease, and that the vacancy should be promptly filled, and filled by a man of energy.   For such a state of affairs there was an obvious solution, and Gambetta, self-confident as ever, did not hesitate to propound it (after he had tactfully offered the post once more to Fourichon and Lefort, the men most certain to refuse it) ; it was simply that he should be Minister of War himself.   However slight his military knowledge, he, the amateur, had the courage to step in where professionals feared to tread.   At least he would show energy in the new duties he proposed to assume, and of energy and enthusiasm great deeds might be born.   Even Danton had never had such an opportunity for complete control : was Gambetta to let it slip when France was crying aloud for a strong man and a saviour ?   Who but he was strong at this moment, and who but he dared aspire to be the saviour or even hope for salvation ?   Oddly enough, while Crémieux and Glais-Bizoin, still nursing resentment against the occupant of the " fatal balloon " strongly opposed his solution, it was Fourichon, the man who had wished to resign because he

[1] J. FAVRE, *Dép.* I, 338.

saw dictatorship dawning, who made its adoption possible.[1]
By the union of civil and military powers in one hand there
might be a last hope of ending their continual conflict ; and,
however that might be, the hand of Gambetta would be less
infirm than that of Crémieux. The Admiral's unexpected
support of Gambetta's proposal was decisive for the consummation of Gambetta's power, and Crémieux and Glais-
Bizoin, neither daring nor wishful to protest by resignation,
bowed before the possessor of the casting vote.[2]

Thus Gambetta's supremacy was sealed. The Minister
of the Interior became Minister of War as well, and within
forty-eight hours of his arrival at Tours had virtually concentrated all power in his own hands. On the evening of
the 10th he despatched a circular to his prefects. " By
decree of the Delegation of the Government of National
Defence established at Tours, drafted on the initiative of
M. Crémieux, and in view of the instructions of the Government of Paris, M. Léon Gambetta, Minister of the Interior,
has taken over the Ministry of War which M. Crémieux had
held since the resignation of Admiral Fourichon." [3] It was
an excellent example of his methods. The skilful administrator conceals every hint of division or of weakness in
governing circles ; he is concerned with the effect rather
than with the truth of his *communiqués*, and so here
Gambetta. If Crémieux was surprised to read of his own
initiative, his surprise was nothing in comparison with the
amazement of the Government at Paris at the result of their
" instructions ".[4] There had been a lengthy discussion as

---

[1] FOURICHON, *Dép.* I, 628.

[2] It is not clear whether the question was actually put to the vote. GLAIS-
BIZOIN (*Dictature de cinq mois*, 86) implies that it was, and that Gambetta used
his casting vote in his own favour. But Gambetta formally denied this (*Dép.*
I, 553).

[3] *D.T.* II, 271.

[4] J. FAVRE, *Gouvernement de la défense nationale*, II, 98 ; TROCHU, *Dép.* I, 284.

to what military powers Gambetta should have on his mission of stimulating the defence,[1] and one of the final sentences of the "instructions"—"So far as concerns military organisation and action, the decisions taken by the Delegation will be executed by the Minister of War and of Marine" [2]—might seem expressly intended to preserve the War Office from the encroachments of the Interior. But the instructions applied to a situation which no longer existed. When Gambetta left Paris, the Government knew nothing of Fourichon's resignation ; ignorant of the problem which had arisen, they could not provide for its solution, though when they learnt that Tours had found its own solution their surprise was comprehensible and also their annoyance. Once again the Delegation appeared to have forgotten that they were only a Delegation (for Fourichon had held the War Ministry as the Delegate of Le Flô and he at least should have been consulted about the appointment of a successor). Once again Gambetta had confronted his colleagues with a *fait accompli,* and once again they were compelled to accept it. A solution, however, had been urgent, and the uncertainty of communications was a strong reason for not delaying to consult the Government of Paris, which was now of all French authorities the least able to judge of the needs of the provinces. If Gambetta's assumption of the Ministry of War was far from being in accordance with the letter of his instructions, he might claim that it was a very realistic interpretation of their spirit, and that he would now still better be able to give the national defence in the provinces that vigorous impulse and unity of control which it was his mission to supply. He was ambitious, and he had seized his opportunity, but there is no reason to doubt that in doing so he believed he was serving the best

[1] DRÉO, *Procès-verbaux,* 181.   [2] See Appendix VIII, p. 299.

interests of his country : for he was possessed of a splendid self-confidence, and that at this moment was a most rare and precious quality.

Nevertheless, Le Flô and his colleagues might pertinently wonder what were the new Minister of War's special qualifications for his post. Inquiry into the past could throw little light : [1] the next four months were to give the answer.

[1] See Appendix IX, p. 301.

IX

GAMBETTA, MINISTER OF WAR

" THE Republic was victorious over the invasion of 1792. The Republic is proclaimed." In these few words of the Government of National Defence's first proclamation lay the key to their [1] notions of the conduct of war. For they did not appeal to the memories of 1792 merely as a means of raising popular morale and stimulating popular enthusiasm ; they firmly believed that the methods which had saved the country in 1792 might also be used with effect against the very different enemy of 1870. Moreover, while they constantly spoke of the great deeds of 1792, they did, in fact, see the events of that year only through a Republican haze ; they knew them not by critical historical study, but by enthusiastic Republican legend, which had simplified the tale of the repulse of the invader greatly to Republican advantage. So for them the victory of 1792 was the victory of the free citizen over the hirelings of tyrants. It demonstrated the superiority of civilians to professional soldiers. It was a triumph of amateur improvisation expressed in the *levée en masse*, in the rising of a whole nation to hurl itself upon the invader in a frenzy of patriotic and democratic enthusiasm. This belief in the virtue of a citizen army accorded with the prevailing Republican distrust of the professional soldier, of the standing army. A citizen army,

[1] Except Trochu.

invincible at home, incapable of carrying war abroad—that was the ideal which had been proclaimed by Jules Simon. The Republican legend of 1792 was quite consistent, therefore, with a Republican philosophy which was anti-militarist, pacifist, internationalist and humanitarian in essence. Now, in 1870, not only was there a remarkable parallel to 1792 in the general situation, but the disasters of the first phase of the war seemed all the more to favour the practice of Republican methods in the second; for to the less discerning Republicans those disasters were a proof that military knowledge was valueless, and that all generals were incapable as well as reactionary. The experts had been tried and found wanting; it was time for the amateur to take control.

And now at Tours the amateur was in control. The lawyer Gambetta was as much an amateur in military matters as the lawyer Danton, and he shared his colleagues' enthusiasm for the achievements of Danton and his contemporaries. The man whose principal military experience hitherto had been the precipitate arming of the citizens of Paris was virtually master of France, more supreme than ever Danton had been, and as eager as he to save a nation and drive out an invader. How did the Republican of 1870 propose to set about his tremendous task?

The chief simple ideas by which he was guided were revealed in the stirring proclamation to the " Citizens of the Departments " which he issued immediately after his arrival at Tours.[1] This was Gambetta's vigorous interpretation of the policy of Paris which it was his mission to execute, and it showed very clearly how strongly he was influenced by Republican tradition. It was an explanation of his own policy, and at the same time a good example of his methods. The ideas were not novel, but they had never been set forth

[1] Cit. J. CLARETIE, *Histoire de la révolution de 1870-71*, 304.

with such vigour and clarity. Paris was the heart of the
defence, the centre of all hopes and fears, the city which
had given France her Government and sent her Gambetta,
and accordingly a glowing account of the state of Paris and
of the courage and resolution of its defenders was Gambetta's
point of departure. But if the truth of his conclusion—
" Paris is impregnable ; it can neither be taken nor surprised "—had yet to be proved, it was none the less true that
the situation and efforts of the capital imposed very definite
obligations upon the citizens of the departments : of these
the first he declared to be to wage war to the knife, the
second—" to accept as a father's the commands of Republican authority which has sprung from necessity and from
right." In fact now, as in 1792, there was a political as
well as a military object to be achieved through the defence,
an object which Gambetta, as he went on to define more
clearly the nature of this Republican authority, denied
and affirmed in the same breath. In the single sentence
of definition lay the whole secret of his policy and of his conduct during the next four months. " This power could not
without forfeiting its title be used to profit any ambition ;
it has only one passion and only one title—to rescue France
from the abyss into which the monarchy has plunged it ;
once that has been achieved the Republic will be founded
and secure from conspirators and from reactionaries." The
second half of the sentence disclosed the ambition which the
first half denied, the ambition to found the Republic by
means of the defence and to transform what was admittedly
provisional into a permanent and unquestioned reality.
Thus the defence was not merely another stage in the
historic struggle between Gaul and Teuton ; it was inseparable from an internal problem of great moment, from
the constantly recurring problem of the form of government

in France. Now, as in 1792, the fate of the Republic seemed
to depend upon the success of the defence, and the regime
which in 1870 could repeat the miracles of 1792 and drive
the invader from the soil must be assured of a continued and
glorious existence. The very desperateness of the situation
offered certain advantages which Republicans were quick to
seize ; it gave them a redoubtable weapon with which to
beat an enemy whom many feared as much as the Prussian,
the loyal supporters of the House of Bonaparte, and it gave
them an opportunity to identify the Republic with the nation
more completely than could ever otherwise have been
possible. No one made more thorough use of these advantages than Gambetta. He seldom missed an opportunity to
discredit the fallen regime,[1] and in every public utterance
and proclamation he emphasised the unity of nation and
Republic. Thus the national defence was a convenient
cloak for Republican action, and a remarkable opportunity
for the Republican party to extend its influence and to
strengthen its hold upon the country. But to those who
were unable to appreciate the identification of the nation
with the Republic Gambetta's claim that the national
defence was his sole preoccupation not unnaturally seemed
a patent falsehood, a perfect illustration of his colleague
Rochefort's cynicism : " To govern is to lie ".

After thus demonstrating the disinterestedness of paternal
Republican authority, Gambetta concluded his proclamation
with an eloquent appeal to all the citizens of the departments.
" The Republic appeals for the aid of all citizens ; her
Government will consider it a duty to employ every brave
man and to make use of every talent. It is her tradition to

---

[1] E.g. in this proclamation when he said that the supplies of arms had all
been sent to " Sedan, Metz, and Strasbourg ; as though by a last criminal
stratagem the author of all our disasters wished in his fall to deprive us of
every means of repairing our ruin ".

arm young leaders ; we shall find them. . . . No, it is impossible that the genius of France should be veiled for ever, that the great nation should be deprived of its place in the world by an invasion of 500,000 men. Let us rise up, then, *en masse*, and die rather than undergo the humiliation of dismemberment. Through all our disasters and beneath the blows of ill fortune we still preserve the idea of French unity and the indivisibility of the Republic." To sum up, there was to be war to the knife under the conduct of Republican authorities, the " awakened populations " of the departments were to "worry, harass, and pursue" the invaders, young leaders were to be improvised, and the nation was to rise up *en masse* in defence of the indivisibility of the Republic. It was a simple Republican programme, and the source of its inspiration was clear.

The new Minister of War, however, was not to be dependent only upon the ideas of 1792, nor upon his own powers of improvisation for the conduct of the defence. Despite his quick intelligence, his remarkable powers of assimilation, and the speed with which he was able to master the complexities of an unfamiliar subject, it was, as he at once realised, impossible for him " to enter into the thousand details of a complicated and absorbing administration " such as the Ministry of War.[1] The same difficulty had faced Crémieux after the dissolution of the short-lived War Committee, and he had been on the point of solving it by the nomination of a deputy who would relieve him of the main burden of the office. Now Gambetta, in his turn, sought for a deputy, a man on whom he could rely, and who would " know his thoughts and be capable of putting them into execution ".[2] He found the man already designated by Crémieux, no military expert, but a little-known civil

[1] FREYCINET, *Souvenirs*, I, 126.   [2] Ibid.

engineer, Charles de Freycinet, a man whom he had only seen once before when, in strange circumstances, he had appointed him to be prefect of Tarn et Garonne. The engineer's prefectorial career had been short and inglorious. Once an official candidate for the departmental council, he was looked upon as a monstrous reactionary by a self-appointed departmental commission of true Republicans ; his prefecture had been invaded, and, yielding to pressure which was backed by force, he had resigned.[1]   He had then proceeded at once to Tours in the hope of finding some more congenial task, and had been attached to the Armaments Commission, of which part had been newly transferred from Paris.   Here he soon found scope for his critical faculties, and in conjunction with Jules Le Cesne, the President of the Commission, composed a memorandum in which he made suggestions for a thorough reform of the War Office.   Less than a month later, in circumstances which, according to his own account, were no less peculiar and dramatic than those of his nomination to the prefecture of Tarn et Garonne, he was appointed " Delegate of the Minister for the War Department, and charged with the direction of the services in his stead and within the limit to be traced for him by the Minister " :—a courtesy call and " the simple formality of leaving a card decided my destiny ".[2]   More probably, however, the factors which determined Gambetta's choice and Freycinet's destiny were the recommendations of Crémieux and of Steenackers [3] and perusal of Freycinet

[1] *D.T.* II, 120, 121 ; cp. FREYCINET, *Souvenirs*, I, 116, where he dismisses the unpleasing experience in one sentence.

[2] Ibid. I, 124, 125.

[3] Ibid. I, 130. It is odd, however, that Steenackers and Le Goff, in their history, make no mention of the part Steenackers apparently played in bringing Freycinet to Gambetta's notice, the more odd since Freycinet was one of the " finds " of his time, and became an important Republican personage. They merely say (II, 40) that Gambetta intuitively divined the man he needed.

and Le Cesne's memorandum on War Office reform,[1] for Gambetta was soon to give effect to many of its proposals. Perhaps, too, he was personally attracted and impressed by this man who, despite his consent to be Gambetta's *alter ego*, contrasted with him no less completely in temperament than in appearance.[2] "I well understand Gambetta's fondness for Trochu," wrote Madame Adam, ". . . Gambetta who is uneasy about his own temper and takes the greatest pains never to lose his self-control, has confidence in this general who is so correct, so well fitted for the daily round, one who would rather turn monk than take the devil aboard." [3] So, too, he could feel confidence in Freycinet, whose frigid, methodical, cautious, and calculating nature was not disguised by " smiling courtesy and exquisite manners ".[4]

Thus the civilians and the " young men "—Freycinet was not more than 42—were now in power at the War Office, and the work of reorganisation according to the new Delegate's plans began apace. Within three days of Gambetta's arrival the military element, which Fourichon had been sent especially to represent in the Council of Government, had been almost wholly superseded. After a brief experience of the new civil direction, General Lefort resigned, ostensibly on the grounds of ill-health, and Freycinet, relieved at the departure of an official whose adherence to military traditions and formalities he had so often criticised, moved from a small dark office into the spacious apartment vacated by the General. " Now," said Gambetta, " we can see the chief," and chief the Delegate was in fact.[5] " It is to him," later declared General Borel, " that we owe the improvisation of our armies ".[6] Gambetta

---

[1] P. Deschanel, *Gambetta*, 66.   [2] Freycinet, op. cit. I, 126.

[3] Mme Adam, *Mes illusions et nos souffrances pendant le siège de Paris*, 97.

[4] H. Pessard, *Mes petits papiers*, 108.

[5] Freycinet, op. cit. 133.   [6] *Dép.* III, 489.

gave his Delegate entire freedom to proceed with his plans of reorganisation, and bade him spare neither men nor money in the interests of the defence.[1] It was Freycinet who reformed the War Office, enlarging it and creating new departments to correspond with the " immense extension of the forces of the national defence," which was Gambetta's aim. It was Freycinet who was responsible for the most important measures for the organisation and training of the new levies. " When M. Gambetta was present either at Tours or at Bordeaux, I was accustomed to visit him at the prefecture . . . to inform him of the events of the day and to discuss important measures," he wrote later.[2] It was at the prefecture that Gambetta lived, and the Ministry of the Interior was still his immediate care. Of measures which Freycinet did not choose to consider important, the Minister of War, in whose name they were executed, might never be informed ;[3] when Gambetta was away Freycinet's control at the War Office was absolute and the Delegate sent the Minister as many orders as he received.[4] As Gambetta admitted later, he himself was rather " a will supplying an impetus " than a specialist in military matters.[5] The specialist, civilian though he was, " the real director of military affairs," as Trochu declared,[6] was Freycinet. But this by no means implied that Gambetta was a mere figurehead, or that he had assumed the Ministry of War only to abdicate. Far from it ; he remained the responsible Minister ; with him lay the ultimate decision in all questions of paramount

---

[1] FREYCINET, *Souvenirs*, I, 139.   [2] Ibid. 159.

[3] Cp. FOURICHON, *Dép.* I, 643.

[4] Cp. COLMAR V. DER GOLTZ, *Gambetta und seine Armeen*, 94 ; *D.T.* II, Nov. 22 ; to G.

[5] *Annales de l'Assemblée Nationale*, VI, annexe 59, cit. H. DUTRAIT-CROZON, 156.

[6] A. CHUQUET, *Le Général Chanzy*, 191.

importance and, as it happened, his decision was by no means invariably in accordance with the advice of his Delegate.[1]

Moreover, the existence of a " will " which could supply an impetus was all important in a country where apathy and defeatism reigned. The war had never roused much enthusiasm among the mass of the French peasantry, whose greatest interest was in the maintenance of peace and prosperity. The idea of the " Patrie " had been subordinated by Socialist and masonic bodies to that of universal brotherhood. The nation as a whole was comprehensibly appalled by the hopelessness of the military prospect after the great defeats of August and September. The forces of discouragement against which Gambetta had to contend were indeed immense. " The nation believed in its power, and has been mightily deceived, lulled to sleep as it was under a coverlet of prosperity and withered laurels," wrote Metternich to a friend at the end of September. " I assure you that the awakening is very interesting." [2] Still more interesting, and far more real and rapid, was he to find it now that the " Sleeping Beauty " had discovered her prince. Not only was a civilian and a young man now at the helm, but as an amateur in military matters he was possessed of a freshness of outlook and a broad-mindedness which were probably invaluable under the circumstances. He had come, he said, to remedy the vices of the situation " without taking account of difficulties and opposition, and to make up for lack of time by force of activity ".[3] In a short while he had agreed to a series of reforming decrees brought to him

---

[1] E.g. concerning the maintenance of Bourbaki.

[2] Sept. 26, private letter, cit. H. SALOMON, *L'ambassade de Richard de Metternich à Paris*, 276.

[3] Proclamation to the Citizens of the Departments, cit. J. CLARETIE, *Histoire de la Révolution de 1870-71*, 304.

by his Delegate, "which," said Freycinet, "probably no
military Minister would have signed ".[1]   He was bound by
no traditions of routine or respect for military hierarchy ;
he knew that an extraordinary situation demanded extraordinary efforts, and he was determined that those efforts
should be made and prepared to take risks in making them.
If the national defence in the provinces was to achieve anything, it could be only by swift action, action that could be
effectively felt before the fall of Paris irretrievably determined the country's fate.   Rapid organisation of the available resources was therefore essential, and this was what
Gambetta recognised.   It was very easy for critics to point
out the many defects of the new war machine, and lay them
to the charge of ignorant civilian control, but, too often,
they forgot to take account of the circumstances in which the
machine had to be constructed.   The problem of the national
defence could not be isolated from the general military and
political situation, and of this Gambetta, the politician newly
come from Paris, was probably as good a judge as any
soldier.   The question is not whether the new war machine
would not have been more efficient if it had been built up
under professional direction, but whether it would ever have
been built to any purpose without the energy and driving
power of civilians unhampered by military traditions.   And
this is very doubtful, in view of the conditions which prevailed in the War Office at Tours when Gambetta arrived,
and of the qualities and temper of the majority of the generals
then available.   The Ministry of Fourichon and Lefort was
merely a branch cut from the Ministry at Paris ; it had but
three departments instead of ten, and its personnel was no
more than a quarter the War Ministry's normal peace-time

[1] *Souvenirs*, I, 148.

strength.[1] Sudden change in routine did not make for increased efficiency, and it was hampered all the more by lack of archives and material which had been left in the capital, and upon which its smooth running depended. Even six weeks after Sedan there were still generals who had no maps by which to conduct their operations.[2] Such a state of affairs was no tribute either to the foresight of the Ministry at Paris, or to the initiative of the Ministry at Tours. Thus the War Office at Tours by its very nature was totally inadequate to meet the exceptional demands of a perilous situation and, although it was by no means inactive, and had organised an army corps and more by the time that Gambetta arrived, the organisers themselves had no belief in the possibility that the troops that they were raising could ever do more than worry the enemy and create minor diversions. Lefort, for example, stated later that he had not expected that the army of the Loire would be called upon to take any real part in military operations ; he had hastened its organisation because he thought that its existence might weigh in France's favour during the negotiations for peace.[3] Moreover, the generals who remained at the disposal of the Delegation were the oldest or least distinguished officers of their rank in the Imperial armies, men who for the most part resembled the colleagues whom Thiers had found on the Committee of Defence at the end of August—" veteran officers bound down by routine and attached to their slow regular habits. They are distressed and dazed if they are asked to hurry ".[4] When their more brilliant or more favoured comrades had met with such disaster in the field,

---

[1] *Revue d'Histoire ; La défense nationale en province ; Mesures générales d'organisation*, 13 ; FREYCINET, op. cit. I, 118.

[2] *Revue d'Histoire ;* FREYCINET, *Guerre en province*, 19 ff.   [3] *Dép.* III, 74.

[4] Cit. R. DREYFUS, *M. Thiers contre l'Empire, la Guerre et la Commune*, 119.

it would not have been surprising if they had had little
confidence in success, even at the head of well-trained troops ;
they could feel no confidence at all in the new levies which
were so hastily being raised.   Such men were incapable of
conceiving the kind of national crusade which was Gambetta's
ideal.   It was contrary to their temperament and contrary
to their traditions, and they could not inspire in others the
enthusiasm they so signally lacked themselves.

But, if the impetus of a civilian like Gambetta was under
the circumstances essential to any great effort of national
defence in the provinces, it was none the less true that
civilian direction was not by any means all sufficing ; they
were hampered in their organisation by that very lack of
outstanding military men which had enabled them so easily
to seize control, and handicapped by their own prejudices as
Republicans.   " There was a lack of military competence,"
said Freycinet, in criticism of the Tours War Committee,
of which he had been a member ; [1] and the same criticism
applied to the War Office after he had reorganised it,[2] and,
indeed, to the whole national defence in the provinces.   The
need for military competence to instruct and lead the new
levies was crying, and made itself felt all the more now that
Gambetta and Freycinet proposed to organise the defence on
a vastly extended scale.   " I have determined to quit the
usual paths," proclaimed the new Minister of War, in an
address to the army.   " I wish to give you young and active
chiefs capable by their intelligence and by their energy of
renewing the prodigies of 1792.   Therefore I have no hesitation in breaking with the old administrative traditions." [3]
The result had been a decree of October 14, which was

[1] *Souvenirs*, I, 122.

[2] *Revue d'Histoire ; La guerre de 1870-71 ; La défense nationale en province ;
Mesures d'organisation*, 77-90.

[3] *Dép. circ.*, etc., I, 46.

hailed by Republicans as " the announcement of a new military era and the pledge of a frankly Republican programme inspired by the traditions of 1792 ".[1]   It created an auxiliary army of all the forces not belonging to the regular army, and placed them on an equality with the regulars as regarded rank and pay.   At the same time, the ordinary rules of promotion were suspended in order to encourage youth and talent, and commands in the two armies were made interchangeable.   The Minister had appealed to the memories of 1792, the appeal which he and his countrymen best understood ; but the Delegate who was responsible for this decree had drawn his inspiration from the example of the American Civil War rather than from the precedents of French Revolution, and the creation of the auxiliary army, like the later establishment of regional training camps, was a conscious imitation of a measure adopted by the Northerners in the latest of " People's Wars ".[2]   But it had needed three years for the Northerners to produce great generals, and while Freycinet sought his model in America, he could not be certain of prolonging the war in France as much even as three months.   If the decree of October 14 produced a quantity of officers, it could not ensure quality, and sometimes led to the promotion of men who were wholly incompetent.[3]   Its disadvantages were soon clear, but the whole period of the war was too short to enable its full advantages to be reaped ; time and experience were necessary for the " young and active chiefs," whom Gambetta sought, to reveal and prove themselves.   In the meanwhile, he had to be content with the existing generals, men whose

---

[1] A. RIVIÈRE, *Trois mois de dictature en province*, 109.

[2] FREYCINET, op. cit. I, 149 ; cp. Appendix X, p. 303.

[3] Cp. A. CHUQUET, *Etudes d'histoire*, 8e série (Paris, 1905), 328 ; L. HALÉVY, *L'invasion*, 139.

aid was often of great value in training and organisation, but whose consciousness of the defects of the troops under their command inclined them all the more to a pessimism which the conduct of their civilian directors only served to strengthen. If it was a misfortune to have to command men who were raw and inexperienced, it was a calamity to have to obey them. Not only were the orders which issued from the War Office open to criticism and sometimes in-executable, but they ignored the rules and prejudices of hierarchy which have such an important place in the life of a permanent army. The union of military and civil authority in the hands of Gambetta by no means ended their conflict, but rather encouraged the pretensions of the civilians, while it increased the misgivings of the professionals. To these, indeed, the first dealings of the Minister himself with a provincial general must have seemed a bad omen.

General La Motte Rouge, who was in command of the 15th army corps, which was still in formation, had been ordered by the Delegation, on October 5, to transfer his headquarters from Bourges to Orléans. Here, two days after Gambetta's arrival at Tours, he was attacked by von der Tann's Bavarians. Before the engagement was over, Gambetta received a telegram from Cochery, a former deputy for Orléans, censuring the general's conduct, and im-plying that he had abandoned his troops, who were still resisting.[1] Gambetta needed no further proof, or more qualified appreciation of the battle ; he replied to Cochery the same evening : " I share your opinion about La Motte Rouge. He is replaced by General D'Aurelle de Paladines." This summary execution was no doubt the result partly of

---

[1] For a modern French military opinion on this engagement see Lt.-Col. GUIGUE in *Revue militaire française*, June, 1932, *Le Gouvernement de la défense nationale*.

vexation and partly of the desire to make an example, and to show that a new spirit of decision and energy now reigned at the War Office, but the reason Gambetta gave to Lefort, whom he requested to arraign La Motte Rouge before a court-martial, cannot have been reassuring : " It was I who sent him the order to advance and to be victorious ".[1] Later Gambetta wrote to Favre in praise of the " sound method " of the Prussians who deprived their generals of their commands as soon as they were defeated.[2] He had been quick to adopt the method himself, and its application in this first instance seemed to have a more than Prussian harshness when the question whether the orders he had given were executable was not allowed to be relevant.   But the evacuation of Orléans and the defeat of the first organised troops of the army of the Loire in their first serious encounter were, in fact, particularly unfortunate for Gambetta, because they occurred at the moment when he was most in need of success, when he had but just taken over the Ministry of War, and when success, however slight, would have been such a powerful reinforcement of his efforts to rouse widespread enthusiasm for the war.   Gambetta had to begin his career as Minister of War under the shadow of fresh defeat, and La Motte Rouge was the victim of his irritation.   But his sacrifice of a general to satisfy his resentment and propitiate public opinion did not reassure the professional soldiers as to the capacity or intentions of their new civilian chief.

[1] LEFORT, *Dép.* III, 76.   [2] *D.T.* II, 453.

X

RESOURCES AND THE MILITARY PROBLEM

" WHEN I arrived in the provinces," wrote Gambetta to
Jules Favre on November 26, 1870, " nothing existed, no
ammunition, no men, no officers, no artillery material, no
cavalry. . . . In forty-seven days I have created an army
of 150,000 men, perfectly organised, very well equipped,
and furnished with artillery and cavalry such as no army of
the Empire ever possessed." [1] A proud boast indeed, but
what was its truth ? and what of the letter which he wrote
a whole month before, on October 24, exactly a fortnight
after his assumption of the Ministry of War : " I have
supplied M. Thiers with positive information concerning the
position and state of our troops. . . . He has been able to
convince himself that an army of the Loire of 110,000 men,
well armed and well equipped really does exist ? " [2] Was
this the achievement of a fortnight, due entirely to Gambetta's
organising genius ? The exaggeration of the later despatch
was manifest ; as usual, he was not a reliable interpreter
of his own activities ; optimistic on the eve of his grand
offensive he was easily led to magnify what he himself
had done, and perhaps, too, there was a purpose in his

[1] *D.T.* II, 215—in another part of this despatch he referred to " this army
which on my arrival here counted scarce 18,000 men, disunited and lacking
in determination ".

[2] Cit. GLAIS-BIZOIN, *Dictature de cinq mois*, 37 ; cp. THIERS, *Notes et
Souvenirs*, 64.

exaggeration, the purpose to hearten the defenders of Paris and to check any pacifist influences.

In fact, the army of the Loire was by no means a myth at the beginning of October ; still less was it true that " nothing existed " when Gambetta arrived at Tours. The organisation of an army on the Loire had been contemplated by the Palikao ministry,[1] but it was left for the Government of National Defence to translate the plan into action. The Tours War Office had, indeed, been slow in its work, hampered as it was by the defects of its composition, and above all by the shortage of officers and of equipment : nevertheless, Lefort claimed that 70,000 men were being trained at the end of September and that the 15th army corps was fully organised, the formation of the 16th well advanced by the time Gambetta came on the scene.[2]   Nor were the men on the Loire the only forces which had been raised in the provinces since Sedan.   The organisation of an army in the south, also contemplated by the Imperial authorities, had been taken in hand, and 35,000 men were in the Vosges to protect the Rhône valley and to threaten the German lines of communication. In addition, there were 30,000 Gardes Mobiles in the west, various garrisons in the north, and numerous small local troops of volunteers and franc-tireurs.[3]   Nevertheless, such forces seemed little to oppose to Moltke's disciplined hosts.   " In all forty thousand regular troops, as many national gardes mobiles, five to six thousand cavalry and a hundred cannon . . . such was the sum of our resources with which to repulse an invading army which already disposed of from seven to eight hundred thousand soldiers in perfect organisation, two thousand cannon not including siege batteries and powerful

---

[1] *Revue d'histoire ; Guerre de 1870-71 ; Mesures d'organisation,* 66 ; *H.H.u.S.A.,* METTERNICH to BEUST, Aug. 22 and Sept. 2.

[2] *Dép.* III, 74.   [3] FREYCINET, *Souvenirs,* I, 170.

reserves on the Rhine." [1] Such was Gambetta's task, as described by Freycinet, and it seemed truly stupendous, the more so because a part of these forces was disorganised at the outset, the 15th army corps by its repulse at Orléans, and the army of the East by the failure of its operations in the Vosges, which led to a demoralising retreat upon Besançon. Freycinet's description, however, was misleading; for, while he included all the besiegers in his estimate of German might, he made no mention of the besieged in his reckoning of those who were to repel the invader : the provincial armies never had to oppose the whole strength of Germany unaided.   Moreover, if the figures he gave represented the sum of the resources already organised, they took no account of those still in process of being organised, or still available for organisation ; and as far as concerned man power these, as Gambetta himself recognised, were immense.[2] Merely by the full application of the series of measures which the Imperial Government had passed to mobilise the reserves, increase the effective forces, and raise the Gardes Mobiles, there was available an effective of 750,000 men.[3] Although this effective of the active army and of the Garde Mobile was, as has been pointed out, greater than the number of men actually made use of in Gambetta's armies,[4] the Republican Government, inspired by the legends of 1792, proceeded hastily to augment these resources by the enrolment " of universal suffrage ". It sought to martial the vast potential army of citizens, the " live forces of the country " provided by the newly re-established National Guard. The mobilisation of the National Guard was expected to be the great military

---

[1] FREYCINET, *Souvenirs*, I, 170.

[2] Procl. to Citizens of Departments, Oct. 9 ; Appendix XI, p. 308.

[3] Cp. H. DUTRAIT-CROZON, *Gambetta et la défense nationale*, Appendix, 505 ff.

[4] Ibid. 507, 508 ; cp. FREYCINET, *Guerre en province*, 28, 29.

achievement of the Government of National Defence : the new citizen soldiers must show themselves worthy of their ancestors. Gambetta had declared that a nation in arms must be opposed by a nation in arms, and he fully intended to make the phrase a reality. Thus, on September 14, he had decreed that all citizens of 21 to 60 were to be registered for service in the National Guard, and a fortnight later the Delegation had ordered the prefects to enrol all volunteers, unmarried men or childless widowers between the ages of 21 to 40, in companies of mobilised National Guards.[1] No less than 650,000 men were affected by this decree, and Gambetta, nothing daunted by his experiences of organisation in Paris, insistently pressed for its speedy execution ; it must, he declared on October 26, be complete in three weeks' time ;[2] and before those three weeks were past he had issued a new decree calling up all the remaining ablebodied men between 21 and 40, the married and widowers with children to whom the first decree of September 29 had not applied. Republicans were enthusiastic ; now the *levée en masse* was indeed a reality ; now the glorious days of 1792 could not fail to be repeated, and Gambetta himself informed Jules Favre that this measure would provide " a reservoir of nearly two million men ".[3]

Thus Gambetta could enrol a nation for resistance, but it was much more difficult to make it a nation in arms, really and adequately equipped for resistance. " The truth is," Laurier had written, as early as October 5, " that we are encumbered with men, and that we are short of arms," [4] and four days later Gambetta himself declared : " there is no lack of men . . . it is arms which have been lacking since the shameful capitulation of Sedan ".[5] This shortage,

---

[1] *Mobilisés.* [2] *Dép.* I, 370, 371. [3] Ibid. I, 124.
[4] *D.T.* II, 268. [5] Procl. to Citizens of Departments, Oct. 9.

and the no less serious shortage of officers and men able to
train the new levies, were to preoccupy the War Office
throughout the national defence, and none of the measures
designed to relieve the situation, the acceleration of home
munition manufacture, the purchase of arms abroad, and
the creation of an auxiliary army, proved a complete remedy,
for the truth was that, as George Sand said, the Government
had " many too many men to have enough soldiers ".[1]   It
asked for every kind of sacrifice at the same time, without
realising that one paralysed another, and the attempt to
equip and train so many men in so short a time with inadequate means led only to confusion and discontent.   It is
questionable which were most to be pitied, the men who
were herded together, exposed to the rigours of a bitter
winter, often without proper shelter or clothing, in training
camps where there were not enough arms with which to
train,[2] or the men who were sent into action with weapons
which were entirely unserviceable, the purchase of un-
discerning armament commissions.[3]   Under such conditions
numerical strength was far from breeding the enthusiasm
Gambetta required, and later it certainly contributed greatly
to the war weariness which he was so anxious to avoid.
From the military point of view the hasty *levée en masse* was
undoubtedly a mistake.   In fact, it proved quite impossible
for Gambetta's decrees concerning the mobilisation of the
National Guard to be executed in the time he wished.   The
chief burden and expense of organisation fell upon the local
authorities, and even where they were most enthusiastic and
strenuous in addressing themselves to the task, the difficulties
which they experienced in obtaining competent instructors

---

[1] *Journal d'un voyageur pendant la guerre*, 131.

[2] The camps of Conlie and of Les Alpines were the most tragic examples.

[3] E. A. VIZETELLY, *Republican France*, 18.

and good material for clothing and equipment were very great.[1] The number of *Mobilisés* handed over to the Minister of War by the end of November was not 650,000 but 133,000, and the number serving with the armies by the time of the armistice just under 250,000.[2] This did, indeed, represent a very considerable effort, far short of Gambetta's intentions though it fell, but the military value of these citizen soldiers was slight, and in the short time they had to show their worth, they were by no means the crowning glory of the national defence. " Unhappily," reported Admiral Jauréguiberry, who had proved himself one of the most spirited of Gambetta's commanders, " one is forced to admit that in general they have rendered scarcely any service, and that their ignorance of the business of war, their indiscipline and want of steadiness in presence of the enemy have frequently been the cause of serious repulses ".[3]

It is, then, a fair criticism of Gambetta's administration that it much exaggerated the value of the National Guard, that it was misled by its reading of 1792, and that it tended to sacrifice efficiency to numbers. But it must also be admitted that the deliberate way in which Gambetta aimed at raising the largest possible armies in the shortest possible time showed how clearly he appreciated the magnitude of his task ; and it must be remembered that if he had had his way the war would not have ended when it did. By mobilising all the available resources of the country, he was prepared to maintain resistance indefinitely, convinced that it would be possible thus to exhaust even the best army in Europe. Moreover, if he did put mistaken faith in the

---

[1] Cp. the vivid account of the clothing of the *Mobilisés* of Creuse in *Frazer's Magazine*, Nov. 1872.

[2] DUTRAIT-CROZON, *Gambetta et la défense nationale*, 152.

[3] Report to Assemblée Nationale, cit. DUTRAIT-CROZON, 509.

strength of mere numbers, there were other reasons not purely military which may well have seemed to make numbers desirable ; the identification of every citizen with the defence would also identify him indirectly with the cause of the Republic ; at the same time, it would make the defence more really national and act as a sort of moral purge after eighteen years of Bonapartist lethargy. But no doubt the most important reason was military, and the strategy adopted by the new Minister of War did from the outset require the employment of large forces.

The system of defensive warfare which should be adopted had, said Edgar Quinet, " the evidence of a geometric truth. . . . From the circumference let the whole of France, armed and organised, close in upon the centre which remains fixed." [1] The relief of Paris was the one obvious, compelling objective ; it was natural that the besieged should consider that the provincial forces were created to that end ; equally natural that Gambetta and the provincials should consider it their supreme concern. The presence of the majority of the Government within the city made its claims to relief all the more pressing, and bound the fate of the country still more closely to that of the capital ; but even had the Government all been free at Tours, Paris must surely still have been the magnet inexorably controlling their strategy. This siege of a city of 2,000,000 inhabitants was indeed, as Gambetta declared, " an unique spectacle," [2] and the heroic resistance of the Parisians made a moral demand upon the provincials which it was impossible to withstand. If the Delegation had been disposed to ignore this demand, public opinion would probably have forced it to act against its better judgment. Instead of " à Berlin," " à Paris " was now the cry.

[1] *Le Siècle*, Sept. 26, 1870.
[2] Procl. to Citizens of Departments, Oct. 9.

But the success of any attempt to relieve Paris depended upon two requirements which under the circumstances seemed almost incompatible ; speedy execution, and the employment of a large army, well disciplined and well equipped. The relief of Paris was a problem which had to be solved within a time limit, the limit of Parisian resistance, and the length of this would be determined by the amount of provisions which the besieged still had in store. This was the outside limit, but there was also an inner limit which made rapidity all the more essential. The duration of the siege of Metz was a factor of vital importance : at the moment, the great bulk of the German troops were immobilised in siege work before Metz, before Paris, and before Belfort ; the forces available for offensive against the new French levies in the provinces were comparatively small, and unimportant. But the fall of Metz would release 100,000 men, and must entirely alter the prospects of a campaign for the relief of Paris. Scarcely less important than the actual duration of both sieges was the estimate of their duration made by the authorities at Tours. According to Freycinet, Gambetta left Paris under the impression that its food supplies would hold out until December 15. But it was clear that the city would be obliged to capitulate before then, and in view of this, he and Freycinet decided that its effective resistance could not be expected to last beyond December 1.[1] This allowed little more than six weeks for the necessary preparations and for the execution of a plan of relief ; by December 1 Paris must have been freed or irretrievably lost. As it turned out, this estimate was based upon a complete miscalculation ; the Parisian authorities had considerably under-estimated the time their provisions would last ; the siege of Paris was to continue

[1] FREYCINET, *Souvenirs*, I, 172.

until January 28, and Gambetta and Freycinet could safely have reckoned upon an effective resistance of another twelve weeks instead of six.

Much less was known of the situation of Metz. Rumours of a sortie by the " glorious Bazaine " had filled the press from time to time, but they had received no confirmation in fact, and it is very doubtful whether a sortie could have been of such advantage to the national defence as Gambetta later declared. The army of Metz, weakened after the hardships of a long siege, and issuing into a country which the invader had stripped of its resources, would most probably have been cut off and annihilated before it could effect a junction with any other French forces, or find a secure base in which to recuperate.[1] The greatest service which Bazaine could render was to prolong his resistance to the utmost. But how long that would be, the authorities at Tours had at first no certain means of calculating. " As nothing gave us reason to suspect the treachery of Bazaine," wrote Freycinet later, " our period of respite was measured by the duration of the siege of Paris," [2]—that is to say, that it was estimated at six weeks, and the implication seemed to be that Bazaine was expected to hold out at least so long. But the Marshal himself had held no communication with the Government of National Defence, and his name had been connected with certain incidents and rumours of incidents which might have led a prudent strategist to foresee the worst. " Bazaine does not belong to you," Bismarck had told Jules Favre at Ferrières. " I have strong reasons for believing that he remains faithful to the Emperor, and therefore would not obey you," [3] and in the second interview he had shown

---

[1] Cp. C. v. DER GOLTZ, *Léon Gambetta und seine Armeen*, 24.

[2] *Souvenirs*, I, 171, but cp. *Guerre en province*, 74.

[3] J. FAVRE, *Gouvernement de la défense nationale*, I, 180.

him Régnier's passport and the Hastings photograph.[1] But Favre had supposed that the wily Prussian was trying to frighten him into concession, and put no faith in his evidence. Nevertheless, Bourbaki's mysterious visit to Hastings was an indication that it was genuine, and when Bourbaki himself came to Tours on October 15 and informed the Delegation that during the fortnight before his departure from Metz the army there still recognised the Emperor,[2] it was clear that there could be no reliance on Bazaine's loyalty to a Republican Government. It might have been supposed that Bourbaki would also have given the authorities at Tours some estimate of the probable duration of Metz's resistance, but of this there seems to be no record, and if he did give one, it did not apparently affect their calculations. As it was, the six weeks which they allowed for the effective resistance of Paris were none too long for the preparations necessary in order to attempt its relief.

Once Paris had been approved as the objective, it was clearly desirable to concert a plan of approach with the defenders, so that they could prepare and muster all their forces for a sortie in the direction of the relieving army's advance. The question had already been studied in Paris, and Trochu had approved a plan of Ducrot for a sortie to be made towards Pontoise and Rouen. The co-operation of provincial forces in Normandy would obviously

---

[1] Régnier was an adventurer who sought to act as an intermediary between the Empress and Bazaine. In this intention he went to Hastings and obtained possession of a signed photograph of the Prince Imperial. He then presented himself to Bismarck who gave him a safe-conduct to Metz. As a result of this self-imposed mission of an adventurer Bazaine decided to send Bourbaki to Hastings. The Empress who knew nothing of Régnier's activities was astonished by the general's arrival and would not hear of treating with Bismarck.

[2] *F.O.* 146, 1481, LYONS to GRANVILLE, Oct. 18. The news of the Revolution of September 4 reached Metz on the 10th, Bourbaki left on the 25th.

contribute to the success of such an enterprise, but Trochu attached such importance to secrecy that he hesitated to make any communication to the provincial authorities until his own preparations were well advanced.   Unfortunately for the future of his plan, it was not until a few days after Gambetta's departure that he decided to disclose it to one of his colleagues, Favre, in his capacity as Vice-President of the Government.   Favre at once expressed his regret that Gambetta had been allowed to go in ignorance, and persuaded the general to transmit the plan verbally to him by means of Ranc, Gambetta's friend, who was about to leave for Tours by balloon.   That Ranc fulfilled his mission there is no doubt, for on October 19 Gambetta wrote to Favre of " the combination of General Trochu which would consist in reorganising the revictualling of Paris by way of Le Havre and the right bank of the Seine " ; [1] but he also foreshadowed its rejection, or at least its postponement, for the same reasons which had weighed against an expedition to cut German communications in the east : " the actual position of our troops, which are required to cover Bourges, Dijon, and Lyons, does not seem to me to allow us to think of realising this combination for some time ".   It was the need of covering Tours no less than Bourges which had already determined an advance upon Paris by the direct route. Bourges and also Nevers were important arsenals ; Tours was the seat of Government, and the Delegation dared not dishearten the public by abandoning it before it was clearly untenable.   Moreover, since time pressed, the direct route was to be favoured simply because it was the direct route, and the recapture of Orléans, which must be a first stage on the way to Paris, would be likely to kindle great popular enthusiasm.

[1] *D.T.* II, 278.

Trochu's famous plan was, in fact, rejected ; by personal persuasion he might have induced Gambetta to transfer a part at least of the army of the Loire to the valley of the lower Seine, but after October 7 the opportunity was lost. The despatch to Favre already quoted, and the fact that Bourbaki, Thiers, and Fourichon were all consulted, prove that the plan was seriously considered.[1]   Yet later, Gambetta and Ranc both attempted to deny that anything so definite as a plan had ever been proposed.   Gambetta seemed to recall that Ranc had reported a " conversation " with Trochu, during which the general had spoken of a great effort to be made by Paris at the end of October, " and then if there were forces to be had in the provinces they should advance towards Paris from Le Havre ".   Gambetta could not take that for a plan.[2]   The complaints of Trochu and the misunderstandings which arose between Paris and Tours can account for these subsequent evasions.   It seems clear that Gambetta omitted to inform Trochu of the definite rejection of his plan, and that for some time at any rate the general could expect no help from troops in Normandy ; his only intimation of this was the personal opinion expressed in the despatch to Favre on October 19, and as this was before the formal discussion of the plan it could not be regarded as final.

Trochu and Favre, on the other hand, appeared to consider the concurrence of Tours as certain, and to take it for granted that every effort would be made to execute the wishes of the President and Vice-President of the Government Council.   On the 21st Gambetta received a despatch from Favre, dated the 17th, announcing that in twenty days'

---

[1] BOURBAKI, *Dép.* III, 347 ; R. DREYFUS, *M. Thiers contre l'Empire*, etc., 233-234 ; cp. RANC, *Souvenirs et Correspondance*, 169 ; FREYCINET, *La Guerre en province*, 77, 78.

[2] *Dép.* I, 561.

time Trochu, reckoning on the support of a provincial
expedition, would be ready to attempt a great sortie,
" passing over the bodies of the enemy ". " As a result,"
said Freycinet, " our plans were suddenly changed. It was
no longer a question of marching on Paris with two hundred
thousand men at the beginning of December (*sic*), but of
attempting a demonstration at the beginning of November
with whatever forces were available ".[1] But the line of
advance was to be the same : Paris was still the ultimate
goal, and the greater need for prompt action was a still
more cogent argument in favour of the direct route.   Yet
further despatches showed unmistakably that the co-operation on which Trochu was counting was, in accordance with
his plan, the co-operation of forces advancing up the valley
of the Seine.   " M. Ranc has told you what is necessary,
and you know how to act," wrote Favre on the 19th, and
again on the 23rd : " General Trochu's plan seems to me to
be excellent, we must make an effort to put it into execution.
. . . I think you can bring 60,000 or 80,000 men to the
point agreed.   If that is done within twenty days under the
command of a good general, we shall solve the problem
victoriously." [2]   The misunderstanding was complete ; but
at Tours it should have been obvious, while at Paris it was
not, and if Gambetta attached real importance to the idea
of concerted operations, he should have undeceived Trochu
at once.

Nevertheless, it was Gambetta who insisted that some
demonstration must be made to help Trochu and to coincide
with his proposed sortie.   Plans for an advance upon
Orléans were drawn up ; two councils of war were held, the
second at Tours in Gambetta's presence, and as a result

---

[1] *Souvenirs*, I, 174, but cp. *La Guerre en province*, 78.
[2] *Rapport* CHAPER, 50.

it was decided that the army of the Loire should begin its advance on the 27th.   Gambetta's will prevailed, but, ominous sign, it had had to overcome the evident reluctance of the Commander-in-Chief.[1]

" There is a cruel lack of generals," wrote Gambetta, on October 24, " and above all of a real soldier capable of reforming and of handling all the forces of which we can dispose." [2]   Such a man, he had hoped to find in Bourbaki, whose offer of his services to the national defence when he was refused permission to return to Metz had been most gladly accepted.   The general had the reputation of being one of the most brilliant officers in the Imperial armies, and Trochu wrote to urge that he should be given an important post.[3]   But Gambetta's hopes that here was the solution to the problem of the chief command of the army of the Loire were quickly disappointed.   A brief inquiry into the condition of the troops that he was invited to command, and into the methods of Gambetta's War Office, convinced Bourbaki both that the task proposed for the army of the Loire was impossible, and that his own position as Commander-in-Chief would be intolerable.   To his professional eye the situation was hopelessly disordered :   " all military officers were in a state of the utmost confusion ; . . . there were no returns of the number of men, or of the amount of materials ; no means of ascertaining where men or materials were, no organisation, no discipline.   To reduce such a chaos into anything like order would require time, and the exercise of unrestricted authority by experienced men.   Such authority," as he told Lord Lyons, " the Government at Tours did not appear disposed to place in his hands : and

---

[1] FREYCINET, *Souvenirs*, I, 175 ff. ; *La Guerre en province*, 79 ff.
[2] *Dép. circ.* I, 94.
[3] *D.T.* II, 282 ; FREYCINET, *La Guerre en province*, 78.

to do any good while military matters were controlled by men without the slightest military capacity or experience would be perfectly impossible. . . . He would confess that he could not reconcile himself to serving under the eye and the immediate control of the men now at Tours." [1]

Since Bourbaki resisted all entreaties, and there had been no time to discover the "young and active chiefs capable by their intelligence and by their energy of renewing the prodigies of 1792," [2] Gambetta had to be content with the man who already held the command of the main body of the Loire army, D'Aurelle de Paladines, whom he himself had chosen to succeed the unfortunate La Motte Rouge.[3] D'Aurelle had won the respect of Gambetta and Freycinet for the competent firmness with which he had set to work to train and organise the 15th and 16th army corps.[4] He was an admirable disciplinarian, but as a professional soldier he was, like Bourbaki, acutely conscious of the defects of his army. He addressed himself with energy to the task of transforming it into an efficient fighting force, but as Bourbaki recognised, that task required time, and D'Aurelle, who was naturally cautious, was far from wishing to court defeat before his work of organisation was complete. Consequently, he did not readily appreciate Gambetta's desire for speedy action. His army was his concern, and he had little confidence in the military direction of civilians. Excellent as an organiser, he was nevertheless too much the professional, imbued with what Republicans denounced as

---

[1] *F.O.* 146, 1481, LYONS to GRANVILLE, Oct. 18.

[2] Cp. Procl. to the army ; *Dép. circ.* I, 46.

[3] Gambetta had met D'Aurelle on his way from Amiens to Tours, and it is significant that the fact that the general had been an object of suspicion to the extreme Republicans of Marseilles was no more a hindrance to his promotion than was expulsion from the prefecture of Tarn et Garonne an obstacle to Freycinet's nomination as Gambetta's Delegate.

[4] *Dép. circ.* I, 147.

the " old spirit of regularity," to adapt himself completely to the essential irregularity of the new conditions of warfare, or to co-operate cordially with civilians for whose opinions on military matters he could have little respect. As a result, like Bourbaki and like so many of his fellow-generals, he lacked the supreme necessity for a general who was to lead the new armies into battle, an indomitable confidence, and his initiative was soon paralysed by the conditions in which he was required to act.

It was natural, then, that D'Aurelle should have opposed any immediate advance of the army of the Loire, but his objections had been overruled, and it was arranged that the forward movement should begin on the 27th, with the object of reaching Orléans by November 1. The grand campaign, the " serious operations " which Gambetta had striven so hard to make possible, now seemed to be launched. The provincial forces and the civilian War Office were about to prove their worth, the efforts of the past fortnight to receive their justification, and hopes and expectations were high at Tours. Great then was the dismay when a telegram from D'Aurelle arrived on the evening of the 28th announcing that owing to bad weather, bad roads, and the defective equipment of part of the Garde Mobile, he had decided to suspend operations.[1]   Most reluctantly Gambetta felt obliged

---

[1] D'Aurelle, *La première armée de la Loire*, 60, says that he telegraphed that he would have to suspend his advance " for a day ". But he does not give the text of this telegram and it has not been published. Lehautcourt (*Campagne de la Loire*, I, 101) accepts D'Aurelle's statement, and assumes that he intended to renew his advance on October 30. If this is so, then the responsibility for further delay must rest entirely with Gambetta and the War Office, and it would seem that Gambetta must really have been impressed by Thiers' arguments. This is suggested, too, by the phrase in Gambetta's reply to Freycinet's letter of November 4 : " Nous avons eu le malheur de voir une première fois notre plan offensif, si sagement combiné, entravé par l'intervention de M. Thiers. Il faut reprendre notre ligne de conduite. . . ." (Freycinet, *Souvenirs*, I, 185 ; in *La Guerre en province*, 88, Thiers' name is

to acquiesce in this delay, although he informed D'Aurelle that his opinion of the excellence of the plan of campaign had by no means changed.

Meanwhile, a distant event had completely altered the military situation. Ever since October 18 the air had been filled with disquieting rumours about Bazaine—rumours that he had concluded peace, that Bismarck had agreed to restore the Empire, and that Bazaine was to be Regent—and contradictory reports that he had made a brilliant sortie by no means allayed the uneasiness. On the 25th Thiers had come to the Council of the Delegation and announced the fall of Metz as an accomplished fact. Gambetta was overwhelmed by the news, and when it lacked confirmation desperately attempted to believe that it was also groundless, and that an appeal to Bazaine from Bourbaki might yet save all. But official confirmation followed only too soon. The news was but too true : Metz had capitulated, and with it three Marshals of France and an army of 173,000 men. It was a terrible blow : the prospects of the national defence were suddenly darkened just when they were for the first time showing gleams of brightness. The effect on the army of the Loire was to be decisive. It was very significant that D'Aurelle's telegram announcing the suspension of his advance was sent shortly after the general had received the official news of the fall of Metz ; no less significant that on the same evening M. Thiers had passed through his lines

omitted.) If this is correct, and it was primarily the political issue, the question of armistice negotiations, which led Gambetta to suspend the army of the Loire's advance, he is open to strong criticism for agreeing to resume it before he had heard the result of the negotiations ; the delay was a mere waste of time.

It is to be noted, however, that if D'Aurelle had intended to resume his advance on the 30th he seems very readily to have acquiesced in its indefinite suspension. As I have pointed out, many reasons made him anxious to gain time and to run no risks.

on the way to discuss armistice proposals at Paris and Versailles. If the War Office was still determined on its plan to assist Trochu, the fall of Metz made its rapid execution all the more essential, so that the French could strike their blow before the German troops released from Metz could be brought against them. But the coincidence of Bazaine's capitulation with the beginning of Thiers' negotiations introduced weighty considerations of quite another kind. D'Aurelle had no wish to risk compromising his army unnecessarily if an armistice was to follow, while Thiers was insistent that no offensive of D'Aurelle should prejudice the success of his attempts to obtain an armistice.[1] It was difficult for Gambetta to resist the combined pressure of soldier and statesman, and for a week, an all-important week, the army of the Loire was allowed to remain inactive. Finally, Freycinet intervened, and wrote Gambetta a formal letter to clear his own responsibility for any consequences of the interference of political considerations with his military plans. He requested a categorical answer to the question whether the army of the Loire was to continue its advance at once, or whether in view of an armistice it should retire : for the maintenance of its actual positions, he said, would be disastrous.[2] Although the result of Thiers' negotiations was not yet known, Gambetta had no difficulty in returning a plain answer to a plain question : " I do not know if the Government of the Hôtel de Ville is disposed to treat. For myself, I know only my mandate and my duty, which is to continue war to the knife. Consequently, notwithstanding false manœuvres and bad management on the part of the diplomatists or of anyone else, do not allow yourself to be

---

[1] FREYCINET, *Souvenirs*, I, 181, implies that the cessation of this advance was directly due to Thiers' representations. But D'Aurelle might well have had the wit to see for himself that the situation was now wholly altered.

[2] *La Guerre en province*, 86.

arrested or hindered by attempts at negotiation for which I
disclaim all responsibility.   We have had the misfortune to
see our cleverly conceived plan of offensive endangered once
already by the intervention of M. Thiers.   We must recover
from the effects of this interference.   I shall empower you
to take measures of the greatest energy, and if fortune can
be won by determination, study, and devotion, the country
will have nothing with which to reproach us.   So it is war !
Forward, without losing a minute."

Provoked by Freycinet, Gambetta thus vigorously re-
asserted his own policy.   This letter was written on November 4.   Three days later the army of the Loire resumed its
advance ; on the 9th it defeated the Bavarians at Coulmiers,
and on the 10th its troops re-entered Orléans.   It was the
first time during the whole war that French soldiers had
gained a victory of any significance, and that victory had
been won by the " rabble of men " which Bourbaki had
regarded with such scorn.   Tours was jubilant : Gambetta's
optimism and the policy of war to the knife seemed to be
completely and triumphantly justified.   But the triumph had
been achieved at a high price, for the " striking revenge "
for the reverse of October 11 had been won only on November 10 instead of on the 1st, as originally planned.   The
army of the Loire had been retarded in its advance by ten
days at a time when each day gained was of quite exceptional value.   The diplomatic and political negotiations
of the last ten days of October had been of the utmost
importance for the future course of the war ; Gambetta had
disclaimed responsibility for them, but he was unable to
prevent them, and they showed that powerful as was his
influence in the Delegation, his supremacy was not unquestioned.   With the fall of Metz they had a marked effect
upon his whole policy, internal as well as military.

XI

GAMBETTA *V.* THIERS : A DIPLOMATIC
CONTEST

THE siege of Paris had created a remarkable diplomatic situation, of which the peculiarities were described by none better than by the diplomatists themselves. " There has been created at Paris," wrote Bismarck to the Papal Nuncio, " a state of things to which modern history furnishes no precise analogy in (from ?) the point of view of international law. A Government, at war with a Power which has not yet recognised it, shuts itself up in a besieged fortress, and finds itself there surrounded by a part of the diplomatists who were accredited to a Government which has been superseded by the Government of National Defence." [1] To the other part of the diplomatic corps, which had preferred to leave Paris before the investment was completed, the state of things at Tours appeared no less anomalous, as Lord Lyons pointed out to Chaudordy when he heard that elections were to be postponed indefinitely. " Not only was the origin of the Government simply (so to speak) fortuitous, but it was difficult to say what the Government of France was at this moment, or even where it was to be found. A part of it was at Paris, and a part of it was at Tours ; the two parts had very scanty communication with each other, and it naturally followed that, as in the case before us, they

---

[1] Cit. E. B. WASHBURNE, *Recollections of a Minister to France*, I, 166, 167.

were often at cross purposes. The Representatives of the principal neutral Powers of Europe had, at the suggestion of the Minister for Foreign Affairs, come to Tours as the place at which they could best hold communication at the same time with their own Governments and the Government of France. But was there anyone at Tours who could speak authoritatively in the name of the whole Government ? Was there anyone at Paris who could do so ? . . . " [1]

The answer was in the negative. However authoritative Gambetta's position was at Tours, his assumption of the Ministry of War was only one of several acts which showed that he was by no means an infallible interpreter of the wishes of his colleagues at Paris. Diplomatically, the situation was still further complicated by the fact that Chaudordy at Tours was only the delegate of Favre at Paris. Thus his initiative was limited, every important point of policy had to be submitted to the Minister in the besieged city, and the Government was not bound to support him. If this had its advantages in so far as it allowed him to speak freely and to " treat what he had said according to circumstances as pledging or not pledging the Government," [2] it also had its disadvantages in that he was likely to have to reconcile different policies and to try and serve two masters instead of one. When the Government Council at Paris met to determine the powers to be given to Gambetta, it had taken care expressly to reaffirm Jules Favre's exclusive control over the department of Foreign Affairs. [3] The members of the Delegation, however, had not appreciated the effect. Crémieux had already complained that he was too little informed and consulted by Favre's *alter ego*, as he called

[1] *B.S.P.* LXXI, no. 197, LYONS to GRANVILLE, Oct. 9.
[2] NEWTON, *Life of Lord Lyons*, I, 339.
[3] DRÉO, *Procès-verbaux*, 181.

Chaudordy.[1] Still less was he informed and consulted after Gambetta's arrival at Tours,[2] while Gambetta himself wrote to Favre on October 25 that " the cipher despatches which are sent to you by M. de Chaudordy are never submitted to me, and I do not know what is in them ".[3] Chaudordy, however, knew very well that, if as delegate of Favre, he was bound to follow instructions from Paris, as delegate at Tours he could not ignore the Government there, and particularly Gambetta. He did not hesitate to acquaint Gambetta with the essentials of whatever diplomatic negotiations were in progress. Diplomacy was not the least important aspect of the national defence, and Gambetta recognised Chaudordy's ability, and the value of a man who was no Republican amateur but a diplomat by profession. He made little attempt to interfere with Chaudordy's freedom of action, but in order to maintain the unity of his general policy, he laid down certain fundamental principles which the delegate was instructed scrupulously to observe. Of these, the most important was that he should never breathe a word to suggest that France would consent to a cession of territory.[4] Chaudordy had no difficulty in reconciling this with his instructions from the author of the famous circular of September 6 ;[5] territorial integrity was a fundamental for Paris no less than for Tours.

The first diplomatic efforts of Favre and his delegate had been to seek possible allies and material aid ; but they had met with no success. The only help of this kind which came or was offered from abroad was either useless or unwelcome. The arrival of a veteran crippled Garibaldi was poor and embarrassing compensation for the disappointment of hopes at one time entertained of the co-operation

---

[1] *D.T.* II, 323, 419.   [2] CRÉMIEUX, *Actes de la Délégation*, 10.
[3] *D.T.* II, 283.   [4] CHAUDORDY, *Dép.* II, 9.   [5] Cp. above, p. 78.

of 60,000 Italian regular troops.[1] No more valuable was
Castelar and Orense's offer of 25,000 Spaniards, unarmed
and unequipped. As Gambetta said, there were men enough
in France ; what lacked were arms and officers ; when
Frenchmen were without them they could scarcely be
spared for ill-disciplined foreigners. Gambetta was not to
be deceived by any illusory advantages of alliance with
unsettled Spain.[2]

As no better material aid was forthcoming, the hopes of
the diplomatists now turned upon the ability of M. Thiers
to secure the good offices of the Great Powers, and when the
elderly statesman returned from his grand tour there was a
sudden renewal of diplomatic activity. His coquetry with
St. Petersburg had roused London, and while he was at
the Delegation's second Council on October 21 Chaudordy
entered with a proposal which he had just received from
Lord Lyons. England now offered to suggest an armistice
on her own initiative to enable France to elect a National
Assembly ; at the same time, she would invite the other
neutral Powers to do likewise. Thiers was in admiration of
Chaudordy's diplomatic skill which had induced England so
far to depart from her attitude of prudent reserve ; nevertheless, he still had a preference for the diplomacy of
M. Thiers, and a mistaken belief in his own power to
achieve great things with the aid of Russia rather than
with that of England. However, the English proposal won
the warm support of all the Council except Gambetta, who
at first reserved his opinion, then voted against an armistice,
and finally agreed to support his colleagues in the Delegation

[1] J. FAVRE, Gouvernement de la défense nationale, I, 305 ; H.H.u.S.A., METTER-
NICH to BEUST, Oct. 1.

[2] GLAIS-BIZOIN, Dictature de cinq mois, 237 ; Rapport DE RAINNEVILLE, 66 ;
STEENACKERS and LE GOFF, Histoire du gouvernement de la défense nationale en
province, II, 16.

if the approval of the Government at Paris could be obtained
for the English proposal. By imposing this condition, he
hoped at least to delay the negotiation ; for an armistice
which would have the express object of facilitating elections
was far from his desire. The proposal ran counter to his
whole policy, internal as well as military ; he had not yet
carried out his work of republicanisation so thoroughly as to
ensure the return of a Republican majority, and the election
of an Assembly which was not wholly Republican might
gravely interfere with his conduct of the war.

But Gambetta's attempt to hamper negotiations by an
appeal to Paris was Thiers' opportunity to forward them by
an appeal to Russia. At St. Petersburg Gortschakoff had
proposed that the Tsar should demand a safe-conduct to
enable Thiers to confer with the Government at Paris, and
to leave again at once, thus " favouring the opportunity of
entering into relations with the German Headquarters ".
While England proposed a mediation which might lead to
the settlement of the terms of peace by the neutral Powers,
Russia proposed an armistice which would lead merely
to direct negotiations between the two belligerents.[1] The
English proposal, won by the efforts of Chaudordy, was far
more favourable to the interests of France, and might have
been highly disconcerting to Bismarck, but Thiers at this
time had a personal preference for Russia and a grudge
against England ; he favoured direct negotiation with the
enemy, particularly when he saw himself as the negotiator,
and he flattered himself that he could manage the terrible
Bismarck far more skilfully than Favre. Thus Gambetta's
stipulation for the consent of the Government at Paris was
Thiers' chance to urge acceptance of Gortschakoff's suggestion and to propose himself as negotiator. He represented

---

[1] A. SOREL, *Histoire diplomatique de la guerre franco-allemande*, II, 46.

its advantages in glowing terms, and the Delegation unanimously agreed that he should request a safe-conduct from St. Petersburg. The proposal was approved by all, but for different reasons : by Gambetta because he believed the negotiation would come to nothing,[1] and by the rest of the Delegation because they were loth to risk incurring the wrath of Paris once again by acting on their own initiative in a matter of such importance. Thus the English offer of mediation was virtually rejected, and Thiers, pinning false hopes on Russia, remained in Tours to await his safe-conduct.

The two most remarkable personalities in French politics, and the two men who were to make the greatest positive contributions to the secure establishment of the Third Republic, were now in close contact. Their opinions on the vital question of war or peace were diametrically opposed, and the opposition was soon to lead to a long and momentous estrangement. Thiers was anxious for an Assembly not merely because he believed that universal suffrage should exercise its privilege ; he desired it above all as a necessary preliminary to the conclusion of peace, and of the necessity of peace he was now entirely convinced. For him the continuation of the war must be the ruin of France. The resistance of Paris had lasted beyond all expectation, and by now the country's honour had been amply saved ; to prolong the struggle further was to make an unnecessary sacrifice of life and treasure. As for the armies of the provinces he had no belief in the possibility of their success, and his experience of life at Tours surely did not convert him to optimism. The streets of this temporary capital were crowded with every variety of warrior, " the most extraordinary masquerade of which any town ever afforded the spectacle," wrote a young officer of the Camo column

[1] THIERS, *Notes et Souvenirs*, 51.

who was in the town at this time, " soldiers of all arms and of all badges mixed up together, covered with stripes from head to foot ; uniforms which would tend to make one think that the papal zouaves had turned into the zouaves of old Crémieux . . . red shirts of an earlier date than those of Garibaldi's bands, suddenly revived and followed by the usual termagants ; all sorts and conditions of volunteers, from the west, the south, the south-west, from every point of the compass, their chests bristling with enormous daggers gleaming in the midst of embroidered blood-stained Sacred Hearts ; all moving about in the height of arrogance among the wounded and the small-pox patients squatting in the railway station or on the threshold of the churches ! This town no longer looks like a city in time of war, but like a mad house. . . . I feel profoundly discouraged." [1] Nor was the experienced M. Thiers likely to be heartened by such a scene of animated confusion, at the hub of which he found the Delegation, a body with little authority, " well intentioned but feeble, with the exception, however, of the juvenile, uncultivated (*sic*), and inexperienced enthusiasm of M. Gambetta ".[2] In the enthusiasm of such youthful inexperience he had no confidence : " Thiers does not like me," said Gambetta, " I confuse and upset him, but we never lose our tempers. When I see him on the point of becoming irritable I bring him maps and consult him upon strategy. He grows radiant at once." [3]

But to encourage Thiers' belief in his own military genius was to encourage him to interfere with the direction of operations at a critical moment, and Thiers was to irritate

---

[1] Marquis de CASTELLANE, *Men and Things of My Time*, 83 ; cp. L. HALÉVY, *L'Invasion*, VIII, for a vivid picture of the dining-room of L'Hôtel du Faisan ; and Mgr. CHEVALIER, *Tours capitale*, 44-52.

[2] *H.H.u.S.A.*, METTERNICH to BEUST, Oct. 23.

[3] Comte de FALLOUX, *Mémoires d'un royaliste*, II, 440.

Gambetta as much as Gambetta irritated Thiers. On the 22nd he heard rumours of an advance on Beaugency ; at once he requested Fourichon to convey his fears to the Minister of War : such an attack was not only imprudent, for if the French were defeated the enemy might march on Tours, but it was also " in flagrant contradiction with a proposal for an armistice ".[1] Again, he spent part of an evening in an attempt to persuade Freycinet that the continuance of hostilities, and particularly the projected march upon Orléans, was useless as well as inopportune.[2] It was then not surprising that when that march was delayed so soon after the passage of Thiers through D'Aurelle's lines, Freycinet and Gambetta were convinced that Thiers was directly responsible.

No less clearly defined than that of Thiers was the attitude of Gambetta. He had thrown all his energies into the prosecution of this national war. The great efforts of a fortnight's intensive organisation were beginning to bear fruit, and the different parts of the vast war machine which he aimed at constructing were beginning to take shape and consistence. The durability and offensive powers of the machine had as yet to be fully tested, and therefore everything might be hoped from it. For him the truly national defence was now only on the point of beginning, and the future of all that he held most dear, both as patriot and partisan, depended on its continuance to a successful conclusion ; for to him, the natural optimist buoyed up by the deceptive precedents of 1792 in France and of 1864 in America, success was by no means a sheer impossibility. But at the very outset he found the realisation of these high hopes and ambitions endangered by the activities of M. Thiers. The negotiations of these last days of October

---

[1] THIERS, *Notes et Souvenirs*, 51.　　[2] FREYCINET, *Souvenirs*, I, 181.

and first days of November were to see a great battle of wits in which each of the protagonists appealed to the Government of Paris as arbiter.

On October 25 M. Thiers received a safe-conduct which, in purposeful error, had been made out for Versailles instead of for Paris. When he announced to the Council of the Delegation that he was returning it Gambetta paid him the tribute of being " correctness itself " ; whereupon Thiers seized the opportunity offered by this exceptional harmony to read the young man who was Minister of War a lengthy lecture upon the strategy he ought to adopt. Gambetta had not the slightest intention of following these " grandes instructions " which were the opposite of his own ideas, but to humour M. Thiers he tactfully expressed approval, and admitted that to make their execution possible an armistice would, indeed, be necessary. Thiers seized on the admission : " Since you agree, write it for me and I will take your letter to Paris. I insisted ; everyone insisted. Impossible to extract one word from M. Gambetta." [1] But M. Gambetta was not long at a loss ; pressed to reply, he said that he had already written to Paris, and would send Thiers a copy of the letter. With this Thiers had to be content. When the copy was brought to him later he pronounced it to be " quite insignificant " ; it was, in fact, a mere summary of the meeting at which the proposal for an armistice had first been discussed.

But Thiers would have used another adjective than " insignificant " had he seen the whole of Gambetta's letter, for the " copy " which Gambetta sent him was an innocent extract merely. Elsewhere there was a passage which would have concerned M. Thiers far more deeply, since he himself was its subject. " He believes France exhausted and

---

[1] THIERS, op. cit. 54, 55.

incapable of victory," Gambetta had written. " He desires
peace and, fearing the responsibility which must be incurred
by those who sign this peace,[1] seeks to provoke the constitution of an Assembly which would take the burden of ensuring
it upon itself. To persuade people to share this way of
looking at things, M. Thiers is inclined to exaggerate the
present insufficiency of our military forces on the one hand
and on the other the alleged demand of public opinion for
elections." [2] Thus Gambetta had stolen a march on Thiers,
and prepared the Government at Paris by a skilful and
by no means inaccurate description of Thiers' attitude.
He anticipated correctly : at Paris Thiers was to declare
that he had found a unanimous desire for peace in the
departments ; that although the army of the Loire would
soon number 110,000, it was not so much an army as a
collection of men without leaders ; and that Gambetta
no more than anyone else believed that it could stand a
campaign, for it had not the confidence born of success.[3]
Since Thiers' acquaintance with provincial opinion was
limited to the impressions gathered during a week at Tours,
and on the journey between Tours and Paris, it may well be
that his interpretation of it was coloured by the dye of his
own strong desires, desires which were shared by " all the
guard and rear-guard of the Orléanists of France " who had
assembled at Tours, and still looked to him as a leader.[4]
But if Thiers exaggerated his countrymen's war weariness,
Gambetta was inclined to exaggerate their aversion from

[1] This, as M. DREYFUS (*M. Thiers contre l'Empire*, etc., 192) has pointed
out, was certainly unjust. The year 1871 was to show that Thiers had the
courage to assume responsibility.

[2] *Rapport* DARU, 266. This despatch was sent on Oct. 24 and reached
Paris on the 26th.

[3] THIERS, *Notes et souvenirs*, 64 ; J. FAVRE, *Gouvernement de la défense nationale*,
I, 317, 319.

[4] *H.H.u.S.A.*, METTERNICH to BEUST, Oct. 23.

elections. It was probably true that, as he said, the Republican party " with the exception of one or two ultra moderates " [1] was " unanimous in regarding elections as a dangerous diversion from the necessities of the war ". What was very much less certain was that the Republican party at this time represented the wishes of the majority of Frenchmen. Moreover, since the elections were to take place during an armistice, the diversion feared by Gambetta would be less harmfully distracting than if they were held without any cessation of hostilities. His despatches to Favre show that it was especially the uncertainty as to the return of a Republican majority which caused him to oppose elections so strenuously, and the rivals he feared were his old enemies, the Bonapartists. A purely military armistice without elections he was very ready to admit, since it would allow the army of the Loire to complete its preparations ; but to an armistice in order to hold elections, he would not consent, except upon conditions which it would probably be impossible either for Bismarck or for the Government at Paris to accept. These conditions were " the revictualling of all the besieged towns and the convocation of all the electors . . . under the formal reserve of exclusion from the Assembly of all the former Ministers of Napoleon III since the foundation of the Empire, of the Senators, Councillors of State, and of all those who have been official candidates since 1852 ". [2] These, said Gambetta, were the necessary conditions for the constitution of an Assembly which would represent France " freely and completely ". It was the first definite formulation of the famous ineligibility thesis, which had, however, been in Gambetta's mind even before he left Paris,[3] and it augured

[1] E.g. Jules Grévy and his son-in-law, Daniel Wilson (NEWTON, *Life of Lord Lyons*, I, 328).

[2] *Rapport* DARU, 266 ; J. FAVRE, op. cit. I, 284 ff.

[3] FAVRE, ibid.

ill for the liberty which would obtain under Gambetta's Republic. It was not proposed merely in order to place another obstacle in the way of elections, but as a measure which Gambetta seriously considered to be essential to the Republican interest : " I dare assert that without this precaution the general elections will be equivalent to a renunciation of the Republican party, and I must say that for myself I should find it impossible to admit them and to urge them forward ".[1] There can be little doubt that he grossly overestimated the strength of the old Bonapartist enemy in its day of misfortune, but as it happened there were at this moment particular circumstances which did seem to give some ground for dread of a Bonapartist revival, and which were probably an inducement to Gambetta to formulate the ineligibility thesis just then.

There had been disquieting rumours about Metz, and later revelations were to show that Bismarck's negotiations with the Empress had been more than mere bluff. The possibility that he might treat with the Bonapartes seemed for a moment a very real danger to the authorities at Tours.[2] It was an additional reason for M. Thiers to hasten his visit to Paris, and to enter into relations with Bismarck as the accredited representative of the Government of National Defence. Bismarck, on the other hand, purposely sent Thiers a safe-conduct which had been incorrectly made out, in order to delay his visit until the capitulation of Metz was an accomplished fact, likely to weigh heavily in favour of Prussia and of peace in the expected negotiations.

The news of the great disaster reached Tours shortly after Thiers had left it. Though many signs had prepared

---

[1] *Dép. circ.* I, 98.
[2] Cp. also *H.H.u.S.A.*, METTERNICH to BEUST, Oct. 23, for Orléanist anxiety at rumours of Bonapartist restoration.

him for the bad news, now that it was a certainty Gambetta gave way to uncontrollable fury, and his fury was reflected in a proclamation which openly denounced Bazaine as a traitor, and declared that despite the heroism of their soldiers, the French armies had " been engulfed in the disasters of the country through the treason of their generals ".[1] At Versailles a few days later Bismarck indignantly confronted Thiers with this " abominable " proclamation ; M. Thiers read it and agreed : " it was in fact absurd. It related to the capitulation of Metz and was extremely violent, calculated perhaps by M. Gambetta to make the armistice impossible." [2] The breach between the two French statesmen was complete. Once again Thiers saw himself justified as a prophet. Was not Gambetta, by his ruinous militarism, proving himself a most terrible " political and social danger ? " [3]

If Thiers was malicious in suggesting that the proclamation was intended to make an armistice impossible it is nevertheless very probable that he was right. Calculation most certainly had a part as well as fury. While the great disaster in no wise altered Gambetta's determination to continue the war, it was certain to be used as a powerful argument in favour of peace by M. Thiers and all those who, like him, had no confidence in the new armies. As a counter move Gambetta's much criticised proclamation was a skilful appeal to popular indignation and will to wipe out the stain of a second humiliation. But its chief and really valid defence was that it was the only way to keep up the morale of the country, and to prevent a wave of war weariness and defeatism : " If I had not uttered the cry of vengeance,"

[1] *Dép. circ.* I, 49.

[2] THIERS, *Notes et Souvenirs*, 85, 86 ; Marquis de CASTELLANE, *Men and Things of My Time*, 80.

[3] Cp. above, p. 14.

said Gambetta, " our unhappy country, constantly deceived and betrayed, would have run the risk of giving way to despair ".[1] The facts that Bazaine's treachery had yet to be proved and that, even if it was indubitable, it had yet to be established by a court martial, were immaterial. His treason was at the moment necessary to the Republic, and justice yielded to political expediency, despite the protests of Fourichon, who refused to sign the proclamation.[2] And there was, of course, a further inducement in that the disaster was an unrivalled opportunity to deal a fresh blow at the fallen Empire, and to ensure the ruin of the party which Gambetta still seemed to think the most formidable enemy of the Republic. So, after the man of Sedan the man of Metz.

At the same time, in order to check the pacifist influence of Thiers, it was essential that the Paris Government should be in no doubt as to the effect of the capitulation upon public opinion in the provinces. " The party in favour of war to the knife," Gambetta wrote to Favre on the same day on which he published his proclamation, " has definitely gained the upper hand, and reveals itself in two ways ; on the one hand, there is mistrust and anger against the former Generals of the Empire who are nearly everywhere, especially in the south and east, the objects of hostile demonstrations ; on the other hand, a great need is felt for the concentration of power and for measures of the utmost energy. . . . From all this you may gather that the spirit of peace and proposals for an armistice have markedly lost ground, and if M. Thiers were still with us he would be able to see for himself that we

---

[1] *Dép. circ.* I, 157.

[2] CRÉMIEUX, *Les Actes de la Délégation*, 31, says that Gambetta issued the proclamation without communicating it to his colleagues. But Fourichon must have known of it to have refused his signature, and it appeared over the names of the other three members of the Delegation.

are on the verge of a war of despair." [1] Such a war Gambetta was doing his best to provoke, and most skilfully he made use of the Metz catastrophe to further his own policy. However unfortunate his proclamation in its effect upon morale and discipline in his own armies in which Bonapartist generals still served [2]—and he found it necessary to issue a special address to the troops in order to remove its painful impressions—politically it attained his object : it left the Bonapartists more than ever discredited, while for the despair which might only too easily have swept the whole country it substituted exaltation [3] and, among the more vocal parts of the population at least, a real will to continue the war at all costs.

" In order to undertake this sublime war and sustain it to the end," pursued Gambetta, in his despatch to Favre, " France, always unhappily drawn towards dictatorship, demands a concentration of powers daily more extreme. People go as far as submitting plans for a plebiscite on peace, on war, on Committees of Public Safety, on the creation of an exceptional temporary magistracy which would have the task and the responsibility of saving the country. It goes without saying that I refuse to lend myself to anything of the kind, but all this shows you the state of people's minds, and enjoins upon me a conduct exempt from all weakness and from half measures. I mean to preserve the supremacy and the command for Paris, and for you who can draw constant inspiration from the lawful aspirations of Paris." By a strange irony, the inspiration which the Government of Paris drew from its alarming experiences on this day of October 31, when it nearly succumbed to a revolutionary

---

[1] *D.T.* II, 288. [2] *D.T.* I, 197, 288, 555 ; II, 136.

[3] G. SAND, *Journal d'un voyageur pendant la guerre*, Nov. 4 ; *H.H.u.S.A.*, METTERNICH to BEUST, Nov. 5.

Commune, was to strengthen its authority by the very means which Gambetta had so emphatically rejected,—by a plebiscite. When Gambetta heard of this intention, he roundly condemned it, not, as might have been expected, because a plebiscite was an essentially Bonapartist device, a misleading appeal to an ill-informed people, but because of the motive with which his colleagues prefaced their decree—" the popular acclamation of September 4 no longer suffices ". If that was so, and it no longer sufficed in Paris, how much less must it suffice in the provinces where the population had never been invited to ratify an acclamation in which it had had no part ? A plebiscite in Paris was a danger to authority at Tours : on all sides, said Gambetta, he would be asked to consent to " the same baptism," but he himself would never submit to such pressure of which the most terrible effect would be " to bring on civil war under " Prussian guns " [1]. Thus Gambetta, on October 31 ; but his disapproval did not prevent the Paris plebiscite from taking place, and the news that the Government had obtained a decisive majority, followed by the report that the armistice negotiations had failed, placed the matter in a wholly different light. What had seemed perilous might now prove profitable, and, as ever adaptable to circumstances, he promptly wrote to Favre, expressing his pleasure that the Prussians had for the second time put themselves in the wrong in the eyes of Europe and inquiring : " now that the war must be our one passion, do you approve that we should, within forty-eight hours, ask the whole of France the question you have asked at Paris ? " [2] And the next day he was insistent : a plebiscite was "indispensable after the Paris manifestation ".[3] But the forty-eight hours elapsed without any reply ; the despatch of the 8th did not reach

[1] *D.T.* II, 293.　　　[2] *D.T.* II, 298.　　　[3] *Dép. circ.* I, 119.

Paris until November 14, that of the 7th until December 16. In the meantime, the army of the Loire had regained Orléans, and Coulmiers was a better and surer confirmation of the " Dictator's " authority than any appeal to popular vote. The orator of April 5 abandoned his short-lived enthusiasm for a plebiscite in November, and the idea lapsed.[1] It does not seem to have received encouragement from Paris, nor did the " adversaries in the departments " press their advantage and clamour for a plebiscite in the way Gambetta had feared.

When the armistice proposals had been discussed at Tours there was one point on which Gambetta and Thiers had cordially agreed : the capital must be revictualled : " Otherwise Paris would be captured with an armistice ".[2] But this question of revictualling proved to be the rock on which Thiers' negotiations were wrecked. Everything pointed to their successful conclusion when Bismarck, as at Ferrières, insisted on a guarantee in the shape of a fort commanding the city. Thiers, convinced more than ever that the prolongation of the war would be ruinous, offered, despite the agreement at Tours, to try and persuade the Government at Paris to consent to an armistice without revictualling ; and when Favre refused to hear of such a suggestion, he then warmly urged that elections should be held without an armistice. It would be impossible for France to escape a large cession of territory and a heavy indemnity, and the more she delayed coming to terms, the more Bismarck's demands would increase. " To-day," Thiers asserted confidently, " we should obtain peace for Alsace and two milliards " [3] : and later he declared that a great opportunity had been lost. But it now seems beyond a

---

[1] April 5, cp. above p. 28.   [2] THIERS, *Notes et Souvenirs*, 50.

[3] DUCROT, *Dép.* III, 95 ; J. FAVRE, *Gouvernement de la défense nationale*, II, 24.

doubt that Thiers had allowed himself to be deceived by
suggestions from Bismarck which were merely a bait to
induce him to continue his efforts to persuade the Government of National Defence to permit some arrangement
which would bring nearer the prospect of peace.[1] Bismarck
was almost as anxious as Thiers for a speedy peace by direct
negotiation, since every day's delay increased the risk of
interference by the neutral Powers (at Tours Metternich
was already writing to Beust that a congress would settle
the Franco-German dispute [2]), but there is no convincing
evidence that Prussia would, much that she would not,[3] have
been content with anything less than Alsace and Lorraine.
The man who truly diagnosed the Prussian attitude was not
Thiers but Gambetta ; and the failure of Thiers' negotiations
at Paris was the triumph of the policy of the young man at
Tours, who believed that " happen what will, Prussia cannot
demand more of France than the Provinces of Alsace and
Lorraine, and that therefore as she demands those Provinces
now, France has nothing to lose by resisting to the last
extremity ".[4]

Thiers had failed to secure an armistice ; his attempts to
secure elections without an armistice were equally unsuccessful. After much discussion, Favre's colleagues vehemently
rejected the proposal, agreeing with Trochu that such
elections " would disorganise the defence, humiliate France,
discredit those who were elected, and serve only the interests
of a handful of bankers and of bourgeois mad with fear ".[5]

[1] Thiers, *Notes et Souvenirs*, 96 ; *F.O.* 146, 1530, Lyons to Granville, Jan.
12, 1871 ; R. Dreyfus, *M. Thiers contre l'Empire, etc.*, 215, 216.

[2] *H.H.u.S.A.*, to Beust, Nov. 5.

[3] E.g. (i) Moltke's conversation with Mgr. Chigi on Oct. 17 ; (ii) the
King of Prussia's letter to the Empress Eugénie on Oct. 26 ; (iii) the official
pronouncement in the *Staatsanzeiger* of Oct. 30.

[4] *F.O.* 146, 1482, Lyons to Granville, Oct. 31.

[5] Dréo, *Procès-verbaux*, 309.

Meanwhile, the " vieux petit bourgeois " had returned to Tours, and Gambetta reported to Favre on November 13 that under his inspiration " the Legitimist and Orléanist coteries " persisted in demanding elections without an armistice.[1] Gambetta himself was unmoved by Thiers' propaganda, but not so his fellow-Delegates, who were glad of an opportunity to show their independence. Crémieux and Glais-Bizoin at least were sympathetic to the idea,[2] and Glais-Bizoin actually proposed to go himself to Paris to dissuade the Government there from its obstinate resolution to reject all compromise. But Gambetta disarmed his elderly colleague by a simple stratagem : he threatened to insert in the *Moniteur Officiel* a note thus worded : " M. Glais-Bizoin, member of the Delegation of the Government of National Defence established at Tours, has to-day conceived the design of proceeding to Paris. This is exclusively personal, and his colleagues are in no way associated with it. This step has no official or governmental character." [3] The elder Delegates dared insist no more. They bowed to the " Dictator's " will ; Glais-Bizoin did not proceed to the capital, and Thiers saw his policy frustrated at Tours, as it had been frustrated at Paris. His young rival had won the first round. Bazaine, Bismarck, and the Government of Paris, had all played into Gambetta's hands : Coulmiers placed his supremacy beyond question. Most opportune, it seemed a final and convincing justification of the policy of war to the knife.[4]

[1] *D.T.* II, 303 ; cp. FRANQUET DE FRANQUEVILLE, *Souvenirs intimes de la vie de mon père*, 351.

[2] *D.T.* II, 323 ; CRÉMIEUX to FAVRE : " He (Gambetta) does not want them. I do, Glais-Bizoin and Kératry also."

[3] *D.T.* II, 307 ; GLAIS-BIZOIN, *Dictature de cinq mois*, 82 ; SOREL, *Histoire diplomatique de la guerre franco-allemande*, II, 199.

[4] Appendix XII, p. 313.

XII

FROM METZ TO ORLEANS

GAMBETTA's proclamation on the fall of Metz was quickly followed by a decree of November 2 completing the *levée en masse*, and the decree by the victory of the army of the Loire at Coulmiers. The value of all three was largely moral. From the military point of view, the effect of the Metz proclamation was unfortunate—the denunciation of the treason of the generals seemed a definite incitement to indiscipline—but from the political point of view it had the same kind of stirring tonic quality as Danton's famous speech, " We must dare and dare and dare again ". "At that sublime and sinister crisis," said Michelet, Danton was " the voice of the Revolution and of France." So now, in another hour of fearful peril, the Republican Gambetta was convinced that he was " giving expression to the depths of French conscience, and was translating the feelings of grief and patriotic determination which escaped from the torn soul of our country." [1] " France," he said, " was never in a graver situation, and yet the resolve to struggle to the bitter end was never more manifest." [2] The action of November 2 was a fitting complement to the words of October 31,[3] the decree raising the remainder of the able-

---

[1] *Dép. circ.* I, 111 ; GAMBETTA to FAVRE, Nov. 26.

[2] *D.T.* II, 288.

[3] *Dép. circ.* I, 124, " nous avons sous le coup de l'émotion publique et des necessités d'une guerre d'extermination organisé," etc.

bodied men between twenty-one and forty was a measure of " the utmost energy " well calculated to demonstrate Gambetta's indomitable spirit and will to wage war to the knife. The military value of these citizen soldiers was to prove slight, the execution of the decree was at times to rouse opposition and discontent, but its promulgation at this moment acted undoubtedly as a moral stimulus. It was a vivid reminder of 1792, and now more than ever the revolutionary legend was invoked as a goad to optimism. The men who appealed to it did not know, or cheerfully ignored, its hollowness ; did not know that the victories of the Annus Mirabilis had been won, as Niel put it, not because of, but in spite of, the *levée en masse*,[1] and that St. Cyr had judged that the greatest misfortune after that of having to fall back on such a means of salvation was that of having to make use of it.[2] In these first days of November there was a blind enthusiasm kindling, and there can be little doubt that it was largely, if not wholly, the creation of Gambetta. The exaltation of Republicans in the south was such that Metternich seriously expected an outbreak of civil war if an armistice was concluded.[3] In districts which were close to the war area, or felt the weight of German occupation, there was less optimism, but a dogged resignation to hardship and, in general, a strong sense of the essential indivisibility of the country. In Champagne, noted Prince Frederick Charles,[4] partisans of the Republic were rare, but Napoleon was unpopular. Everybody desired peace, provided that it meant only an indemnity payment and no cession of territory, and

---

[1] Cit. *Rapport* DARU, 437.

[2] *Moniteur universel*, June 16, 1819, cit. DUTRAIT-CROZON, *Gambetta et la défense nationale*, 17.

[3] *H.H.u.S.A.*, METTERNICH to BEUST, Nov. 5.

[4] Report to the King of Prussia, Nov. 13 ; *Mémoires du Prince Frédéric Charles*, 183, 184.

he added—proof of the influence of Gambetta's proclamation, as well as an indication of national character—that it was rare to hear Frenchmen admit that the French armies had been fairly beaten ; all reverses were attributed to treason.

Yet the spirit of exaltation might easily have subsided, like a pricked bubble, into a void of despair, or sought sustenance in political excess, but for the victory of Coulmiers which gave artificial confidence a sadly needed foundation in reality, and was a real incentive to work and service in the cause of the national defence.   Unfortunately, however, the military importance of the success was negligible in comparison with its moral effect.   Gambetta naturally made the most of the first victory of any significance gained by the French during the whole course of the war, but the actual achievement was from a military point of view more a matter for regrets than for congratulations, since the opportunity to surround the whole Bavarian force had been lost, and the inexperienced French troops were in no condition to follow up their success to advantage.[1]   To the Germans, however, it was a rude awakening.   They, like Bourbaki, had been convinced that the army of the Loire was a mere rabble to be scattered to the winds at the first encounter. " A moment's reflection," wrote Hatzfeldt, one of Bismarck's attachés, on November 7, " must show that the undisciplined and badly armed bands that are called the army of the Loire, and the army of that poor fool Garibaldi, are incapable of struggling against a regular army ; and that Prince Frederick Charles, with his army of more than 200,000 men, can march over the whole of France from north to south and from east to west, driving all these creatures before

---

[1] L. HALE, *The People's War in France, 1870-71*, says (85), " the faintest semblance of a pursuit would have resulted in the capture of the whole force so utterly exhausted was it ".   Cp. C. R. BALLARD, *The Military Genius of Abraham Lincoln* (London, 1926), 59, on the difficulties and rarity of successful pursuit.

him and pillaging the country as he chooses." [1] And a few days later the Prince himself wrote that the enemy was " in his death agony," his feeble effectives " no longer capable of continuing the struggle ".[2] The disillusionment which quickly followed showed that Moltke's diagnosis of French strategy was wholly mistaken.[3] In the new conditions of this second period of the war, faced with irregular armies concerning whom he had no data, the great Prussian was as fallible as any inferior general. Lack of information as to the strength and composition of the French forces, the active hostility of the population in many districts, and the existence of so many small forces of volunteers and franc-tireurs, which might well be mistaken for the outposts of larger bodies of troops, all contributed to produce a veritable fog of war which it was by no means easy to penetrate. When contact with the army of the Loire did cause a momentary rift, the revelations that rift disclosed were a most unwelcome surprise, and the appearance of a French detachment before Houdan, which was only two marches distant from Versailles, caused such alarm that the removal of headquarters was actually contemplated. This incident vividly illustrated the difficulty the Germans had in obtaining reliable information : the Houdan detachment was thought to be part of a large army advancing from Dreux and Chartres ; reinforcements were ordered in haste and the Grand Duke of Mecklenburg-Schwerin was commanded to concentrate his forces to meet the imaginary danger from the army of the West. In reality this " army," so far from threatening to march on Paris, was extended in a cordon over a front of some sixty miles, and numbered no more than 35,000 men.

[1] Count HATZFELDT, *Letters*, Nov. 7.
[2] *Mémoires du Prince Frédéric Charles*, 180-185.
[3] Cp. L. HALE, op. cit. 85.

The circumstances of a " people's war " thus placed the Germans at a real disadvantage ; but fortunately for them, the French never understood how real that disadvantage was. Although decrees such as that issued by Gambetta on October 14, placing each department within 100 kilometres of the enemy in a state of siege, undoubtedly contributed greatly to the thickening of the fog of war, the French authorities did not realise how complete was their enemy's perplexity, and how exceedingly precious was every scrap of information about their own troops' strength and disposition. Yet General von Heinleth could write that, although Coulmiers was tactically unfavourable to the Germans, strategically it was of much importance to them, since it " furnished complete information about the new army of the Loire, and crippled its aggressive power for a long time to come ".

" Had the French a notion of generalship," wrote von Stosch, on November 14, " things might turn out very badly for us," [1] and early in December Prince Frederick Charles declared that if Metz had fallen a day later, or his army had reached the Forest of Orléans a day later, the siege of Paris would have had to be raised : " That is clear, and every one is agreed on that point ".[2] But the French knew nothing of German anxiety ; it was not until three days after the victory that Gambetta and Freycinet went to D'Aurelle's headquarters to congratulate the army of the Loire, and determine the further plans of campaign, and then it was decided that D'Aurelle should fortify Orléans and remain there until reinforcement by three new army corps made him strong enough to resume the advance towards Paris. This

---

[1] A. von STOSCH, *Denkwürdigkeiten*, 206 ; cp. MOLTKE, *Letters*, II, 66.

[2] *Mémoires du Prince Frédéric Charles*, 264 ; cp. Count BEUST, *Memoirs* (London, 1897), II, 209.

failure to follow up the success of Coulmiers has been much criticised, and taken as convincing proof that the French had no "notion of generalship". It was, indeed, true that D'Aurelle was by no means an ideal chief for an army intended for offensive operations ; but there were many weighty reasons besides the natural timidity of the Commander-in-Chief for not continuing the advance immediately. "Our army," wrote the Southern general after the first battle of Bull Run, "was more disorganised by victory than that of the United States by defeat"[1] : the same could be said of the army of the Loire after the battle of Coulmiers, for its men were raw and inexperienced, and this for many of them was their first action, and a most exhausting experience. D'Aurelle was insistent that they must have time in which to rest, and be reorganised before undertaking any further offensive, and Gambetta and Freycinet, who were able to see for themselves the condition of the troops, seem to have been fairly convinced by the force of his arguments.[2] On the other hand, D'Aurelle admitted that the morale of his troops had improved tenfold,[3] and a bolder commander, less acutely conscious of every point in which his men were inferior to the regular troops he had been accustomed to handle, might have made a more vigorous effort to profit by this improvement. The need for rapid action was no less pressing than before : victory on the Loire could not increase the supplies in besieged Paris by a single day. But there was another reason, and a very cogent reason, for remaining on the defensive until further reinforcements were forthcoming. Gambetta, Freycinet, and the generals all apparently accepted as true a report, attributed by Freycinet to Thiers,[4]

[1] Cp. C. R. BALLARD, *The Military Genius of Abraham Lincoln*, 59.
[2] Cp. DUTRAIT-CROZON, *Gambetta et la défense nationale*, 255 ff.
[3] P. LEHAUTCOURT, *Campagne de la Loire, 1870-71*, I, 154.
[4] FREYCINET, *La Guerre en province*, 102 ; cp. *D.T.* II, Nov. 13.

that a German army 80,000 strong was advancing from Paris in the direction of Orléans. Actually, this was double the strength of the combined forces of the Grand-Duke of Mecklenburg-Schwerin and of von der Tann, the only possible opponents of D'Aurelle's army on November 12. The acceptance of this report was no tribute to the efficacy of Gambetta's decree of October 24, in which he had ordered local authorities to transmit to the War Office any and every piece of information concerning the numbers and movements of the enemy,[1] or to the discernment of Freycinet's vaunted [2] intelligence service which had the task of sifting and piecing together the information thus received : but, grossly erroneous as it was, its acceptance certainly was a decisive argument against a resumption of the offensive until the army of the Loire had been reorganised and reinforced.

Gambetta's men had made their demonstration, but there had been no news of Trochu passing victorious from Paris " over the bodies of the enemy ".   In fact, he had not yet attempted to do so ; his preparations were still incomplete when an appeal from Gambetta that he should make vigorous assaults in the direction of the Orléans road,[3] followed by the news of Coulmiers, showed him beyond a doubt that his own plan for combined operations in the Seine valley had been ignored by the provincial authorities. As he considered a junction with relieving forces an essential for the success of a sortie, and as he could not change the direction of the army of the Loire's march even if he wished, he reluctantly abandoned his long-cherished plan, and began to study the possibilities of breaking the investing lines on

---

[1] But it is in point of fact exceedingly difficult to obtain reliable estimates of numbers from untrained observers ; cp. G. F. R. HENDERSON, *Stonewall Jackson and the American Civil War* (London, 1902).

[2] *Souvenirs*, I, 158.   [3] Sent Nov. 8, arr. Nov. 14.

the southern side of the city. No sooner had he abandoned it than by a strange irony, the advance of the army of the Loire now being suspended and a counter offensive feared, Gambetta wrote suggesting that he might make a diversion by means of a vigorous attack in the direction of Normandy.[1] But it was too late ; this despatch which, a week earlier might have had decisive results, was now of no effect. In the meantime, while Trochu was hastily making new plans Favre, eager to spur on the provincial armies to action, reminded Gambetta that Paris could not hold out indefinitely : although it had food enough to last until January, December 15 should be regarded as the outside limit of effective resistance.[2] His despatch was immediately effective in rousing the War Ministry at Tours. The army of the Loire had now had a full week's rest since its re-entry into Orléans, and although some of Prince Frederick Charles' men were beginning to make their appearance, there had as yet been no sign of the expected offensive of 80,000 Germans. Upon receipt of Favre's reminder, Freycinet at once invited D'Aurelle to consider plans for a march to " join Trochu " : " We cannot remain at Orléans for ever. Paris is hungry and clamours for us ; "[3] and he informed the general that he could expect to dispose of 250,000 men. At the same time, the War Office at Tours was also studying a plan of advance. But D'Aurelle showed no enthusiasm for a renewal of offensive. He replied that Freycinet's figures were illusory : " it would be dangerous to trust to the deceptive mirage of figures grouped on paper, and to take them for a reality," and he objected that he could not devise a plan for a junction with Trochu without some knowledge of Trochu's

---

[1] *D.T.* II, 303 ; Nov. 12, GAMBETTA to FAVRE, written immediately after the conference at D'Aurelle's H.Q., arr. Nov. 18.

[2] FREYCINET, *Souvenirs*, I, 192.

[3] FREYCINET, *Guerre en province*, 112 ff.

movements. Gambetta answered that it was enough for D'Aurelle's purpose to suppose that Paris was aware of his presence at Orléans, and that it was " on the arc of the circle of which Orléans was the median point that the Parisians would necessarily be compelled to act ". The surmise was perfectly correct, but D'Aurelle was none the more rapid in devising a plan ; perhaps he hoped that the long-expected German offensive would soon demonstrate, more forcibly than any argument of his, the folly of imagining that it was possible to march on Paris. But Prince Frederick Charles had come to the conclusion that he was faced by the whole army of the Loire, and that the assembling of such large forces meant that rash though the enterprise seemed, the French, " obeying lawyer's commands," were determined to relieve Paris at any cost.[1] He, too, was expecting his adversary to take the offensive : and, despite D'Aurelle, he judged correctly. D'Aurelle's hesitation was Freycinet's chance to prove his own skill as a strategist. The Grand Duke of Mecklenburg had quite erroneously supposed that the army of the Loire was contemplating a turning movement in conjunction with the forces of the west towards Chartres and Dreux, and in this belief he had directly turned his back on the main French troops and marched westward in the direction of Le Mans.[2] Freycinet believed that Le Mans was seriously threatened, and imagined a diversion to be executed by the army of the Loire in order to draw the Germans away from Le Mans. But before the diversion could be executed the Grand Duke had been ordered to retire and co-operate with the army of Prince Frederick Charles in front of Orléans. Meanwhile, Gambetta had hastened to Le Mans to bring courage to the inhabitants and to inspire the defence with

---

[1] *Mémoires du Prince Frédéric Charles*, 198, 211.
[2] L. HALE, *The People's War*, ch. 6.

new vigour by his energy and optimism. His arrival almost coincided with the beginning of the Grand Duke's withdrawal. The inference was obvious, and Gambetta wrote with elation : " As a result of this journey the Prussians evidently thought there was a considerable concentration of troops on Le Mans and retreated. . . . I am convinced that I have saved Le Mans." [1] After displaying his energy by replacing Fiereck as commander of the forces of the west, visiting the camp of Conlie, and reorganising the new 23rd army corps under Jaurès, he returned to Tours. The grievance against Fiereck was that " he had compromised everything by his inertia . . . had not known how either to organise or to discipline his troops, and had scattered them over too long a line ".[2] The value of that long line in thickening the fog of war and mystifying Moltke no less than the Grand Duke of Mecklenburg entirely escaped the Minister of the Interior and of War.

Freycinet was not to be deterred from the execution of his diversion by the fact that its primary *raison d'être* no longer existed. It could serve as the first move on the way to " join Trochu," since D'Aurelle would produce no plan himself : " necessities of a superior order force us to do something, and in consequence to leave Orléans " ; [3] and they forced Freycinet not merely to desire the execution of his own plan, but to direct the advance of the 18th and 20th corps himself from his office at Tours, while General D'Aurelle de Paladines, Commander-in-Chief of the army of the Loire, virtually abdicated his command and remained spectator of movements which he disapproved.[4] He criticised the

[1] *D.T.* II, 316, 317.

[2] *D.T.* II, 316. The general had also been appointed at the request of the League of the West, which was not a very Republican organisation.

[3] FREYCINET, *Guerre en province,* 123.

[4] L. HALE, op. cit. 169.

dispersal of troops involved in Freycinet's scheme of a simul-
taneous advance on Beaumont, Montargis and Pithiviers,
but Freycinet, while he acknowledged the justice of the
criticism, replied that every plan had its risks, " and since
you have proposed no plan, we must suppose that the risks
here are no greater than elsewhere ".[1]   What those risks
were time was soon to show, but they were scarcely greater
than the risks involved in such strained relations between
the War Office and the chief command on the eve of
a series of decisive engagements.   It was intolerable for
Gambetta to have a Commander-in-Chief who would
neither take any initiative of his own, nor resign when he
saw himself virtually superseded and his troops ordered to
execute movements of which he did not approve.   Had
D'Aurelle been defeated like La Motte Rouge or Fiereck,
Gambetta no doubt would not have hesitated to replace
him, but when he was the only victorious general in the
army, and correspondingly popular, he could not well do so
without some more positive justification than a difference of
opinion.   The usual and more weighty pretext of defeat was
to be provided soon and disastrously enough.

The first of the considerable battles to which the movements devised by Freycinet were the prelude, was the battle
of Beaune-la-Rolande on November 28.   The whole strength
of the best part of the 18th and 20th corps was thrown into
the attack, but, after a prolonged struggle and an astonishing
resistance by the German defenders, the French were forced
to retire without taking the village.   " Rarely," said Colonel
Hale, " has an attacking force been so completely overthrown
and rendered so thoroughly incapable for either defence or
offence." [2]   But the significance of the repulse, understood
well enough by the French generals, was not so well ap-

---

[1] FREYCINET, *Guerre en province*, 125.   [2] *The People's War*, 203.

preciated either by the War Office at Tours or by the enemy. The Germans saw only that they had narrowly escaped severe defeat, and instead of following up their advantage, they remained on the defensive, prepared for a repetition of the ordeal. They now over-estimated, after long under-estimating, the strength and discipline of the provincial armies.

Now, indeed, the troops concerned in this engagement required rest and time in which to reform and recover from their losses. But that time was not to be allowed them. On the 30th Gambetta received a despatch from Trochu dated the 24th : " The news from the army of the Loire has naturally determined me to make a sortie by the south and go ahead, cost what it may. I shall complete the preparations, which have been hastened on by night and by day, on Monday (November 28). On Tuesday the 29th the outer army commanded by General Ducrot, the most energetic of us, will attack the enemy's fortified positions. If he captures them, he will push on towards the Loire, probably in the direction of Gien." [1] It was now already Wednesday the 30th. Supreme example of the fatal uncertainty of communication by air,—the balloon carrying Trochu's despatch had been borne far away to the north, and landed in Norway some distance from Christiania, which the aeronaut had been unable to reach before the 29th. On the receipt of this belated telegram there was great excitement, mingled with hope and vexation in the War Office at Tours. Freycinet telegraphed urgently to D'Aurelle to begin a general offensive, and proceeded himself to headquarters at St. Jean de Ruelle, to suggest the adoption of his plan for an advance on Fontainebleau.[2] The generals,

---

[1] Cit. FREYCINET, op. cit. 133.

[2] Although the plan was seriously criticised, no real modifications were permitted. The Ministry might just as well have sent its instructions by post, wrote Chanzy afterwards. A. CHUQUET, *Le Général Chanzy*, 16.

including D'Aurelle, agreed that some attempt should be made to join Ducrot, and the four principal army corps began the forward movement next day. At Tours hopes were high. Another balloon which had left Paris on the 30th came down at Belle-Ile-en-mer on December 1, and a Havas despatch was forwarded to Tours giving a detailed account of the fighting at Paris. Gambetta read it and cried for joy. The sortie, he announced, had succeeded ; Admiral de la Roncière had "advanced on Longjumeau" and " captured the positions of Epinay beyond Longjumeau " ; General Vinoy was expected to continue an attack towards the south that day ; finally, Trochu, with the modesty of a Turenne, made no mention of his own valiant contribution to the victory. The good news was communicated to the departments in a circular to all prefects, sub-prefects, and generals, and Freycinet telegraphed to D'Aurelle that the lines of investment had been " broken and smashed," he must fly to the aid of Ducrot without losing an hour.

Unfortunately, the despatch on which Gambetta based this vision of triumph made no mention of Longjumeau, which lay well to the south of the investing lines : nevertheless, the wish was so much father to the thought that he had immediately jumped to the conclusion that the Epinay referred to was Epinay-sur-Orge, beyond Longjumeau ; instead of which it was Epinay-sur-Seine, a little village close to Saint Denis. The whole tale of a victorious break through rested on this confusion of names, and a careful reading of the despatch should have shown how doubtful was Gambetta's interpretation.[1] He had not the caution of a Palikao, and his optimism led him cruelly to deceive himself and also his country. Disillusionment was

---

[1] Cp. H. DUTRAIT-CROZON, *Gambetta et la défense nationale*, 561, App. E, for full text of this despatch.

to come when the cup of misfortune seemed already full to overflowing.

The army of the Loire continued its operations on December 2, but without gaining any appreciable advantage. Nevertheless, Freycinet professed optimism, and telegraphed to D'Aurelle that, from the information available at the Ministry of War, he should not meet with much resistance, either " at Pithiviers or at the other points," since the bulk of the enemy forces was hastening towards Corbeil to check the victorious Ducrot.[1] He also informed D'Aurelle that, as a result of the operations in progress, he was to resume the strategical direction of all five army corps. On the eve of the decisive battles, Freycinet generously renounced his control, and sought to avoid responsibility. But, far from contemplating an advance on Pithiviers, D'Aurelle found the heritage bequeathed him by Freycinet so precarious, and the exhaustion of the troops so great, that he determined to retire on Orléans. The execution of the retreat was none the easier because Freycinet continued to give orders without the knowledge of D'Aurelle, and frequently in contradiction to the general's own instructions. The enormous defensive advantages of the Forest of Orléans were entirely lost, and Prince Frederick Charles' advance through the Forest, a leap in the dark which, according to probabilities, courted certain disaster, proved a brilliant success.[2] His boldness intimidated troops whose morale was impaired, and who were exhausted by continuous fighting and the hardships of bitterly cold weather. " We must be in Orléans on December 4," said Prince Frederick Charles, and he was. Bad news followed bad news, and D'Aurelle telegraphed to Tours before 4 a.m. that morning that the defence of Orléans was

---

[1] H. DUTRAIT-CROZON, op. cit. 289.
[2] HALE, *The People's War*, 251 ff.

no longer possible.[1] Freycinet was stupefied. He could not
understand the abandonment of a place which had been so
strongly fortified, and which D'Aurelle had originally said
that he hoped to hold against any numbers. However,
when D'Aurelle replied to his expostulations and said that
any attempt to hold the city longer might " result in a great
disaster," Freycinet decided to appeal to Gambetta. The
signature of the Minister of War at the foot of the answer to
D'Aurelle might " produce some effect upon these cowardly
spirits ".[2] But the general who had formerly shown such
fatal lack of initiative now stood firm by his own judgment,
and his resistance was the more stubborn because he felt
that the existence of his whole army was at stake. He
replied that he was on the spot, and therefore in a better
position to judge the situation ; the only means of avoiding
a complete catastrophe was by having the courage to make
a sacrifice while there was still time. The responsibility for
any other decision rested with Freycinet and with Gambetta,
and they dared not bear it alone. The other members of
the Delegation, whose interference in military matters was
ordinarily resented and forbidden by Gambetta, were now
called in to share the burden of admitting grave defeat.
" If the situation had not been so serious," said Glais-
Bizoin, " we should all have replied that since our advice
had not been asked upon the military plans and combinations
which preceded the battle, we had not to pronounce upon
a question of retreat ".[3] However, as the situation was so
serious, they consented to discuss the question and the
decision was in favour of evacuation. A telegram drafted
by Gambetta and signed by all four Delegates threw the

---

[1] Cit. FREYCINET, *La Guerre en province*, 164.

[2] *Dép. circ.* II, 217, cit. DUTRAIT-CROZON, *Gambetta et la défense nationale*, 296.

[3] GLAIS-BIZOIN, *Dictature de cinq mois*, 108, 109.

final responsibility upon D'Aurelle : "Since you say that retreat is necessary . . . the Government leaves to you the task of executing the movements of the retreat on the need of which you insist ".[1] For a moment, however, D'Aurelle thought he might after all hold out, and Gambetta promptly determined to fortify the general's welcome resolution and to save Orléans by his presence, as he had saved Le Mans. But close to Orléans the line was completely blocked, and it was impossible for the Minister to reach the threatened city without risk of capture. The Marquis de Castellane was at Beaugency station that day when " suddenly a shrill whistle sounded. An engine [2] arrived at full speed. There were three men on it : the driver, the stoker, and a third with a goat skin wrapped round his neck. It was Gambetta ! . . . he had just risked his skin dashing down the line before it was quite cut, for the railway was overrun with Bavarians, who shot at him like a hare as he passed." [3]   However, D'Aurelle's hope of resisting proved as illusory as Gambetta's journey was fruitless : at 11 p.m. that night the Germans were once again in possession of Orléans. Two days earlier the sortie at Paris had failed, and Ducrot, without fulfilling his promise, had returned to the city, neither victorious nor dead.[4] Once more the French were faced by defeat on every hand. A month had served to shatter Gambetta's strategical plan and to destroy the bright hopes raised by Coulmiers ; prospects were even gloomier than in the black days after Metz, Paris was growing hungry, and the provincial armies were further than ever from her relief.

[1] FREYCINET, *Souvenirs*, I, 203.

[2] But Gambetta's despatch to prefects on Dec. 5 speaks of a "special train " ; cp. *Murailles politiques françaises*, I, 549.

[3] Marquis de CASTELLANE, *Men and Things of My Time*, 87 ; and *Les hommes d'état français au XIX siécle* (Paris, 1888), 370.

[4] FREYCINET, *La Guerre en province*, 139.

Gambetta's strategy had required confident generalship as well as experienced soldiers, and without either the dice had been heavily loaded against its triumph, for not only was the enemy exceedingly formidable, but also the country through which the army of the Loire was obliged to advance beyond Orléans was, in the opinion of a military expert, " wholly unsuitable to young and inexperienced troops ".[1] " Very different," once wrote the future Marshal Foch, " would have been a programme of national resistance which aimed first at the defence of every foot of territory providing resources, and then at the deliverance of the country.   Its execution would have permitted the employment of the defensive to begin with, the only formation possible for young levies, because it makes use of space, time, and ground, and permits the defenders to refuse to come to conclusions with an adversary who has need of decisive victories in order to break resistance and so to conquer the country.   It would have allowed the use of offensive later with armies which had been hardened and restored to confidence against an enemy whose forces would necessarily have been extended, scattered, and exhausted by sterile efforts and reduced to a wretched plight owing to the length of his communications." [2] Very different indeed, and perhaps much sounder, if the national defence could have been treated as a purely military problem and if the existence òf Paris could have been conveniently ignored.   But the siege of Paris was the prime factor in the defence problem from the outset.   What Government could have adopted Foch's programme of defensive when Paris was crying out for relief?   What enthusiasm could such a programme arouse in a country which, above all, needed some quick result, some striking

[1] Foch, *De la Conduite de la guerre* (3rd edn. Paris, 1915), 17.
[2] Ibid.

success to allow it to hope once more? The plan completely failed to take account of the moral and political requirements of the situation, and those requirements were all important : it was another witness to the truth of the generalisation that soldiers are notoriously bad politicians. There can be no question that Gambetta was right in fixing the relief of Paris as the objective : an attempt at offensive was essential : the tragedy was that the means of execution were imperfect, and that the man who mattered above all, D'Aurelle, had a defensive mentality. By his reluctance to take the initiative and his evident desire to limit his responsibility, he only increased the difficulties of his position and encouraged the interference of the civilian amateurs whose capacity he mistrusted. The result of that interference was disastrous : but had the army of the Loire found a Bonaparte, or even a Chanzy, to command it in November, a man with a vigorous offensive mentality, there would have been no need for civilian strategists to work their havoc, and it might well have achieved the success which was nearly within its grasp.

XIII

A NEW PHASE IN THE WAR

THE situation caused by the defeat of the army of the Loire
and the loss of Orléans was to show Gambetta the man both
at his worst and at his best ; at his worst in his treatment of
D'Aurelle, at his best in his refusal to despair.

General D'Aurelle had now been defeated, and it was to
be expected that he should go the way of beaten commanders ;
indeed, his defects had become so clear during the past ten
days, and his relations with the War Office so strained, that
his retention would scarcely have been feasible or desirable.
But Gambetta was not content with allowing the chief
command of the army of the Loire to lapse simply as a result
of the fact that retreat had divided the army in two. His
troops had met with disaster as a result of the direction of
operations by the War Ministry, but it was the Commander-
in-Chief who was the victim of his anger and disappointment,
and whom the Minister of War designed as the scapegoat for
the sins of civilian strategists. The official account of the
defeat, communicated by Gambetta in a note to all prefects
and sub-prefects on December 5, was skilfully composed to
clear the responsibility of M. le Ministre de la guerre, while
laying the conduct of D'Aurelle open to the gravest suspicions.[1] D'Aurelle, it explained, had suddenly found the
situation of his army disquieting, and proposed to evacuate

---

[1] For the full text see *Les Murailles politiques françaises*, I, 549.

Orléans ; yet that army still consisted of over 200,000 men, and Orléans was a well-fortified camp. "These exceptionally favourable circumstances" ought to have allowed a resistance, and in any case "the most elementary duty of a soldier" demanded an attempt at resistance. "Gambetta added that the retreat was proceeding in good order, but that he was ' without news of General D'Aurelle '." A note so full of innuendo was clearly liable to the worst interpretations ; accordingly, the prefect Gent informed the populace of Marseilles that the evacuation had been ordered " without a fight, without a struggle, without a defeat," and that the army had withdrawn " without being pressed, without even being attacked ".[1] A month after Bazaine, D'Aurelle, too, lost his reputation through the action of Gambetta : but Gambetta could not defend the note of December 5 as he had defended the proclamation of October 30 on the grounds of absolute moral necessity, in order to prevent the country from giving way to despair. It explained too little and suggested too much to be wholly reassuring : moreover, the man whose incompetence alone it represented as responsible for the disaster was his own choice. How was it that the capable victor of Coulmiers should suddenly show such incapacity ? [2]

Nevertheless, unjust and misleading though the note was, it was evidently designed to minimise the importance of the defeat as well as to clear the War Ministry of responsibility. It ended on a note of optimism : the retreat had been carried out " in the best possible conditions. We hope to resume the offensive shortly. The morale of the troops is excellent." [3] Gambetta was as sensible as ever to the importance of maintaining the confidence of the country as a

[1] Cit. C. VON. DER GOLTZ, *Gambetta u. seine Armeen*, 91.
[2] Cp. *D.T.* I, 27 ; II, 75. [3] *Murailles politiques françaises*, I, 549.

whole ; yet without success the task must be increasingly difficult. The loss of Orléans was later judged by Freycinet to have been " the greatest misfortune of the second period of the war and the one which decided the fate of France " ; [1] and close upon it followed the news that the great effort at sortie from Paris had definitely failed. The blow was all the harder to bear after Gambetta's enthusiastic misreading of an earlier despatch. Now Paris and the provinces alike had summoned all their strength in vain. Their weakness in comparison with the enemy had been proved. What could be gained or hoped from a continuation of the struggle ? Moltke thought that its futility must now be obvious, even to the authorities in Paris, and promptly wrote to Trochu informing him of the capture of Orléans and inviting him to send an officer to verify the defeat of the army of the Loire. Clearly it was an indirect overture for peace, and as such it was hailed by General Ducrot.[2] But the Government Council were not all agreed with him in regarding it as a " providential incident ". Trochu believed that this was the beginning of an attempt to compromise him as Bismarck had compromised Bazaine ; and the majority were in a frame of mind which led them to suspect any proposal made by a Prussian. It was now considered a point of honour to resist to the last extremity, and the reply was a brief refusal to enter into any parley.[3] Thus Paris doggedly confirmed its policy of " guerre à outrance " and Gambetta, well pleased, told Trochu that his letter had been " applauded by the whole of France ".[4] If Paris was determined to continue the struggle, still more so was Gambetta ; it was by no means obvious to him that the loss of Orléans had decided the fate

---

[1] *La Guerre en province*, 175.   [2] *Dép.* III, 96.

[3] DRÉO, *Procès-verbaux*, and for Trochu's uncompromising attitude cp. *F.O.* 27, 1829, CLAREMONT to GRANVILLE, Dec. 30.

[4] Cit. SOREL, *Histoire Diplomatique de la guerre franco-allemande*, II, 113, 114.

of the country, and defeat merely impelled him to still greater energy. It was in these dark days of December that he appeared at his greatest as a moral force, a veritable "Tribune of Forlorn Hope," undaunted by misfortune, tireless in his efforts to restore confidence, boldly planning to snatch victory from the jaws of defeat. More vehemently than ever he declared his intention of waging war to the knife. There were still immense reserves of men ; less than half the *Mobilisés* called up by the decree of September 29 had been handed over to the Minister of War as yet, and in addition, there were all those affected by the decree of November 2 which had completed the *levée en masse*. The full effect of much of the new organisation had yet to be shown : for instance, the decree establishing eleven big training camps had been issued only a fortnight before,[1] and had still to prove its value. Before the defeat of Orléans, Gambetta had estimated that the national defence in the provinces would not be fully equipped until January 15 ; then, he told Jules Favre, " we shall really be armed to the teeth ". But by then, too, according to Favre's reckoning, Paris would have been compelled to capitulate. Now, however, the attempt to relieve the city having failed, Paris was no longer to be the all-dominating factor in Gambetta's calculations. He could look elsewhere and beyond the fall of the capital, when its relief seemed outside the bounds of present possibility. That it must fall, he recognised, but he refused to believe that its fall must inevitably decide the country's fate. " Even after the fall of Paris," he wrote, on December 20, " we shall change their insolent and fragile fortune into unheard of disaster ".[2] Moltke's letter might

---

[1] Nov. 25.

[2] *Dép. circ.* I, 157 ; cp. I, 155, Nov. 26. It was Freycinet who on Dec. 18 first proposed that " on renoncerait quant à présent à marcher sur Paris ". *Revue d'Histoire, Campagne de Général Bourbaki dans l'Est*, I, 49.

well encourage him in the optimistic belief that it would be impossible for the Germans to occupy French soil for another six months and remain victorious. The idea of a war of " lassitude " was no new conception, but it emerged much more clearly now that the army of the Loire had met with defeat.[1]

The loss of Orléans marked the beginning of a second phase in the second period of the Franco-German war, and this phase was distinguished from the first not only by a different grouping of the French forces and by a different strategy, but also by a change of the seat of government. The Delegation had soon found that Tours was uncomfortably close to the theatre of war ; but though removal had, since the end of September, often been discussed, it had as often been postponed.[2]   Now, however, it was an unavoidable consequence of defeat, and the gravity of that defeat was but thinly disguised by the explanation that the presence of the Government at Tours " embarrassed the movements of the armies ".[3]   Wisely the Delegates removed to a city far away from the fighting area.   The strategy of the armies on the Loire was not likely to be confused by the necessity for covering Bordeaux ; and the wisdom of the choice of Bordeaux as the new capital was confirmed by another generation.[4]   Forty-four years later a French Government was compelled to quit Paris owing to a fresh German menace,

---

[1] See Appendix XIII, p. 315.

[2] For a description of Tours on the eve of the Delegation's departure, see G. SCHLUMBERGER, Mes Souvenirs, I, 125.

[3] Though this was, of course, true.   F.O. 146, 1483, LYONS to GRANVILLE, Dec. 8.

[4] Several other towns had been suggested.   Fourichon favoured Périgueux, Gambetta preferred Clermont-Ferrand, Ranc and Spuller urged the claims of Lyons, D.T. II, Oct. 15 ; DRÉO, Procès-verbaux, 247, Oct. 26 ; FRANQUET DE FRANQUEVILLE, Souvenirs intimes de la vie de mon père, 340, 345 ; RANC, Souvenirs et Correspondance, 176.

and to the insistence of the Higher Command, which was determined that the great error of government in 1870 should not be repeated in 1914. It proceeded directly to Bordeaux, and President Poincaré was housed in the Prefecture which once had sheltered Gambetta.

Gambetta, however, did not go immediately to his new capital. During the past two months there had been only two occasions on which he was absent from Tours for more than a day at a time : the first, a flying visit to Besançon in October to assist in the reorganisation of the army of the Vosges ; the second, the journey a month later to "save Le Mans" and to reorganise the army of the West. At Tours the Minister of War was close to the main scene of operations, and could easily exert his personal influence, but at Bordeaux he must be far removed, and that at a time when, as it seemed to him, his presence was all the more necessary to give a fresh impetus to the forces of the national defence after they had just experienced such a grave set-back. By now Freycinet had proved his worth, and the Delegate who had the Minister's entire confidence could be trusted to continue the direction of the War Office unaided. Nor were there any diplomatic or internal questions so important as to require Gambetta's presence at Bordeaux. He was free to carry out the duties of a War Minister after his own fashion, to visit the armies, to reorganise scattered troops, to revive courage and to maintain enthusiasm by means of personal contacts. Thus, of the fifty-one days between the arrival of the Delegation at Bordeaux and the signing of the armistice, he spent only twenty-two with his colleagues, and his first visit to the new seat of government did not take place until December 28.

The army of the Loire had been cut in two as a result of its defeat and so, as Gambetta cheerfully pointed out to

Favre, there were now two armies where before there had been only one.[1] The 16th and 17th corps, which were retreating westward along the right bank of the Loire towards Vendôme, now formed the Second Army of the Loire, under the command of Chanzy, in Gambetta's opinion " the one real soldier revealed by these last events " [2] : the 18th and 20th corps were to reform under Bourbaki at Bourges, where they were soon joined by the 15th under Des Pallières. It was this, the First Army, which was to need all Gambetta's attention, and after a brief visit to Chanzy at Josnes on December 9, the day of the Government's departure for Bordeaux, he left for Bourges accompanied, as always, by his faithful Achates, Eugène Spuller.[3] The retreat of the corps composing the First Army was far from being the retreat in good order of which Gambetta had spoken in his note of December 5. The commanders of the 15th and 20th corps had reported the utter exhaustion of their men, and their lack of the most necessary clothing and equipment. Gambetta at once saw for himself how true these reports were, and hastened to enlighten Freycinet, whose tendency was to attribute any complaints to the " poor spirit " of the generals, and to regard war as a mathematical problem in which the disturbing human factor need not be taken into account. His own report entirely agreed with that of Bourbaki, the most pessimistic of generals : the troops, he told Freycinet, were in a " vèritable state of disorganisation " ; it was the saddest thing he had yet seen.[4]

By his choice of Chanzy to command the Second Army of the Loire, Gambetta showed that he could recognise a

[1] *Dép. circ.* I, 178, 179.

[2] *D.T.* II, 375. For the horrors of the retreat on Vendôme, see G. SCHLUM-BERGER, *Mes Souvenirs*, I, 128 ff.

[3] Cp. Appendix XIV, p. 318.   [4] *D.T.* II, 342.

good general when he saw one ; by his choice of Bourbaki to command the First Army he proved, as he had already proved in the nomination of D'Aurelle, that the interests of the national defence were by no means invariably subordinated to the demands of Republican politics. But in the appointment of Bourbaki he displayed much less sound judgment than in the promotion of Chanzy. After failing to organise a strong force in the north, largely owing to the opposition of the civil authorities, who suspected him as an Imperialist and a supposed accomplice in the " treason " of Bazaine, Bourbaki had been removed from this post at the instance of Freycinet,[1] and had returned to Tours very discontented with the Government as a result of his experiences. But the Government, too, was disappointed : " Bourbaki is not exactly an organiser," Gambetta told Favre, " and he showed little energy in hurrying on the recruitment of his forces in spite of the fact that he was given a blank cheque as regards ways and means. His ill-disguised discouragement and the detestable entourage he had formed on his staff . . . were too many pretexts for mistrust and suspicion. . . . All our efforts to restore his confidence have been powerless." [2] Yet, despite this very clear sense of his shortcomings, Gambetta seems still to have been dazzled by Bourbaki's reputation, and good generals were not so common that he could afford to dispense with the services of a single one. Bourbaki had failed as an organiser ; he had yet to be proved in battle. Gambetta, therefore, had made every effort to persuade him to accept the command of a corps [3] in the army of the Loire ; at length the general had accepted on condition that he should no longer be treated with suspicion. The promise was readily, no doubt sincerely,

[1] *D.T.* II, 304.   [2] *D.T.* II, 317, Nov. 26.
[3] The 18th A.C.   He did not take over command until Dec. 2.

given by Gambetta, who assured him of his entire confidence : [1] but it did not hold good for Freycinet, who had
no such veneration for " old military glories ".[2] He justly
regretted that Bourbaki should have been promoted to the
chief command of an army after the fall of Orléans, and he
did not hesitate to try and provoke his resignation.   In this
the Delegate was more clear-sighted than the Minister :
Bourbaki, as Freycinet recognised,[3] might have done excellent service as the subordinate commander of an army
corps, but the example of D'Aurelle had fully proved the
disadvantages of a Commander-in-Chief who was pessimistic, and had no belief in the possibilities of victory.
Chanzy, whom Freycinet held up to Bourbaki as a model,
was right when he said that confidence was essential for
success in war.   Yet Gambetta was unwilling to provoke the
resignation of the man whom Trochu had recommended to
him as capable of saving France.   Moreover, he wished to
give Bourbaki a chance of justifying the confidence he had
promised to show him, and his determination to maintain
Bourbaki in spite of Freycinet was perhaps strengthened by
a momentary difference of opinion with the Delegate upon
the new plan of campaign.   Nevertheless, the suspicions of
Freycinet made their impression on Gambetta, and the impression could not fail to be strengthened by Bourbaki's
discouragement which Gambetta described as " heart-
rending ".   The ultimate decision with regard to the
command of the First Army was an unhappy compromise.
Bourbaki was maintained, but De Serres,[4] Freycinet's
" confidant ", yet by no means a faithful interpreter of

---

[1] *Dép.* III, 368.

[2] *Rapport* PERROT, 480, 489, cit. DUTRAIT-CROZON, *Gambetta et la défense
nationale*, 318, 319 ; FREYCINET, *Souvenirs*, I, 232.

[3] *Souvenirs*, I, 196.

[4] A Pole, born Wieczffinski ; cp. DUTRAIT-CROZON, op. cit. 53.

his master's instructions,[1] was attached to the general as " Delegate " of the Minister of War, and the decline of Gambetta's " entire confidence " in Bourbaki was measured by the terms of De Serres' mission—" to keep a watch on everything and never to hesitate to take extreme measures if there is need ".[2] Extreme measures meant the production of an undated decree which De Serres carried with him, and which deprived the Commander-in-Chief of the First Army of his command.[3]

The division of the army of the Loire, brought about by necessity, was in itself strategically sound, since it puzzled the Germans and also simplified the problems of supply, but it led to a division of opinion as to the plan of campaign, and particularly as to the use of the First Army. Chanzy was urgent that it should be employed to create diversions which would relieve his own retreat, and he and Freycinet both wished Bourbaki to retire westwards towards Amboise. At the same time, Chanzy pressed for the eventual reunion of the armies, and as he was now Freycinet's model commander, there were many who expected that he would be given the chief command of both.[4] But those who counted upon Freycinet's favour reckoned without Gambetta. For one thing, the First Army was for several days incapable of any movement whatsoever, and when the work of reorganisation had made some progress, Gambetta had his own plan of campaign. The best strategy, he said, was to take the offensive in the east, and so " relieve every one, Chanzy as well as Paris ".[5] He proposed, then, that the scattered forces in the

---

[1] Cp. *Revue d'Histoire, Campagne de Bourbaki dans l'Est*, I, 59 ff.

[2] *Rapport* PERROT, 565, cit. DUTRAIT-CROZON, *Gambetta et la défense nationale*, 365.

[3] *Revue d'Histoire, Campagne de Bourbaki dans l'Est*, I, 86.

[4] *F.O.* 146, 1483, FEILDING to LYONS, Dec. 14.

[5] *Dép. circ.* I, 280.

east should rally and, after an advance on Dijon, proceed
to attempt the relief of Belfort, and to cut the German communications ; [1] meanwhile the First Army should march
upon Montargis and Fontainebleau. This plan was a combination of the two which had originally been considered on
Gambetta's arrival at Tours in October ; he revived the
idea of an expedition to the east, but at the same time he
clung to the notion of an advance in the direction of Paris.
No sooner was the plan conceived than Gambetta was
impatient to put it into execution ; the interests of the
Republic and of France, as well as General Bourbaki's
reputation, demanded its immediate trial, and the departure of Bourbaki's army was fixed for December 19. But
Freycinet, too, was a strategist, and he and De Serres,
abandoning the idea of a reunion of the two chief armies,
had worked out a plan of their own. Gambetta's plan,
which reached them on the 18th, appeared by no means
satisfactory, and De Serres was sent in all haste to Bourges
to point out that the advance upon Montargis was both
useless and dangerous, and to induce Gambetta to adopt
their plan which proposed to transfer operations wholly to
the east. Gambetta was at length impressed by De Serres'
arguments, and agreed to accept this change of programme
if it was approved by Bourbaki. The decision now lay with
the general, and it was not difficult for De Serres to persuade
a man who had already lost his power of initiative. Too
readily, Bourbaki agreed to De Serres' verbal proposals,
which proved to be a distortion of Freycinet's real plan.
The "confidant" returned in triumph to Bourges, and
Gambetta telegraphed that all had been arranged to the
general satisfaction. Two days later he informed Freycinet

---

[1] GAMBETTA to FAVRE, Dec. 14, cit. *Revue d'Histoire, Campagne de Bourbaki
dans l'Est*, I, 46.

that, knowing that De Serres was completely in his confidence, he had given him full powers " pour tout diriger ".[1] Thus, within a few hours, the intervention of Freycinet had entirely altered the situation, checked the opening movements of the First Army's new campaign, and supplied that army with an entirely new objective. The expedition to the east on which so much depended was launched in haste, its details imperfectly worked out, and the means of execution unprepared. It was directed and organised principally by its authors Freycinet and De Serres, but unfortunately the one was to prove a very loose interpreter of the ideas of the other.[2]

According to all the specialists, wrote Freycinet later, this campaign in the east was bound to have " great results," and an offensive in the east, Gambetta had said, would relieve " every one, Chanzy, as well as Paris ". Of these, Paris was clearly the most important. Yet Chanzy was horrified when he heard of this plan to relieve Belfort ; even if it did succeed he thought the success would be too remote to have any effect upon the capital. And now still more than ever speed was an essential in any plan devised to assist Paris. The plan for the expedition to the east was not adopted until after the date originally mentioned by Favre as the ultimate term of Parisian resistance, December 15. The most sanguine reckoners did not think that the city could possibly hold out longer than the end of January, so that Gambetta could not safely count on much more than a month in which " to do something for Paris ". Prompt success was essential. Yet of prompt success there was never any question. The army of Bourbaki was the victim of misunderstanding and miscalculation from the day it left

[1] *Revue d'Histoire, Campagne de Bourbaki dans l'Est*, I, 87.
[2] Ibid. 48 ff.

Bourges. Freycinet's plan, bold and seductive at first sight, was the plan of an arm-chair strategist, for it ignored certain simple but all-important facts ; it overlooked the great difficulties of transport, for which no adequate preparation had been made ; it ignored the nature of the country in which the army was required to operate, a district unsuitable at any time for the movement of large masses, and particularly unsuitable for a large mass of inexperienced troops with a low standard of morale in the depths of an exceptionally bitter winter. It was precisely these factors, difficulties of transport, country, and weather, none of them wholly incalculable,[1] which were to prevent the possibility of speed. Freycinet overlooked them : but so did Gambetta and Bourbaki, when they accepted his plan. They, too, must share the responsibility, for they were under no compulsion to adopt it, particularly when another movement was already under weigh. The difficulties of the grand expedition to the east multiplied as soon as its execution began ; there were blockage and confusion on the railway lines, uncertainty as to the forces available, uncertainty even as to the real objectives of the campaign. De Serres, Freycinet, and Gambetta all gave orders from different places, and in the midst of the confusion was the Commander-in-Chief, Bourbaki, as unfit an instrument as ever for the execution of a bold plan. The auspices were, indeed, unfavourable.

Meanwhile, the Second Army was being forced back from position to position. But Chanzy's retreat was by no means the rout which his adversary, Prince Frederick Charles, had been led to expect from his observations of the Loire army in the battles of Orléans ; [2] it was a masterly with-

---

[1] For snow was a common occurrence in E. France in mid-winter.
[2] *Mémoires du Prince Frédéric Charles*, II, 264.

drawal by stages to Le Mans, where he set to work to re-organise. He reached Le Mans on December 20 ; by the end of the month his troops, after reinforcement, numbered 130,000, and on January 8, 1871, he declared his readiness to make a new attempt to relieve Paris. But his optimism was speedily to be quenched. Frederick Charles, whose atten-tion had for a time been diverted, owing to the uncertainty of headquarters as to the whereabouts of Bourbaki, now advanced once more against the Second Army of the Loire. Some Breton *Mobilisés* abandoned an important position and, after severe fighting, Le Mans fell into German hands. This marked the end of the Prince's westward advance ; his army was too fatigued and too much reduced in numbers for the pursuit to the Atlantic of which he had dreamt : but it was also the end of Chanzy's hopes of offensive, although his confidence was indomitable, and he wished to retire on Alençon instead of on Laval, because it was six miles nearer Paris.[1] This time the retreat of the Second Army of the Loire did very nearly resemble a rout. Raw *Mobilisés* had broken in panic and the panic had spread ; the hardships of the retreat were increased by a Siberian temperature, and Colonel Feilding, writing from Laval on the 17th, estimated the number of " stragglers and runaways " at no less than 70,000.[2] It was clear that Chanzy's forces must be incap-able of further action for some time to come, and that his hopes of relieving Paris were chimerical, for the fall of the city was now expected to be imminent. Defeat, too, met the army of the North, which had become a reality under Faidherbe, and had made valuable, and sometimes successful, diversions since the beginning of September. " I wonder," said Feilding, " when the French will be tired of seeing their

[1] *F.O.* 146, 1530, FEILDING to LYONS, Jan. 17.
[2] Ibid.

armies strategically mismanaged by the personnel of the
Minister of War." [1]   The answer was soon to be given.
The last hope of the national defence in the provinces now
rested upon the expedition to the east, an expedition planned
by a Freycinet, distorted by a De Serres, and executed by a
Bourbaki.

[1] *F.O.* 146, 1530.

XIV

THE LONDON CONFERENCE AND THE LAST
EFFORTS AT RESISTANCE

" The adversaries of the Republic," Gambetta told Favre
on December 14, " talk incessantly of peace, of the impotence
of our efforts, and of the sterility of the struggle " ; [1] and it
was easy for them to represent the man who talked incessantly
of war, who was supreme in the Delegation, and refused to
admit the exercise of universal suffrage, as nothing better
than an ambitious adventurer who desired merely to prolong
his enjoyment of power and to establish a personal dictatorship. Dictator Gambetta was, in fact, though he later
repudiated the title with indignation, and there can be little
doubt that a man of his temperament did enjoy the exercise
of unlimited authority. But that authority he exercised,
not merely to gratify a love of power for its own sake, but to
realise a far greater aim in the salvation of the country and
the Republic. His attitude to the London Conference is
in itself a conclusive refutation of the charge that he aimed
simply at dictatorship for dictatorship's sake.

Although Gambetta had so strenuously opposed armistice
negotiations which might lead to elections, he was, as Lord
Lyons pointed out, ready " to take advantage of any accidents
which might occur ".[2] Russia's denunciation of Article 2 of

---

[1] *D.T.* II, 351.
[2] *F.O.* 146, 1482, Lyons to Granville, Oct. 31.

the Treaty of Paris (1856) was such an " accident ".[1]   The
clause regulated the neutralisation of the Black Sea, imposed
on Russia after the Crimean War, and there were great
hopes in France that its denunciation would rouse England,
and that the incident would create a diversion which would
be advantageous to France, even if a general war did not
follow.   Gambetta summed up the possibilities of the situation very clearly in a despatch to Favre on November 13 : [2]
England, the Power most affected and offended by Russia's
action, would, he said, either submit, in which case any
precipitate action by France would alienate Russia, or act
vigorously, aided by Italy, Austria, and Spain, which would
be very advantageous for France ; or, again, there might be
a congress of the signatory Powers.   The Gladstone ministry,
however, was far from bellicose, and inclined to the third
suggestion of a congress.   Tours was disappointed : " as a
kindler of discord," noted Metternich, Russia's action had
been welcomed ; " as a subject for lengthy discussion," it
gave far less pleasure,[3] all the less (moreover), because the
proposal for a congress originated with the enemy, Prussia.

Odo Russell's bluff and threats of war had, in fact,
induced Bismarck to undertake to propose a conference as
the one solution which could avert an European conflagra-
tion and save England's face.[4]   Bismarck had no wish for a
conference in which France, as a signatory to the Paris Treaty,
would be entitled to take part ; it might be highly inconvenient, but not so inconvenient as a generalisation of the war,
and he could not afford to throw England into the arms of
France.   But to the suspicious Favre the conference seemed

---

[1] The eventful day of Oct. 31 was the day she chose for this action.
[2] *D.T.* II, 304.
[3] *H.H.u.S.A.*, METTERNICH to BEUST, Nov. 21.
[4] Cp. MORLEY, *Life of Gladstone*, II, 352 ; FITZMAURICE, *Life of Lord
Granville*, II, 73.

a snare merely because it was proposed by Bismarck, and the Prussian Minister was soon able to turn his mistrustful hesitancy to good account. The sentimental Frenchman was " revolted " at the thought of a diplomatic conversation about the Black Sea, in which the French representative would gravely discuss the estuaries of the Danube, while " his Prussian neighbour would open a despatch announcing that Paris was in flames ".[1] The hysterical atmosphere of the capital was, as Gambetta realised, quite unsuited to the cool conduct of diplomacy, and although he spoke warmly of Chaudordy as " an important and capable representative, fully aware of the value of prudence," he had urged, even before a congress had definitely been proposed, that Favre would best solve the weighty problems arising from the Gortschakoff circular by leaving Paris himself : Thiers was discredited by two failures, and the French diplomatic agents abroad he considered woefully inadequate ; the presence of Favre at Tours would be most valuable.[2] But the diplomatic possibilities of the situation, clearly seen by Gambetta and Chaudordy, were lost on the Minister for Foreign Affairs. By participation in the conference France could not impair her military position, she could scarcely make her diplomatic position more unfavourable, while by skilful management she might succeed, as did Talleyrand in 1814 and Cavour in 1856, in reaping great advantage. It was not until December 17 that Favre yielded to the urgent appeals of Chaudordy, and to the considered opinion of Gambetta, that France should accept the invitation to London without attempting to impose any preliminary conditions.

[1] FAVRE, *Gouvernement de la défense nationale*, II, 253, FAVRE to CHAUDORDY, Dec. 5.
[2] *D.T.* II, 304, Nov. 13.

" If a congress should result," wrote Metternich on November 21, " which might lead to a peace which would be honourable for France and a germ of future alliances, they would be very glad—but if Prussia, playing a double game, simply caused the negotiations to be dragged out interminably, people here would think of it no more." [1] Unfortunately, although the diplomats at Tours and Paris rightly suspected " the double game," they did not foresee how it would work out or realise in time how Bismarck intended " to set in action external influences and those of the country to prevent the presence " [2] of a French representative at the London Conference. So far from thwarting him they played into his hands by their choice of a delegate. Favre's hesitation to accept the invitation to London had already lost a fortnight : now his decision to go there himself provided Bismarck with the desired opportunity to prevent French participation. That decision, however, was due to the pressure of Chaudordy and Gambetta. Clearly the occasion of the conference must be seized as an opportunity to plead the cause of France before Europe, and for this no mere *Chargé d'Affaires* could suffice : [3] the French delegate must be a man of real authority worthy to represent the nation on such an errand, in short, no less a person than the Minister for Foreign Affairs himself.[4] Chaudordy's arguments were reinforced by Gambetta. There were reasons of internal policy as well : not only could Favre, once at the conference, " escape from its miserable programme " and speak of the war, of France, and of Paris, but once out of Paris he could see for himself the magnitude of

[1] *H.H.u.S.A.*, to BEUST, Nov. 21.

[2] BISMARCK, *Gedanken und Erinnerungen*, II, 374.

[3] *F.O.* 146, 1530, LYONS to GRANVILLE, Jan. 16. Favre considered Tissot, the *Chargé d'Affaires* in London, unsuitable under any circumstances.

[4] FAVRE, *Gouvernement de la défense nationale*, II, 262 ff.

the military effort of the provinces, gain a true view of the state of the country, " recognise its resources and visit its armies. . . . You will lend us your authority for the solution of political questions and the ratification of our financial operations. . . . And lastly, you will help us to maintain the national spirit and to pursue the war to a victorious end even after the fall of Paris. . . ." [1] This sincere desire to strengthen the Government in the provinces by the presence of the Vice-President showed how far Gambetta was from any thought of personal tyranny ; and it was all the more significant because, although Gambetta no doubt hoped to win Favre's full support for his policy, Favre was indisputably one of the more moderate members of the Government. It was Favre who, in September, had been one of those most in favour of early elections ; it was he who had suggested that Picard might accompany him to the provinces, he who just recently had advised the acceptance of Moltke's overture ; [2] as Lyons pointed out to Granville : " It might be very useful in certain contingencies that he (Favre) should be out of Paris to act as a counterpoise to Gambetta ". [3] For this reason, indeed, his coming would surely have been welcomed by the other Delegates ; besides, the addition of Favre to the Council would have deprived Gambetta of his casting vote. If, however, Gambetta could have converted Favre to a resolute policy of war to the knife, even after the fall of Paris, the situation at the end of January, when that great catastrophe did occur, would have been still more remarkable than it was. Whatever the influence of the London Conference, with Favre out of Paris it is doubtful whether the remnant of the Government in the city would have

---

[1] GAMBETTA to FAVRE, Dec. 31, cit. J. SIMON, *Souvenirs du 4 septembre*, II, 270. This despatch did not reach Paris until Jan. 9.
[2] DRÉO, *Procès-verbaux*, 380, 381.   [3] *F.O.* 146, 1483, Dec. 31.

ventured to treat on behalf of the whole country without reference to the Delegation when Favre was one of its members.

But Favre hesitated ; and when at last he had overcome his doubts and fears, it was Bismarck's turn to be obstructive. The formal invitation was despatched by Granville on December 29 : but it did not reach Paris until January 10, and the conference was due to begin on the 17th.[1] For ten days Bismarck had refused to transmit any diplomatic correspondence on the convenient pretext that French outposts had fired on German " parlementaires ". Meanwhile, the bombardment of Paris, so long delayed, began on January 5. Diplomatically, its effect was as great as Bismarck could wish : on the 9th Favre told his colleagues that he believed his presence at the conference was indispensable, but that he was resolved not to leave Paris unless " this abominable bombardment " was stopped. It was not until the following day, when Granville's invitation at last arrived, that he had any suspicion that he had been caught in a trap. Then he proposed that some one else should go in his stead, but his colleagues could not agree upon a substitute, and they reached the unsatisfactory conclusion that he should accept the invitation on principle, but proceed no further " in view of the circumstances ".[2] Nevertheless, on the 13th, vainly hoping that diplomatic protests would lead to the cessation of the bombardment, Favre decided to request Bismarck for a safe-conduct. The Prussian Minister referred him to the military authorities, and added significantly that he doubted whether it was advisable for Favre to leave Paris in order " to take part in person at a conference on the Black Sea at a moment when there are interests at stake at Paris which

---

[1] J. FAVRE, *Gouvernement de la défense nationale*, II, 285, 298.
[2] Ibid. 294 ; DRÉO, *Procès-verbaux*, 509.

are more important for France and for Germany than Article XI of the treaty of 1856 ".[1]   This was two days before the opening of the conference.   Yet even thus late Gambetta persisted in his entreaties : " You can.   You ought to go. . . . I attach the same importance to your presence at London as to the immediate sortie of General Trochu from the capital.   And in fact the same interest is at stake—the salvation of the country." [2]   And on the 27th he still pleaded with Favre : " Europe wants you.   Europe demands you. M. de Chaudordy and my colleagues of the Delegation even think that I should do well to go and spend some days in London to gather the fruits in the interest of our country. . . . I am opposed to taking a place which belongs only to you.   In the midst of the difficulties which are about to beset us, it seems almost illusory for me to think of such a journey ; but I still hope to see it undertaken by you." [3] But that hope, too, was illusory : by then Favre had discovered the significance of Bismarck's advice, and was already at Versailles negotiating, not the salvation of the country, but the capitulation of Paris.   The great event so long expected, so long dreaded, and so long delayed, was about to become a reality.

" It is the business of free governments to draw their inspiration from public opinion," [4] said Gambetta, on December 30, addressing the officers of the National Guard and the municipality of Bordeaux.   But although he later expressed the belief that, whereas the majority of the people had been opposed to elections until the middle of December, from then on they had desired them,[5] he did not venture to risk this surest method of ascertaining public opinion.   Nor

---

[1] FAVRE, op. cit. II, 306.   [2] DRÉO, op. cit. 546.   [3] D.T. II, 477 ff.
[4] Dép. circ., etc., I, 64.   [5] Dép. I, 553.

did he point out that if elections were desired, it was certainly as a means to peace. If at the time he observed the change in opinion he doggedly refused to be inspired by it. The darker the outlook, the more emphatic he was in declaring his intention to fight to the bitter end, the more energetic in attempting to rouse flagging courage and to sustain morale. " Some days of struggle yet," he declared on December 30, " another two months of energetic efforts and the defeat of the Prussian army is certain," [1] and at Laval nearly three weeks later he said that France would fight on for months, even for years if necessary, " convinced that Germany would tire sooner . . . of the sacrifices necessary for the prolongation of this gigantic war." [2]

By then, however, the signs that France herself was tiring were unmistakable. Metternich might write on December 19 that every one was behind the Government ; [3] Mr. West of the British Embassy might report that, despite the distrust caused by the dissolution of the departmental councils, not much attention would be paid to the internal policy of the Delegation so long as the war lasted ; [4] it was still possible for hopes to be high when the army of the Loire was preparing to resume vigorous operations, and when Bourbaki was about to launch his offensive in the east : but when the bombardment of Paris had begun and when Chanzy was beaten and driven from Le Mans in the greatest disorder, the general discouragement was manifest. The circumstances of his defeat were not only calculated to discourage public opinion, but they were evidence of the lack of enthusiasm among the troops. "Last night," reported Feilding on January 11, " every general (except those drawn from the navy) declared that he could

---

[1] *Dép. circ.*, etc., I, 64.   [2] *F.O.* 146, 1530, FEILDING to LYONS.
[3] Cit. SALOMON, *Revue de Paris*, Feb. 15, 1924, 756.
[4] *F.O.* 146, 1530, Jan. 19, 1871.

not count on his troops fighting to-day " ;[1] and after the defeat the enormous number of deserters and stragglers testified to the weariness of Gambetta's citizen soldiers. Cathelineau might assure Feilding that the greater part " of the real gentry of France " were still anxious for the continuance of the war until favourable terms could be obtained from the Germans,[2] but the real gentry were a small minority of the French people, and it was the democracy, the still uneducated democracy, which was deserting its champion, who was also the champion of war to the knife. Industries were crippled and commerce disorganised by mobilisation and the difficulties of access to markets. The country people especially were weary of a war which seemed both hopeless and ruinous : the harvest had been indifferent, agriculture was paralysed by shortage of labour, and sons and husbands were sacrificing themselves, serving as *Mobilisés* and submitting to the terrible hardships of the training camps, all apparently to no purpose. By January 15, Gambetta had written in November, France would really be armed to the teeth and ready to achieve a crushing revenge :[3] but when January 15 came he was obliged to admit the shortcomings of his new troops and of his war machine : " They lack solidity and endurance. . . . It is a machine which has been too hastily equipped and manufactured, which can only function for a certain number of days, and which requires periodic repair." [4] Yet the consciousness of its weaknesses by no means daunted his resolution : " We must be determined never to tire and to renew the work of reorganisation and of resistance to the knife after each reverse ".[5] Tireless himself, he hastened from one beaten army to another, from

---

[1] *F.O.* 146, 1530.   [2] Ibid. FEILDING to GRANVILLE, Jan. 17.
[3] *D.T.* II, Nov. 26, to FAVRE.
[4] *D.T.* II, 452, to FAVRE, Jan. 16.   [5] *D.T.* II, 452.

Chanzy at Laval to Faidherbe at Lille. In the north he
found a population which, " as always," required to be
cheered and encouraged, and as a result of Faidherbe's
defeat he said there would be much to do.[1] Nevertheless,
he remained at Lille only two days, and, although his big
speech there was the "finest oratorical display " [2] to which
Dilke ever listened, the warmth of his Republican eloquence
produced little answering glow of enthusiasm.[3] It was
significant of the changing atmosphere that he felt obliged
to defend both himself and the Republican regime, to refute
the charge that the Delegation was prolonging the war to
prolong its own power, and to declare that when the day of
victory arrived it would be seen that if he was possessed of
the democratic passion that could tolerate no foreign invasion,
he was also profoundly animated by the Republican faith
which abhorred dictatorship.[4]

But he seemed a blind optimist, indeed, who could still
talk of the day of victory. It was impossible for the country
to endure reverse upon reverse and rally each time more
cheerfully than before to risk a fresh defeat. The " flame "
that Gambetta bore with him [5] could not kindle spirits which
were damped by four months' bitter experience. And now,
after the middle of January, the clouds of disaster were
gathering black and fast. On the 21st, the day of his
arrival at Lille, a telegram reached Bordeaux announcing
a sortie at Paris. It was the capital's last despairing effort,
and it failed as all previous efforts had failed. It was the
sign that the end was near. Gambetta found the army of

---

[1] *D.T.* II, 466.

[2] GWYNN and TUCKWELL, *Life of Dilke*, I, 23.

[3] FREYCINET, *Souvenirs*, I, 223 ; ABEKEN, *Ein schlichtes Leben in bewegter Zeit*, 489.

[4] *Dép. circ.*, etc., I, 72.   [5] FREYCINET.

" The Sunflower."

GAMBETTA

(Alfred Le Petit : *Fleurs, fruits et légumes du jour,* 1871)

the North disorganised and exhausted by great hardships,[1] clearly incapable of renewing operations for some time to come, and he returned to Bordeaux on the 26th to learn that yet another army was on the brink of catastrophe. After Le Mans, all hopes had been centred on the expedition to the east : Bourbaki alone might be capable of winning a victory, and so stem the tide of ill fortune. But the success of his venture depended upon speed and secrecy, and neither were obtainable. Werder's stubborn resistance during the three days' battle of Héricourt on the Lisaine,[2] determined Bourbaki's failure. His men were exhausted by continuous fighting ; the cold was intense, and provisions were short ; it was necessary to retreat on Besançon. Freycinet, realising that the relief of Belfort could no longer be hoped for, was prompt in devising a fresh plan : the First Army should proceed from Besançon to Nevers, and thence march northwards to join Faidherbe. But the plan was impracticable, and the time for such ambitious combinations was past. A new German army, under Manteuffel, had now arrived, and threatened Bourbaki's communications : the *Mobilisés* of the south, on whose support he had counted, had not come to his relief; in despair, the general decided to retreat upon Pontarlier, close to the Swiss frontier and thence, if possible, to escape into the Rhône valley before he was cut off. " If you do not agree with this plan," he telegraphed to Freycinet, " I really do not know what to do. I assure you that the exercise of command at this moment is a martyrdom." [3] The retreat began on the 26th, and that same evening, overcome by the weight of impending disaster,

---

[1] Cp. GWYNN and TUCKWELL, op. cit. Dilke's vivid description of Faidherbe's men.

[2] Jan. 15-17.

[3] *Rapport* PERROT, cit. DUTRAIT-CROZON, *Gambetta et la défense nationale*, 366.

and disheartened by the control and suspicions of the War Office, the general whom Gambetta had insisted upon placing in command of this army in spite of Freycinet, shot himself.[1] The news of this tragedy crossed a telegram from Bordeaux in which Gambetta, now on Freycinet's advice, replaced him by General Clinchant.[2]

But a change of command at this late hour could not avail to avert disaster. The one faint hope of saving the army of the East lay in the possibility of a diversion by Garibaldi, which would delay Manteuffel's advance to cut Clinchant's line of retreat : but that hope was to be frustrated. The doom of the army of the East was finally sealed neither by the incompetence of its commanders nor by the folly of the War Office, but by the shrewdness of Bismarck and the misunderstanding of Favre. It was at Versailles that the fate of the last of Gambetta's armies was determined, and Gambetta himself was to be an unwitting instrument of its fate. The army of the East was exempted from the general armistice which Favre negotiated with Bismarck, for the Germans wished to complete its destruction, while Favre, ignorant of its true situation, still believed in the possibility of its success. But in his telegram to Gambetta, Favre did not mention this all-important exception and Bismarck, who despatched the telegram, did not attempt to repair the omission. Gambetta naturally inferred that the armistice was general, and ordered the cessation of hostilities on all fronts. The order was obeyed by Garibaldi and Clinchant, while Manteuffel continued to advance, and refused Clinchant's proposal for a thirty-six hours' truce to clear up the misunderstanding. Thus the last hope of escape into the Rhône valley vanished ; the army of the

---

[1] The wound was not fatal, as was at first reported.
[2] Gen. THOUMAS, *Paris, Tours, Bordeaux,* 219, 220.

East saw its communications cut, and retreat across the
frontier was the only alternative to annihilation. On
February 1, the army which had been intended to cut the
German communications and to relieve every one, Chanzy
as well as Paris, exhausted and demoralised, struggled pain-
fully over the border, to seek safety and disarmament in
neutral Switzerland. Sedan, Metz, Paris, Pontarlier : the
cup of bitterness was indeed full to overflowing. Four such
disasters in five months were more than the proudest nation
could bear. Gambetta could turn Sedan and Metz to good
account, but Paris and Pontarlier condemned both himself
and the Government of which he was a member : they
sounded the death-knell of his policy, and he was powerless
to frustrate their effects.

XV

GAMBETTA'S REPUBLIC

" GAMBETTA and his friends," said Jules Simon in 1869,
" have no more love of liberty than Rouher. They would
be more authoritarian than the Empire if they replaced it." [1]
But Gambetta, having replaced the Empire, could claim that
it would be " not the least of the honours of the Government
of National Defence to have wished and known how to give
the entirest liberty in the midst of the most terrible crisis a
people has ever traversed," [2] and declare that in his conduct
as a Minister he had been ruled by the " conviction that the
Government, even in its revolutionary period and under the
fire of the foreigner, should act without having recourse to
intimidation, without violating any law, and without ex-
ceeding its powers ".[3] There was truth both in Simon's
criticism and in Gambetta's claim. It was true that Gambetta was more Republican than Liberal, and had none
of the vague belief in a universal emancipation called
Liberty, which had characterised the democrats of an
earlier age, true that he himself was by nature authoritative.
Moreover, he had come to power in circumstances which
gave him an unrivalled opportunity to display his love of

[1] Mme ADAM, *Mes sentiments et nos idées avant 1870*, 376.
[2] Dec. 20, 1870 ; to officers of National Guard at Bordeaux, *Dép. circ.*,
etc., I, 67.
[3] *Dép.* I, 549.

authority, and made him virtually Dictator outside Paris. He, like Danton, was member of a revolutionary Government at a time of foreign invasion, and the invader of 1870 was far more formidable than the enemy of 1792. But, this being so, his claims to moderation were all the more remarkable ; Danton certainly could not have made good such professions of respect for entire liberty.

In fact, Simon had under-estimated the good sense of the tribune of Belleville. Gambetta had the courage to accept a revolutionary situation, and the wisdom to take advantage of it where possible, but he had no wish unnecessarily to abuse its opportunities, and, above all, he was anxious to avoid violence. A pattern in warfare, the First Republic was a warning in government. Revolutionary terror and the guillotine were no means to found a durable Third Republic in 1870. Nor did the Republican party need those means in order to establish its control. There were no such dangers of royalist conspiracy and civil war as had faced the Ministry of August 10, 1792, and the men of the Convention. Sedan had completed the discomfiture of the Bonapartists as effectively as massacre or proscription, and the other monarchist claimants to power were too weak, unprepared, and patriotic to menace the Republican supremacy of the moment. Although Gambetta's proclamations and correspondence abounded with references to Bonapartist power, intrigue, and treachery, the men who most endangered the preservation of order and threatened his Republican authority were not Bonapartists but Republicans. In the provinces, as in Paris, the most dangerous rivals of the Government of National Defence on and after September 4, 1870, were the extremists of the Left.

As in 1848 two Republican parties stood face to face : one moderate, parliamentary, Liberal, interested above all in the conquest of democratic freedom and of the weapons of political control ; the other extreme, revolutionary, Socialist, eager for a general social as well as political upheaval. It was a far cry from Gambetta, who proclaimed a Republic based upon order and denounced " those who attack the governmental institutions of a country . . . and forget that in a free society we ourselves should be the government," [1] to those whose conception of a " free society " meant " the demolition of the old social order, no more parasites, no more pretexts for exploitation, no more privileged, proprietors or others, that is to say, no more patrons, no more authoritarian State ; consequently no more army or magistrates appointed by authority, no more priests, no more religion, no more God " ! [2] But such views were held by a band of Republicans in the departments as well as in Paris ; the name of Republic was a cloak for all kinds of Utopian aspirations and personal ambitions, and with its proclamation in September the extremists in the big southern towns hoped that the time had come for the realisation of their dreams.

The three chief centres of disturbance were Lyons, Marseilles, and Toulouse ; Lyons, which had long been a centre of anti-clerical and industrial agitation, and was the headquarters of the Republican-Socialist Nouvelle Montagne of 1849-50 ; Marseilles, turbulent seaport and Gambetta's own constituency ; and Toulouse, where extremist activities were deliberately fostered by one of Gambetta's " redder " prefects. On September 4 the Republicans of Lyons had anticipated the Republicans of Paris. The element whose attempt to gain power in Paris Gambetta had himself frustrated, was supreme in the second city of France. The prefect and numerous officials of the Empire had been

---

[1] Cp. above, p. 27.   [2] *Rapport* DE SUGNY, ch. i.

thrown into prison ; a self-constituted Committee of Public Safety had proclaimed the Republic and the " arming of the nation ". " The dangerous idea" with which the new rulers of the city were playing was, as Gambetta informed his colleagues, that of an independent Commune ; [1] they affected to receive the new prefect appointed by Gambetta as a " delegate of the Government of Paris to the Government of Lyons " ; [2] one of their number wrote later that the men in power at Lyons on September 4 might well have issued the declaration of principles which was to appear in the *Journal Officiel* of the Commune at Paris : " The Commune is the sole power, its autonomy is absolute ; it votes the communal budget ; it apportions and collects the taxes ; it chooses the magistrates ; it organises the defence of the city as well as public instruction and administration ; it votes and executes all administrative and economic reforms destined to universalise power and property ".[3]

The Republic established at Lyons was thus the antithesis of the Republic which Gambetta desired to found. If Gambetta's Republic was naturally authoritarian in tendency and freely adopted all the institutions of a centralised state, the peculiar circumstances under which it had come to birth, and the urgent needs of the national defence could serve only to increase that tendency ; they seemed to provide every excuse for a ruthless assertion of authority. But the problem created by the pretensions of the extreme Republicans in the south could not be solved by forcible means ; not only had the new Government at this time no forces with which to attempt suppression, but its position in Paris was too precarious for it to risk denunciation as an arbitrary and tyrannical power false to all its Republican

---

[1] DRÉO, *Procès-verbaux*, 107, Sept. 11.
[2] L. ANDRIEUX, *La Commune à Lyon en 1870-71*, 40.　　　[3] Ibid. 44, 45.

professions of liberty.   Moreover, the Republic was as yet
only provisional, and its secure establishment must sooner or
later depend upon a popular vote.   Election figures had
shown that apart from Paris, the chief strength of the Republican party lay in the towns of the south : Gambetta could
not afford to alienate his southern supporters.   Republican
extremists were proving a thorn in the flesh, but since they
were Republicans, they must be won to obedience by peaceful
means.   Much, then, depended upon Gambetta's choice of
prefects, and one of his first and most urgent tasks as Minister
of the Interior was to find men who would be capable of
maintaining the authority of the central Government in the
troubled cities of Marseilles and Lyons.

His choices were not equally fortunate ; and he confessed later that when he went to Tours he " found the
country in a veritable state of secession," but he added : " In
a very short time I was happy enough to be able to restore
order everywhere ".[1]   By October 9, however, a relative
order had already been established at Lyons.   The climax
of the disturbances in the second city in France had been
reached on September 28, when the Russian Communist,
Bakunin, and the adventurer Cluseret, future War Delegate
in the Paris Commune, had marched upon the Hôtel de
Ville at the head of a mob and proclaimed the Commune at
Lyons.   In his *Letters to a Frenchman*, Bakunin denounced
the Government of National Defence as " delegates of a
bourgeois Republicanism, and as such enemies of Socialism,
enemies of the true people's revolution ".[2]   Nevertheless,
despite the influence of Socialist doctrines at Lyons, the
Nihilist's attempt to replace the authority of the bourgeois
Republicans and to establish the Utopia of a pure social
anarchy with the " annihilation of the principle of authority

[1] *Dép.* I, 548.   [2] *Lettres à un Français*, 36.

in all its forms " and the " complete abolition of the political and juridical State " [1] was destined to fail. The extremists overreached themselves ; the great majority of the National Guard stood firm, and rallied to the support of the prefect and of the municipal council. The revolutionary mob was easily dispersed, and its leaders hastened to shake the dust of Lyons from their feet. The issue was a personal triumph for Gambetta's representative, Challemel-Lacour, and the prefect did his best to take advantage of the situation and to consolidate an authority which hitherto had been exceedingly precarious. Challemel-Lacour was a man of whose capacities Gambetta had the highest opinion ; he was, he had declared a year before, " a statesman, rarissima avis in nostris terris ".[2] Now at Lyons his statesmanship was severely tested, and its triumph was by no means complete. He succeeded in re-establishing a relative order without bloodshed, and the price he paid in pandering to anti-militarist and anti-clerical sentiment cost him little, for those sentiments coincided with his own : [3] but it was only a relative order, and the peace of Lyons remained uncertain ; " throughout the whole of Challemel-Lacour's proconsulate and the first months of his successor's administration," wrote Andrieux, who had been one of the moderate members of the Committee of Public Safety, " we lived in constant alarm. We were on the brink of a disturbance every day." [4] Throughout the period of Challemel's rule, too, even when Gambetta visited the city in December, the red flag flew

---

[1] *Lettres à un Français*, 22.

[2] LAVERTUJON, *Gambetta inconnu*, 21 ; cp. letter of G. to RANC, April 19, 1874, where he uses the same expression " rara avis " with reference to Challemel-Lacour.

[3] Cp. Mme ADAM, *Mes sentiments et nos idées avant 1870*, 323, and the interesting appendix giving a summary of Challemel-Lacour's life in D. HALÉVY, *La Fin des Notables* (Paris, 1930), 285.

[4] *La Commune à Lyon en 1870-71*, 199.

over the Hôtel de Ville, a symbol of the prevailing uncertainty and of the continued influence of the extremists, for, though the municipal council declared that it was merely the ensign of " LA PATRIE EN DANGER," [1] it had originally been hoisted as the banner of the revolutionary Commune.[2] Nevertheless, Challemel-Lacour always retained Gambetta's complete confidence ; he was allowed a free hand, and the Minister never disputed the wisdom of the concessions to extremist feeling which his prefect thought it necessary to make.   Challemel-Lacour never willingly consented to become the mere tool of the extremists as did Esquiros, the journalist and former deputy,[3] whom Gambetta had chosen to assert the authority of the Government of National Defence at Marseilles.   It was, in fact, Marseilles, and not Lyons, which was to be Gambetta's chief source of anxiety after his arrival at Tours.   " The Republic," proclaimed Esquiros, " is above all the Government of the Law.   Let it win honour by breaking with every arbitrary tradition and with political reprisals " ; but at the same time, finding himself in a position similar to that of Challemel-Lacour during his first weeks at Lyons, virtually the prisoner of an extremist " Departmental Commission " and of a Civic Guard composed of the dregs of the populace, he informed Gambetta that order could be maintained only by " wise concessions to revolutionary feeling ".[4]   The result was scarcely a vindication of Esquiros' Republic as a " Government of the Law " ; his wise concessions led him to attempt

[1] *Le Petit Journal Lyonnais*, Sept. 26.   The council disclaimed any intention of disowning the national flag.

[2] L. ANDRIEUX, *La Commune à Lyon en 1870-71* ; DUCARRE, *Dép*. II, 450 ; MARX, *Civil War in France*, 34, calls the red flag " the symbol of the Republic of Labour ".

[3] In the Legislative Assembly of 1848, and in the Legislative Body of 1870.

[4] *Rapport* DE SUGNY, 23 ; cp. ROUVIER, *Dép*. II, 488 ; THOUREL, *Dép*. II, 531.

to force the resignations of magistrates, to decree the expulsion of the Jesuits and to suspend the *Gazette du Midi*, which had been guilty of publishing a letter of the Prince de Joinville and a manifesto of the Comte de Chambord.[1] Gambetta at once intervened : the maintenance of the freedom of the press was a question on which he " could not capitulate " ; he ordered Esquiros to withdraw his decrees, and when the administrator refused, and resigned, he cancelled them himself. The *Gazette du Midi* was authorised to reappear, for it was necessary " to prove that the Republic is the only Government which can tolerate complete freedom of the press and that those who in opposition always favoured this liberty should neither restrict nor mutilate it " ; and the expulsion of members of religious congregations was forbidden, for " if the dissolution of a corporation is legally possible, the individual liberty of the Frenchmen belonging to it and their right to reside in France may not be infringed ".[2] Thus the anti-clerical Gambetta appeared as the protector of the Jesuits ; this was no time to raise a religious issue irrelevant to the national defence, and only too likely to encourage free-thinking fanatics to the worst kind of excess.

The cancellation of Esquiros' decrees did not, however, put an end to the conflict with Marseilles. The choice between the prefectures of Marseilles and Nice, where Gambetta's friend, Baragnon, had been misgoverning, was now offered to Marc Dufraisse, an exile of 1852 ; but when he found himself a prisoner as soon as he entered the prefecture of Marseilles Dufraisse prudently chose Nice, informing Gambetta that " if the Government at Tours was better acquainted with the temper of Marseilles, it would

---

[1] Which declared *inter alia :* " Republican institutions which may correspond to the aspirations of new societies will never take root in our ancient monarchic soil ".

[2] *D.T.* II, 275.

relax the rigour of its principles by reason of the force of facts, and of the necessity of local circumstance ".[1] The prefect, Delpech, and numerous deputations went to lay siege to the Government at Tours ; enthusiasts telegraphed that they had sworn to burn the town rather than let Esquiros go ; the Departmental Commission extended Esquiros' decree of expulsion of the Jesuits to the whole of the Bouches du Rhône ; the former prefect, Labadié, refused to resume office : Marseilles was defiant.[2] The activities of the Socialists redoubled, and the appearance of Cluseret was a certain herald of disorder, to which, as at Paris, the news of the fall of Metz furnished a pretext and a provocation. On October 31, a month after his demonstration at Lyons, Cluseret, accompanied by the usual foreign adventurers,[3] proclaimed the Commune at Marseilles. Departmental Commission and Civic Guards supported him, there was a demand for Esquiros as dictator, and Cluseret was named commander of the armies of the south : for three days the Commune reigned supreme.

But Gambetta had not followed Dufraisse's advice and yielded, nor had he any intention of yielding. He stood publicly committed to uphold his principles and the authority of the Government depended upon his firmness. His difficulty was to find an administrator who would be strong enough to control the situation, and it was not until October 31 that a new prefect was appointed. The arrival at Marseilles of Alphonse Gent, formerly leader of the Nouvelle Montagne movement of 1849-51,[4] a man of great

---

[1] Cit. STEENACKERS and LE GOFF, *Histoire du gouvernement de la défense nationale*, II, 90.

[2] GLAIS-BIZOIN, *Dictature de cinq mois*, 143, 144.

[3] An American named Train was one of the most conspicuous.

[4] P. DE LA GORCE, *Histoire de la seconde République française*, II, 545 ; GLAIS-BIZOIN, op. cit. 148 ff.

influence with Republicans in the south, whose support the Delegation had prudently won by the offer of an important post at Tours, marked the turn of the tide. He was welcomed as a liberator by all the better elements of the population, and although he was shot at and wounded shortly after his entry into the prefecture, because he refused either to resign or to collaborate with Esquiros, the assistance of the National Guard soon enabled him to gain control and re-establish the authority of the Central Government : the Communards dispersed, the Civic Guards evacuated the prefecture of which they had made a " veritable Augean stable," [1] Cluseret disappeared, and Delpech left to join Garibaldi. In a short time Gent, invested with full civil and military powers, both of which he freely used, was supreme in the department ; order was completely restored, and there were no more disturbances at Marseilles.

Gambetta's firmness in resisting the pretensions of Esquiros at Marseilles was in striking contrast to his capitulation before the insolence of his former client, Duportal, at Toulouse. The arbitrary conduct of the prefect of Haute Garonne, who deliberately encouraged the activities of local Republican extremists, exhausted the patience of the Delegation.[2] They invited him to resign, and appointed M. Huc, a law professor, to succeed him. But Duportal had no intention of abandoning his post : it was Huc who was intimidated into resignation, and Duportal replied that, as for his own resignation, any of the Delegates who had ever spent a day in prison for the Republican cause might come and seek it.[3] His defiance succeeded where that of Esquiros had failed : it seemed to imply that he would stubbornly

---

[1] *Rapport* DE SUGNY, 124.

[2] Cp. *Rapport* DE RESSEGUIER, 12, 16, 17 ; *D.T.* I, 287, 288.

[3] *D.T.* I, 291 ; GLAIS-BIZOIN, op. cit. 167 ff. Duportal was in prison at the time of the Empire's fall.

resist any attempt to dislodge him ; to deal with a Duportal a Gent or a body of troops was necessary, but a Gent was not to be had, and the use of troops against Republicans was no part of Gambetta's policy. The Government yielded and hoped that Duportal, being his own master, and not the mere tool of extremists, like Esquiros, would henceforth show more moderation. Thus, Duportal's tactics were victorious, and he clung to his prefecture until March, 1871, when he proclaimed the Commune, and had to be forcibly expelled by his successor, Kératry, the agent of a Government which did not fear to treat Republican extremists with rigour. But the attempt to remove him in November did, in fact, have a sobering effect upon Duportal ; he had gained his principal object, and henceforth he was less anxious to create a Republican order by means of disorder.[1] By the middle of that month the chief disturbances in the provinces were over, and Metternich was able to admire the skilful way in which Gambetta had " without a shot " succeeded in quelling the insubordination of the southern cities, and in re-establishing " a relative but very salutary order ".[2]

Closely connected with the extremist agitation at Marseilles and Toulouse were the Leagues of the South and of the South-West. In September, when preparations for the siege of Paris were the dominant preoccupation of the Government, local authorities had been encouraged to act on their own initiative for the organisation of provincial defence.[3] Amateur defence committees were formed all over the country, and the idea naturally followed of organised regional defence, in which groups of departments

---

[1] GLAIS-BIZOIN, *Dictature de cinq mois*, 170.

[2] *H.H.u.S.A.*, to BEUST, Nov. 21,

[3] Cp. circ. of Sept. 6, cit. STEENACKERS and LE GOFF, *Histoire du gouvernement de la défense nationale*, I, 400 ; *D.T.* I, 312 ; II, 285.

should combine. Such groups or leagues were soon outlined for the greater part of the unoccupied territory, except the north : in Brittany thirteen prefects met to organise a League of the West ; at Toulouse Duportal summoned delegates of thirty departments to form a League of the South-West ;[1] and at Marseilles the notorious Departmental Commission took the initiative in forming a League of the South for " regional and Provençal defence " and " to help the Government of Tours which is powerless to take energetic measures ".[2] Of all these groups, it was this League of the South which was by far the most conspicuous ; Duportal's appeal met with little response, and the League of the West never became an organised reality through lack of Government support, but the organisers of the League of the South continued their activities, despite the refusal of Government patronage. Although it was ostensibly concerned for the national defence, this League soon revealed itself as one of the vehicles by which the extremists were attempting to extend their authority ; for its programme was as much political and social as military. Nevertheless, though it issued many manifestos, held many meetings, and passed many resolutions, its achievements were negligible, since the character and claims of its organisers aroused the suspicions and hostility of neighbouring prefects, as well as of the Government at Tours.[3] The victory of the Commune, and the wave of unrest which followed the fall of Metz, gave it a last momentary flicker of importance ; thus, the extremists of St. Etienne hoisted the red flag at the Hôtel de Ville, and declared the adhesion of the town to the Ligue du Midi—but it was precisely this identification with the Communards

---

[1] *D.T.* I, 284 ; II, 167.   [2] *Rapport,* 53-9.

[3] *D.T.* I, 21 ; CHALLEMEL-LACOUR, *Dép.* II, 465 ; DUCARRE, *Dép.* II, 451.

which sealed its downfall, for the overthrow of the Commune was also its own undoing. After the arrival of Gent and the humiliation of its president, Esquiros, it faded into complete insignificance. It had been a symbol of the unrest which prevailed in the south, but Gambetta exaggerated its importance when he saw in it a movement towards separation.[1] If its leaders wished to spread their social and political doctrines, there is no evidence that they had any idea of establishing a line of the Main in France. Some of them desired extreme decentralisation, but they were no less vigorous in championing French unity, and the maintenance of the Republic " one and indivisible " Their movement was no claim for autonomy in any way comparable with that which was made in recent years in Alsace ; it was dominated by Jacobin and Socialist catchwords, misdirected patriotism and personal ambitions, not by any questions of language or of race, or by any profound theory of federalism.

Gambetta's handling of these provincial disturbances, and more particularly his firmness in dealing with Esquiros, were considerable justification of his claim to be a champion of liberty : but while they demonstrated his prudence and moderation, they also showed the limitations of his authority, his dependence upon his own officials, and the inconvenient shortage of capable Republican administrators. Yet for him the administration also had defects of another kind. The final climax of disorder had followed upon the fall of Metz, and that event was to be the pretext for urging a more vigorous policy of republicanisation. If he desired to respect liberties as far as was possible and politic, he was determined to deprive his political enemies, the Bonapartists, of all influence in politics or administration. But the Government

---

[1] For evidence of the existence of separatist ideas see, however, G. HANO-TAUX, *Mon Temps*, I, *De l'Empire à la République* (Paris, 1933), 182.

of Paris had so far withheld their sanction from his policy of radical purification. Now, on October 31, he returned to the charge : " the system of toleration which had been complacently adopted after the fall of the (imperial) Government should give way to more energetic methods, calculated to disconcert the partisans of the fallen regime, who have recovered from their first alarm, and to accentuate more clearly for the population the change accomplished by the revolution of September 4, not only from the point of view of principle, but also from the point of view of the personnel to whom was entrusted the duty of making the principle prevail ".[1] The great majority of the municipalities were now ruled by provisional councils, composed of the nominees of Republican prefects. They had been purified. But there were still the departmental councils,[2] the only group of elected bodies which now remained to testify to the sovereignty of the democratic principle of universal suffrage. They were concerned purely with departmental administration and finance, and almost without exception they had very readily voted funds for the national defence after the revolution of September 4.[3] Nevertheless, the fact remained that they were a link with the Empire ; they had been elected under the Empire, and there were few of them in which Republicans had the majority. They were thus out of harmony with the general spirit of Gambetta's administration. Some of his prefects had already acted on their own initiative, and dissolved their councils before he came to Tours,[4] and he himself appears to have been in favour of a general dissolution. Now, after the fall of Metz, he urged upon Favre that this was " evidently one of those measures which could

[1] *D.T.* II, 287.   [2] Conseils Généraux.
[3] Cp. e.g. *D.T.* I, 370, Landes ; I, 177, Cantal ; II, 189, Gard.
[4] E.g. Loire, Tarn et Garonne.

no longer be deferred ". Nor were departmental councillors to be the only victims of the more energetic methods which he considered necessary : he reminded Favre that all the old personnel still remained in the Ministries of Finance and of Public Instruction, and even in the consulates, and declared that their maintenance excited " the most violent and legitimate complaints ".[1]

But Gambetta's despatch of October 31 did not reach Paris until December 16, and no authority came to sanction the measures he desired. While prefects were impatient for the dissolution of the departmental councils,[2] his colleagues in the Delegation were reluctant to act without Parisian approval, and it was not until late in December that Gambetta decided that since this was not forthcoming, the Delegation must act independently. He was at Bourges when Cazot reported to him there that Crémieux would vote for the dissolution if he was authorised to place Gambetta's name at the foot of the decree.[3] It would seem that Gambetta had hoped that his colleagues could be persuaded to adopt the measure during his absence, and upon their own responsibility.[4] But this was impossible, for Fourichon and Glais-Bizoin were stubbornly opposed to it ; he could not hold aloof if he really desired the councils to be dissolved before the beginning of a new financial year. Laurier wired urgently : " Telegraph to him (Crémieux) and to me in the most imperative terms so that I may carry off the decree," [5] and Gambetta complied. He sent the message which Crémieux had dictated, requesting that his name should be attached to the decree of dissolution,[6] and added that the

[1] *D.T.* II, 287.　　　　　　　[2] E.g. Prefect of Hérault, Nov. 27.
[3] *D.T.* II, 365, Dec. 18; cp. J. Durieux, *Le ministre Pierre Magne*, II, 255 ff.
[4] Crémieux, *Actes de la Délégation*, 86.
[5] *D.T.* II, 381.　　　　　　　[6] *D.T.* II, 374.

measure was necessary in view of the end of the year, and because it was impossible both for political reasons and on account of the budget of 1871 to " continue to allow life and legality to the worst assemblies of the Empire ". The conclusion was superb : " We are agreed ; the question of opportunity alone separated us ; I think the time has now come, and I insist that this satisfaction be given at last to the rights of universal suffrage and to Republican opinion ".[1] Glais-Bizoin and Fourichon, however, were as far as ever from being agreed, and it was only after a stormy discussion that Laurier was able to " carry off " the decree.[2] Wisely he hastened to communicate it at once to the prefects, for the following day Crémieux had misgivings about this surrender to " that devil Gambetta who dreams of nothing but battles," and asked for the decree to be returned to him : but it was then too late ; as Laurier said, " there was a *fait accompli*. The Government accepted the *consummatum est*." [3]

The decree thus wrested from reluctant Delegates was signed on December 25, and a despatch of Lord Lyons written the same day succinctly demonstrated the " satisfaction " given to " the rights of universal suffrage " : " Your Lordship is aware that under the Imperial Government in the Departments of the Seine and the Rhône . . . commissions named by the Executive Power were substituted for the ' Conseils Généraux ' which in other departments were elected by Universal Suffrage. This system is applied by the new decree to the whole of France. . . . The ' Conseils d'arrondissement' appear to be dissolved without any provision for the appointment of new ones, either by election or by nomination."[4] The Delegation agreed with the prefect of

[1] *D.T.* II, 377.　　[2] FOURICHON, *Dép.* I, 637.　　[3] *D.T.* II, 407.
[4] To GRANVILLE, *F.O.* 146, 1483, Dec. 25.

Lot [1] that these councils were superfluous institutions which there would be no object in replacing. As for the new departmental commissions they, like the provisional municipal councils, were to play their part in the foundation of Gambetta's Republic. One of his telegrams to the prefect of Ain was an illuminating commentary upon the whole episode : " I am glad to tell you that you would disregard your dearest interests if you limited yourself to making a finance council of your departmental commission ; it must breathe the spirit of the Republic. Consequently in the choices you are about to make, consult the interests of the democracy rather than your own administrative convenience ".[2]

Despite Gambetta's assurance to Favre that with the exception of " two or three interested protests " the dissolution of the departmental councils had passed absolutely unnoticed,[3] Republican opinion was by no means unanimous in its " satisfaction ". The division of opinion in the Delegation was reflected elsewhere in the departments,[4] and it was significant as well as irritating. When the prefect of Nièvre protested against the dissolution of a council composed of men of all shades of opinion who had supported him with the greatest goodwill and patriotism, Gambetta removed him from his post,[5] but in the Nord, a district which, though admittedly one of the least Republican parts of the country, was of great importance as the heart of the national defence in the north, despite Gambetta's entreaties, both the prefect and the Commissioner of Defence themselves insisted upon resignation rather than execute a decree which they

[1] *D.T.* I, 419 ; cp. I, 318 ; II, 409.   [2] *D.T.* II, 488, Jan. 7.

[3] *D.T.* II, 424, Dec. 31.

[4] Cp. despatches from Landes, *D.T.* II, 200 ; and from Eure et Loir, *D.T.* I, 275.

[5] Cp. G. SAND, *Journal d'un voyageur pendant la guerre*, 238.

considered injurious both to the interests of the Republic and
of the defence.[1] As Legrand, the prefect said, the decree
substituted " the product of arbitrariness for the product of
universal suffrage even though Imperial in its essence ".[2]
It was really justifiable not by any plea of the needs of the
defence, but by an appeal to what Gambetta called " the
special right arising from revolution ".[3] " Firmness has
nothing in common with arbitrariness," he had informed
Esquiros,[4] and his firmness in maintaining democratic
principles of liberty had disappointed the Republican extremists of Marseilles ; but now it was by arbitrariness
that he alarmed Republican Liberals throughout the country.
And one arbitrary act begot another. Where Republicans
were not agreed, the hostility of other parties was certain.
The decree of December 25 aroused more vigorous protest
than any measure which Gambetta had yet imposed,[5] and
the result was that the man who in October had declared
that it was impossible for him to admit the suspension of
opposition papers, "whatever the nature of their opposition,"[6]
in January suspended the *Union de l'Ouest* for two months
because it had protested against the dissolution of the departmental councils ; such criticisms were " a veritable connivance with the enemy ".[7] On the other hand, the " violence
and injustice " of papers such a *La Commune* demonstrated
their complete powerlessness, and there was no need to take
any action.[8]

This apparent reversal of policy marked all the difference
between October and January, between the time when
Gambetta arrived full of hope to organise a great national

---

[1] *D.T.* I, 501 ; II, 432.   [2] *D.T.* I, 501.
[3] *Dép.* I, 549.   [4] *D.T.* II, 275.
[5] E.g. Daru's letter to Gambetta ; cp. GLAIS-BIZOIN, *Dictature de cinq mois*,
6 ; *F.O.* 146, 1530.
[6] *D.T.* II, 275.   [7] *D.T.* II, 418.   [8] *D.T.* II, 438.

resistance, and the days three months later when, still undaunted but unsuccessful, he was valiantly trying to maintain
the enthusiasm of a nation which had suffered yet another
defeat for war to the knife, even after the fall of Paris.   Now,
the preservation of the country's morale was more than ever
important, and any well-grounded attack upon Gambetta's
policy might help to weaken it.   What was surprising was
not that the " Dictator " should make arbitrary use of his
power, but that under the circumstances he had so long used
it with such restraint.   Once, however, he had effected the
dissolution of the departmental councils without authority
from Paris he was encouraged to continue his offensive against
the " elements of reaction " and himself to complete the
application of the Republican programme he had laid down
in his despatches of October 24 and 31.   Metz had led to
the vigorous formulation of that programme ; December, the
silence of Paris, and the increasing seriousness of the situation,
led to its partial execution on the " Dictator's " own initiative,
and thereby the revolutionary character of his Government
was conspicuously accentuated.   Consciously or not, his
whole policy now appeared to be based upon the doctrine of
Blanqui that a revolutionary Republican Government should
during a preparatory period take the place of any institutions elected by universal suffrage, not in order to do away
with universal suffrage, but in order to free it from the
fetters which prevented it from working democratically and
to educate the electorate.[1]   Having disposed of all such
institutions, Gambetta turned to the education of the electorate.   His appeals to Paris to purify the personnel of the

---

[1] A. ZÉVAÈS, *Auguste Blanqui Socialiste et patriote Français* (Paris, 1920), 144.
But the war had led Blanqui to a more extreme position ; cp. *Rapport* DARU,
147, cit. *La Patrie en Danger*, Sept. 29, in which he declared that representative
assemblies were out of date, condemned not only in times of crisis and of war,
but at all times.

Ministries of Finance and Education had remained unanswered, for none of them reached the capital before
January 8. At length on the 13th, his patience exhausted,
he issued a circular to his prefects authorising them to make
all changes in the teachers' personnel which they considered
expedient "from the political and Republican point of
view," and that they should have no scruples in doing
so he invoked the instructions of the Minister of Public
Instruction at Paris ; but, as those instructions were a
fiction, he wisely took the precaution of adding that the
circular must be treated as "absolutely confidential, and
should remain so between you and the Minister of the
Interior ".[1] Even Silvy, Simon's deputy at Bordeaux, was
apparently to have no voice in the changes. The Republicans had, when in opposition, frequently protested against
the use of schools for political propaganda,[2] so that Gambetta
was well aware how effectively they might be employed on
behalf of the Republic. Another instrument of Republican
education was the *Bulletin de la République*, edited by a notable
Kantian pacifist, Jules Barni, who had presided over the
Congress of Peace at Geneva in 1867 : already, as early as
November 10, the Minister had ordained that schoolmasters
should read the chief articles in this successor to the old
Moniteur des Communes to the assembled inhabitants of their
communes every Sunday, "and even several times in a week if
he can. . . . The schoolmaster will make a particular point
of communicating the articles on matters of history and
doctrine by which the editors design to enlighten the people,
teaching it its political and social rights as well as the duties
which are their corollary, and demonstrating the essential

---

[1] *Dép. circ.* I, 399, cp. MARTIN NADAUD, *Six mois de préfecture*, 45, for an
appeal to Gambetta to "purify" the administrative departments.

[2] SILVY, *Dép.* IV, 546.

truth that the Republic alone is by its institutions capable
of ensuring the freedom, the greatness and the future of
France." [1]   The only prefect who showed great enthusiasm
for this propaganda was Delattre of Mayenne, who reported
that it was meeting with " incredible success in a country
which was thought to be dead ".[2]   The success, however,
was, he explained, due to an inspector who was sent to
enforce Gambetta's instructions :   " If you can send such a
man into each department you will have founded the
Republic in all the countryside in rear of the armies before
two months are over ".   The suggestion was heeded, but it
was not until January 26 that the Minister of the Interior
and of War, who had now virtually assumed the functions
of Minister of Public Instruction as well, authorised prefects
to appoint special school inspectors ; and then it was too
late for them to exert much influence.   The sub-prefect of
St. Malo expressed his satisfaction :   " The intelligent organisation of these tours would certainly ensure the success
of the Republic in the elections ".   Elections, however, were
to come far sooner than either he or Gambetta expected
or desired.   There was to be little time for the intelligent
organisation or execution of these inspections and the result
of the poll was in appearance an overwhelming condemnation
of the Republic of September 4.   Yet appearances were
deceptive ; the seed which Gambetta had sown with such
deliberate care did not all fall on barren soil, and in July,
1871, there was to be a Republican harvest which his
husbandry had undoubtedly helped to prepare.   The
democracy was proving responsive to his education.

[1] *Dép. circ.*, etc., II, 54.   [2] *D.T.* I, 466.

XVI

THE FINAL STRUGGLE : PARIS *V.* BORDEAUX

" If the Communards do not effect a revolution," wrote Favre, at the end of December, " we shall hold out three weeks longer." [1] Already Paris had fulfilled a part of his early boast, defeated all expectations, and held out three months : but she had not conquered, and victory now seemed far beyond her weakening grasp. The German bombardment began on January 5, and in the provinces men generally realised that capitulation could not long be delayed.[2] Clearly, by his more and more frequent references to the continuation of the war " even after the fall of Paris " Gambetta was seeking to prepare public opinion for the calamity. But would this be enough ? The fall of Paris must be a blow to morale still greater than the fall of Metz, and the effects of Metz he had countered by denouncing Bazaine. How could he counter the effects of such a disaster as threatened now ? When the end was in sight, and with it the ruin of such great hopes and ambitions, it was easy to yield to regrets and suspicion because what might have been was not. He hinted that Trochu was, if not another Bazaine, at least as incompetent as D'Aurelle ; he suggested that Paris had not done all it could ; he tried to terrorise his colleagues into a last desperate effort at sortie. Should not Republicans face death rather than undergo a

---

[1] To Gambetta, Dec. 28.   [2] *F.O.* 146, 1530, Feilding to Lyons.

humiliation comparable to that of Sedan or of Metz ? [1] If ten days hence, by the 25th, he had received no news of a sortie, made " without thought of return," he would publish the whole truth : " You must understand that we cannot allow Paris to fall without consoling public opinion and preparing people to endure such a blow ".[2] To maintain the morale of the country, and thereby to make his own policy possible still, he could threaten even the Republican colleagues, whose Delegate he was, with public denunciation.

Whether the threat was the outcome of indignation and despair, or of cool calculation, the appeal was answered ; but answered in vain. The last attempt at sortie was as fruitless as the first ; provisions were failing, and the Government had no choice but to negotiate. The first report of Favre's presence at Versailles had reached Gambetta at St. Malo on the 25th, but it still lacked official confirmation when he returned to Bordeaux next day, and, as with Metz, he desperately hoped against hope that reports were untrue. " But no ! " he exclaimed in a despatch to Favre on the 27th,[3] " you will not give in until a great battle has been lost. Then the task of negotiation will fall upon me who represent you, and who am acquainted with all the needs of the present situation," and he proceeded to examine the conduct to be followed. Paris, he insisted, could capitulate only as a fortress, and not as a Government representing the whole country : not only was it, in fact, Paris, not France, which was compelled to surrender, but the Parisian rulers had no right to treat on behalf of the whole Government ; the division of the Government implied the devolution of power upon the survivors when their colleagues had succumbed to natural or political death. Thus, anything the

---

[1] Cp. *D.T.* II, 426, Dec. 31.
[2] To FAVRE, Jan. 16.　　　　　[3] *D.T.* II, 477 ff.

Government at Paris did which was not concerned solely
with the special interests of Paris, and received no ratification
from the Delegation at Bordeaux would be " null and of no
effect ".   Paris, then, should surrender only as a fortress,
overtures for peace preliminaries should be steadfastly
refused, and its " splendid political personnel " should be
sent out " to galvanise the country ".[1]   Once the capitulation was complete, the Delegation, now the sole Government,
must pursue the war until France was freed, and it must
employ the most sure and regular methods to enable the
continuation of resistance.   Three means occurred to
Gambetta : a plebiscite, an Assembly, the maintenance of
the actual regime.   The first he rejected : a plebiscite
would invite the nation to stain its honour by refusing war,
and—evidently he feared that the invitation might be
accepted—the result would be uncertain.   An Assembly, on
the other hand, might be an " inestimable force for the
development of a national policy," provided always that
elections were held with Gambetta's corrective of Bonapartist ineligibility, which, he affirmed, had now at last been
accepted by his fellow Delegates.   " A Chamber constituted
in this way would deprive M. de Bismarck of the best part
of his schemes for the internal politics of France, and . . .
we should find in this Assembly the energy of a national
Convention."   Lastly, the actual regime might continue
unchanged ; but he feared that the fall of Paris would lead
to a revival of party polemics and increase the demoralising
activity of the partisans of a monarchic restoration.   These
conspiracies could be defeated only by " the substitution of

---

[1] " Despatch officers, engineers, publicists, administrators, diplomats, and,
above all, the authorised leaders of the democracy who have borne the weight
of persecution and exile during the last twenty years."   It does not seem to
have occurred to Gambetta that Bismarck might have something to say about
such an emigration.

a real dictatorship for an authority which is purely moral. This is a means little in harmony with our Republican doctrines and which we should not adopt unless it is certain that there is no other better." He preferred an Assembly, or even a plebiscite, to dictatorship, although he added that he was convinced that the country would still be willing to accept " our direction if it was reinforced by the presence of an eminent member of the Government such as Jules Favre ". This long and able despatch was a most interesting exposition of Gambetta's views at this critical moment. It showed how far he did recognise the change in opinion. It explained much in his attitude during the next few days. But it did not reach Paris until February 2, and it had no influence upon the course of events in the capital. Gambetta and Bismarck were not to negotiate while Paris abdicated, and a meeting between them, of which this was the first suggestion, never took place.

Not two days later, very early on the morning of the 29th, a brief despatch from Favre arrived at Bordeaux. Gambetta was awakened to hear the worst : that Paris had capitulated, that the Government had agreed to an armistice of twenty-one days, and that a National Assembly was to be summoned on February 12. The message added that a member of the Government was about to leave for Bordeaux.[1] Thus the Parisian majority, utterly ignorant of conditions in the provinces, had arrogated to itself the right to act for the whole Government, and to speak in the name of the whole country. The Delegation had been ignored, and Gambetta's policy was set at nought. What of Favre's declaration that, if Paris fell, France, ready at its fall, would continue the struggle until the aggressor perished ? What of Ferry's assurance that Paris was not France, and of his oath that

[1] Cit. SOREL, *Histoire diplomatique de la guerre franco-allemande*, II, 160.

the enemy would find none in the city who would consent to treat for France ?[1] Declarations and promises apparently counted for nothing. Gambetta's immediate impulse was not to resist, but to resign. At once he wrote a letter of resignation to Crémieux, as the doyen of the Delegation ; he recognised that he no more had a right to resist the decisions of Paris than he had a right to execute them : " The disagreement which has arisen as a result of the steps taken at Versailles is fundamental and of the sort upon which compromise is immoral ".[2] But Crémieux was much disturbed ; he saw Lyons and other turbulent cities of the south in open revolt as a protest against Gambetta's withdrawal ; the consequences of this resignation might be calamitous ; and without showing the letter to his colleagues, he hastened to reason with the writer ; he should remain at least until the arrival of the member of the Government at Paris made the situation wholly clear. The request was reasonable, for there were many points which still required explanation, and Gambetta consented thus much ; he would continue in the Delegation until the obscurities arising from Favre's brief communication had all been dissipated.

Meanwhile, he passed on that communication to his prefects, observing that he would maintain the *statu quo* " until the arrival of the personage who left Paris last night ".[3] But when Gambetta sent this circular the " personage," so far from being on his way, had not even been designated. There had been many proposals in the Government Council at Paris, but it was not until the evening of the 29th that it was decided that Simon should go, and go alone ;[4] not until the morning of the 31st that he actually left Paris. At

---

[1] J. FERRY, *Lettres*, Dec. 15.

[2] CRÉMIEUX, *Actes de la Délégation de Tours et de Bordeaux*, 92 ; cp. GAMBETTA, *Dép.* I, 551.

[3] *Dép. circ.* I, 404.   [4] DRÉO, *Procès-verbaux.*

Bordeaux, in the meantime, uncertainty continued to reign, and tension increased, while at Versailles Bismarck was wondering what Gambetta would do : " Gambetta, little leg, in Italian," he mused, " it is the name of a marsh bird of the stork or heron family. He seems to want to reflect on the matter, for he has not yet replied. But I expect that in the end he will give in like the others ; anyhow, if he does not give in it will suit me equally well. A little line of the Main would hardly be disagreeable for us." [1]

Bismarck was soon to have news of Gambetta. On that day, the 30th, Gambetta telegraphed to Favre to complain of his silence. The message went to Versailles, where Bismarck intercepted it, so that Favre did not receive it until the following day. In the meantime, Bismarck chose to answer Gambetta himself, and now for the first time the Minister of War learnt the real terms of the armistice, and the exemption of the army of the East which Favre, through misunderstanding, had neglected to mention. The consequences of that neglect were disastrous and irreparable. Gambetta's anger was stirred to the depths. Here, indeed, was justification for accusing the Parisian Government of " culpable carelessness ".[2] He had consented to remain at his post, but he would no longer be silent. The promised emissary from Paris still did not come ; elections were to be held on February 8 for an Assembly which was to meet on the 12th, there was little more than a week before polling day, and still the Delegation was ignorant of the electoral decree which was to be enforced. Gambetta's colleagues wished simply to re-enact their decree of October 1, but Gambetta refused his signature unless the decree were

---

[1] BUSCH, *Graf Bismarck und seine Leute während des Kriegs mit Frankreich*, II, 204.

[2] Cp. P. DESCHANEL, *Gambetta*, 101.

amended in accordance with his ineligibility thesis. Here, at least, his policy should prevail. If the Parisians chose weakly to surrender, and to do the bidding of Bismarck, Gambetta would frustrate them and Bismarck by imposing conditions of election which would ensure a Republican Assembly pledged to continue the war. Moreover, it was by no means certain that the Government at Paris was as absolutely opposed to Bonapartist ineligibility as it had been in October. Gambetta had been Favre's chief informant as to the state of opinion in the provinces, and by dint of repetition and a threat of resignation,[1] he had caused the incorruptible Republican to waver. " I am beginning to be shaken," Favre had written in December, replying to a despatch from Gambetta of November 4. " At bay as we are, without means of enlightening our fellow citizens, still at the mercy of the old administration which has continued to exist in its entirety, it would perhaps be our duty, in order to pronounce upon the question of peace or war, to set aside those whose servile docility has plunged us into the abyss of misfortune in which we now are. It would be a great deviation from principle, but it might be justified by necessity although nothing at the moment indicates the opportunity of such a discussion." [2] There was now no question of its opportunity while in Gambetta's opinion the necessity was urgent. " What France needs," he declared to his prefects, " is an Assembly which wants war, and is determined to do everything to carry it on. . . . The policy maintained and pursued by the Minister of the Interior and of War is the same as always : war to the knife, resistance until complete exhaustion. . . . We shall take advantage of the armistice period to reinforce our three armies with men, munitions,

---

[1] Cp. J. FAVRE, *Gouvernement de la défense nationale,* II, 75.

[2] Ibid. 185.

and provisions." [1]   In face of this determination, his fellow
Delegates had no option but to sign the decree as he would
have it.   A decree of their own unsigned by Gambetta
would not be recognised or obeyed if it were published, while
if they refused their signatures to Gambetta's decree there
would be no elections at all, and then, as Crémieux asked,
what would become of the armistice ? [2]

The decree was immediately posted up at Bordeaux
and communicated to the departments.   It was Gambetta's
final blow at the carcass of Bonapartism, and it framed all
those exclusions which he had outlined in October. [3]   The
method of election, too, the same as that prescribed by
the Delegation on October 1 with voting by cantons and
" scrutin de liste " was carefully designed in the Republican
interest.   " The object of these changes," as Lord Lyons
explained, " was supposed to be to throw impediments in
the way of bringing the Rural Population to the Poll, and
thus to increase the influence of the voters in the towns, who
constitute the principal support of the Party now in power." [4]
At the same time the usual interdict upon the candidature
of prefects was removed.   It was a very thorough attempt,
this attempt of Gambetta, to serve the " great party of the
French Revolution ".   Simultaneously with the publication
of the decree he issued a stirring proclamation in its defence :
" Nobody comes from Paris and the treacherous combinations of France's enemies must at all costs be thwarted.   In
place of the cowardly and reactionary Chamber which is
the enemy's dream "—a skilful hint at connivance between
Bismarck and the Bonapartists—" let us set up a truly
national Republican Assembly. . . .   " We must all (—all
classes and parties, Legitimist and bourgeois, workers and

---

[1] *Dép. circ.*, etc., I, 407.
[2] CRÉMIEUX, *Actes de la Délégation de Tours et de Bordeaux*, 90.
[3] Cp. above, p. 169.   [4] *F.O.* 146, 1531.

peasants) rally round the Republic. . . . To arms. To arms ! " [1]

At 4.40 that day, January 31, Favre telegraphed to Gambetta : " Our misfortune is great but our honour is safe. Now we must avoid divisions. . . . I count on your loyalty." [2] But the appeal had come too late. Gambetta had published his decree, and the first division was already made. He had withheld his resignation in order not to provoke a conflict in the provinces ; now the reticence of the Government at Paris threatened to provoke a conflict no less serious between it and the Delegation. The " personage from Paris " who arrived at Bordeaux on February 1, after a tedious journey of thirty-two hours, was to find that his worst fears had been realised, and that Gambetta had already acted. On the way from the station to the prefecture he saw and read the Delegation's election decree, and with him he bore full powers to ensure the execution of the decree of the Government at Paris, a decree in which there was no ineligibility clause. A struggle seemed inevitable, for Gambetta surely would not yield to Simon as in October the Delegation had yielded to Gambetta.

The Delegates were assembled in council when Jules Simon came to join them and to explain his mission. Gambetta listened impatiently, and the fact that Simon was the emissary probably made him none the more conciliatory, for after Picard Simon was one of the colleagues with whom he was least in sympathy. The election question quickly led to a stormy debate, which continued after a deputation from the municipality of Bordeaux had been introduced into the council room. [3] If the former deputy

---

[1] *D.T.* II, 493.
[2] *D.T.* II, 489.
[3] SIMON, *Dép.* I, 505 ; FOURICHON, *Dép.* I, 638 ; CRÉMIEUX, *Actes de la Délégation*, 92.

of Bordeaux was eloquent,[1] so was its present hero, and
the mayor marvelled at the magnificent oratorical duel ;
but M. Fourcand was also concerned for the preservation
of order in his city, and his colleagues openly sympathised
with Gambetta. He told Simon that he could not ensure
the execution of the Paris decree ; there would be civil
war if Gambetta resigned : he himself could recognise no
Government other than that which had so long been
residing at Bordeaux.[2]   These opinions were reinforced
by two other deputations, one from Lyons and the other
from Aveyron and Toulouse.[3]   There is no evidence that
Gambetta himself had arranged the introduction of these
outsiders, though their presence at this particular moment
was significant ; but if it was arranged, it failed in its object.
Simon was completely isolated—the other Delegates remained true to their signatures and loyal to Gambetta—
but he was not intimidated.   He would not yield ; his
instructions were definite and he had been invested with
full authority to ensure their execution.   As a result, the
meeting broke up in anger, Gambetta striding from the
room, hurling bitter accusations against his Paris colleagues,
crying, "You are no Republicans ! You are no Republicans ! " while Glais-Bizoin hurried after to pacify him.[4]

Thus matters were at a deadlock, and the situation
seemed as serious as it could be without actual civil war.
Of the danger of that Simon had been warned, and despite
his full powers, he dreaded the responsibility of provoking
a conflict by their premature use.   He telegraphed to Paris
to ask whether the Government would modify its decisions
in view of the grave situation ;[5] he sent Liouville back to the

[1] Simon had been elected for Bordeaux in 1869.   This was presumably
one of the reasons for his choice for this mission.

[2] FOURCAND, Dép. I, 638.   [3] D.T. II, 495.
[4] SILVY, Dép. IV, 551.   [5] D.T. II, 495.

capital to give a detailed account of the state of Bordeaux ; [1] and he tried to succeed informally where formally he had failed, and to win the lesser members of the Delegation by private persuasion. They were obdurate, but Glais-Bizoin hinted that he would yield if there was at Bordeaux a majority of the Government in favour of the Parisian decree.[2] It was the first suggestion of the final solution, and Simon recalled it when he was consulting M. Thiers. Thiers advocated vigorous methods : " You must publish your decree. You have no time to wait. You will have the support of one legion of the National Guard and the neutrality perhaps of the others. You must sound General Billot's army.[3] Make use of me. If my name or presence can be of any service, I am ready." [4] But Simon was not so ready, and such prompt and forcible measures, which in Sorel's opinion would have wholly succeeded,[5] were not to his taste. He waited for Thiers to calm himself, and then suggested, could not governmental reinforcements be brought from Paris ? The idea found favour. M. Thiers agreed ; it would be possible, and the sooner the better ; and he forthwith despatched his trusty agent, Cochery, to Paris to convince the Government there of the necessity of this measure. Therein, Simon hoped, lay the solution. His policy was now to await the arrival of colleagues from Paris, and to restrain the Delegation from any precipitate action by the promise of a full explanation with other members of the Government of National Defence.

Bismarck was supremely indifferent to the justice or

---

[1] FAVRE, *Gouvernement de la défense nationale*, III, 18 ; DRÉO, *Procès-verbaux*, 607.

[2] J. SIMON, *Le Gouvernement de M. Thiers*, I, 20, 23.

[3] Billot was in command of an army corps being trained near Poitiers.

[4] J. SIMON, op. cit. I, 22.

[5] SOREL, *Histoire diplomatique de la guerre franco-allemande*, II, 199.

injustice of French electoral methods, but he was interested in the results. A little line of the Main might not be dis- agreeable, but he did not wish to risk the return of a violent Assembly pledged to the continuance of a war which in German opinion had already lasted far too long ; the Assembly he desired was one which would most truly re- present the French nation, and thus be the surest guarantee of the peace terms he intended to exact. Hence a clause in the armistice convention had stipulated that the elections must be free, and when he received Gambetta's decree, Bismarck was moved to strong protest. He wrote to Favre, hinting not obscurely at the risk of rupture, and he despatched a telegram of protest to " Monsieur Léon Gambetta " [1] : " In the name of the freedom of elections stipulated by the armistice convention, I protest against the measure taken in your name to deprive numerous categories of French citizens of the right of being elected to the Assembly. Elections held under a regime of arbitrary oppression cannot confer the rights which the armistice convention allows to deputies who are freely elected." [2] But Gambetta promptly and adroitly seized this German intervention as a pretext to strengthen his own case. On the 3rd, Bismarck's telegram was posted up throughout Bordeaux, and with it a brief proclamation, which denounced it as an unwarrantable interference in French internal affairs, and a proof that the Germans wanted to procure an Assembly composed of the " allies of M. de Bismarck," and of the " accomplices of the fallen dynasty ".[3]

For four days the deadlock continued. Simon remained in Bordeaux unmolested, but his telegrams to Paris were liable to be intercepted by Gambetta's friend Steenackers,

---

[1] Whereas he addressed Favre as " M. le Ministre ".
[2] *D.T.* II, 505.   [3] Ibid.

and every effort was made to frustrate his attempts to secure the publication of the Paris decree. A notice which he had had posted, announcing his mission and his determination to execute it, was promptly removed on Gambetta's orders,[1] and fourteen newspapers which consented to publish the decree were seized by Ranc and Allain-Targé, acting on instructions approved by the whole Delegation.[2]

The success or maintenance of Gambetta's policy depended now upon the extent to which he could intimidate the Government at Paris, and upon the amount of support which he received from the country. But the attempt to intimidate Simon had failed, while Bismarck's protest was potent in stiffening the resolution of the Government of Paris : Favre, who most feared the consequences of Bismarck's wrath, threatened to resign if the Bordeaux decree were not withdrawn and Gambetta replaced.[3] He and his colleagues readily agreed to the proposal brought by Cochery, and at a special session on the morning of the 4th it was decided that Simon should be reinforced by Garnier-Pagès, Arago, and Pelletan. Before they left Paris Liouville had arrived and painted a gloomy picture of the state of Bordeaux, of Gambetta's power, and the possibility of his successful resistance, but this did not alter the Government's decision to assert its authority ; it merely determined that if the worst came to the worst it would remove to Poitiers with the Assembly.[4] Thus the Government at Paris was inflexible, and prepared to maintain its decree even at the risk of civil war. What would Gambetta do in the face of such opposition, and what was the attitude of the country in general to

---

[1] GLAIS-BIZOIN, *Dictature de cinq mois*, 213.

[2] RANC, *Dép.* II, 66, and letter in *L'Indépendance Belge*, Oct. 17, 1873 ; cp. MONTFERRIER, *Le Gouvernement de Bordeaux* (Paris, 1872), 78 ; SIMON, *Le Gouvernement de M. Thiers*, I, 28.

[3] DRÉO, *Procès-verbaux*, 652.   [4] Ibid. 661.

this conflict between the two parts of the Government of National Defence ?

Gambetta lacked neither advice nor approval. Counsel was showered upon him by ardent Republicans : several of his prefects urged him to make himself dictator ; a deputation came from Lyons to persuade him to remove thither, to the city which, the prefect of Basses-Alpes declared, was " the real seat of Government at such a moment ".[1] But Gambetta was by nature averse from desperate courses : he had preached the peaceful accession of the Republic simply by the exercise of universal suffrage ; he had deliberately eschewed the use of violence to suppress the disorders at Lyons and Marseilles ; and now, on January 29, he had withdrawn his resignation in order to prevent fresh outbreaks. His clear review of the situation in the despatch of the 27th showed that he was by no means anxious to bear the burden of dictatorship alone, and that he was aware of a change in public opinion. The change had been accentuated all the more by the fall of Paris and by the disaster of the army of the East, and reports of discouragement and opposition to the war came in from the opposite poles of France : [2] if twenty-five prefects, expressing their personal opinions, or reflecting the views of their Republican entourages, endorsed Gambetta's policy and welcomed the ineligibility decree, seven plainly expressed their disapproval, and hesitated to obey the instructions of their Minister.[3] Significant, too, was the attitude of troops and generals on whom Gambetta must rely, both for success in an armed conflict with Paris, and for the continuation of the war : " You ruin the defence and prepare civil war," wrote General Masure, and Jauréguiberry declared that Gambetta's action had had a

---

[1] *D.T.* I, 28. [2] E.g. Ardèche, Creuse, Nord.
[3] Cp. *D.T.*, Jan. 29 and following days.

very bad effect on the army of the Loire. Rumours there were of a *coup d'état* ; Gambetta would become dictator, Simon and " reactionaries " like Thiers and Fourichon would be arrested : Simon thought it prudent to sleep at a friend's house.[1] Noisy meetings were held by Republican extremists demanding a Committee of Public Safety, the indefinite adjournment of elections of all kinds and the prosecution of war to the knife. But the rumours were untrue, if not unfounded, and the demands of the extremists were without effect. If Gambetta considered the proposals, such as dictatorship and removal to Lyons, it was only to reject them. He was still far too much of a realist to allow himself to be blinded by dangerous illusions as to the strength of his position. He could scarcely wish to become the tool of the noisy demagogues of Lyons. At thirty-two he had a political future to care for ; there was every prospect that it would be long, presumably he also wished that it should be glorious. At Lyons it was unlikely to be either. Nor was Challemel-Lacour's account of that city encouraging for those who wished to make it the centre of successful rebellion and of continued resistance to the foreigner : " I ought to warn you that if the enemy marches on Lyons he will find a town without troops, provisions, or courage. To defend us we shall have 600 sailors, of whom half are ill, and a handful of Republicans from the suburbs." [2]

In fact, Gambetta's refusal to withdraw his decree was very far from implying any intention to " prepare civil war " —that he must have known would be fatal to the two causes he had most at heart, the defence of the country and of the

---

[1] SIMON, *Dép.* I, 507 ; FOURICHON, *Dép.* I, 637 ; SILVY, *Dép.* IV, 551 ; ANATOLE CLAVEAU, *Souvenirs politiques et parlementaires d'un témoin*, I, 372 ; P.-B. DES VALADES, *Martial Delpit, député à l'Assemblée nationale, Journal et correspondance* (Paris, 1897), 77.

[2] *D.T.* II, 49, Feb. 4 ; cp. ANDRIEUX, *La Commune à Lyon en 1870-71*, 96.

Republic—but he stood publicly committed to the decree, and he clearly hoped that a show of inflexible opposition would induce his colleagues of Paris to yield, and once more to accept a *fait accompli* of his devising. Perhaps, too, he calculated that, if he held out long enough, elections would be impossible on February 8 ; if Bismarck then chose to denounce the armistice convention there would be no option but to continue the war to the knife as he, Gambetta, desired. Moreover, although Simon was obdurate, he could still hope to persuade other members of the Paris Government, a hope which was reflected in a new proclamation on February 4 : " The Government of Paris has been besieged for four months and cut off from all contact with public opinion. Nothing shows that it would not have agreed with the Government of Bordeaux, had it been better informed : no more does anything, apart from the mission assigned in general terms to M. Jules Simon to proceed to the holding of elections, show that it intended to determine the special case of incompatibility in an absolute and definite fashion." As evidence of this conviction that the Government at Paris needed enlightening, Crémieux was authorised to repair to Paris himself to reason with his colleagues. He set out on the 5th, but went no further than Vierzon, for there he encountered Simon's reinforcements bound for Bordeaux. He at once abandoned his journey to Paris, and returned with them to Bordeaux. The numbers of the Delegation were now doubled, and the Government of Paris, fortified by the mighty figure of Bismarck which loomed in the background, inexorably maintained the authority of its own decree. The drama was nearing an end, and on this occasion Gambetta's *fait accompli* was destined to fail.

The climax of excitement at Bordeaux was reached that

Sunday afternoon when the extremer Republicans organised a monster demonstration and clamoured for Gambetta to assume the dictatorship. " Immense crowds," wrote Lord Lyons, " collected by the supporters of these views, but composed probably in great measure of persons attracted by mere curiosity, have gathered round the Prefecture at which M. Gambetta resides. They have been addressed shortly by the Prefect, and some other officials, but M. Gambetta has not shown himself. Up to the hour (6 p.m.) at which I am writing, no serious disorder has taken place." [1] Nor did any occur ; nor did Gambetta appear. He rejected the temptation, if temptation it was, to be the idol of a mob ; he refused to be a pretext for disorder or to be forced by popular enthusiasm into slippery paths which he was anxious to avoid. From the point of view of its Republican organisers, the manifestation was a dismal failure.

There remained the last round, the contest with the new arrivals from Paris at the council of the Delegation next morning. It was to be brief. A warm debate soon convinced Gambetta that there could no longer be any doubt of the resolution of the Government of Paris nor any hope of overcoming it. Another meeting had been fixed for the afternoon, but before it assembled Gambetta had sent in his resignation. The obscurities arising from Favre's first telegram had now wholly been dissipated. Gambetta had striven his utmost to assert his own policy, but the attempt had failed. There was nothing to do but withdraw in accordance with his original intention. Further resistance was only likely to lead to humiliation, and to throw him into the arms of the extremists, whom he knew how to humour, but with whom he had little sympathy. It was well, he told Freycinet, that " the man who is accused of exercising

[1] *F.O.* 146, 1531, Feb. 5, Lyons to Granville.

a dictatorship " should voluntarily disappear from the
scene.[1] But he retired, he said, bearing with him as " an
apanage of our party the grand idea of national resistance ".[2]
A grand idea, and one of worth ; in days to come it was to
be a most valuable political asset.

The resignation of the Minister of Interior and of War
was thankfully accepted by his colleagues, this time without
fear of civil war ; Bordeaux and the other southern cities
remained quiet, and Arago peacefully assumed the interim
administration of both his offices.   The prefects now received
instructions couched in very different language : " Anyone
can be elected. . . . The important thing is that the elections
should take place, and that they should be free." [3]   Despite
the short notice, they did everywhere take place, and they
were the freest elections held in France for twenty years.
There was no time for any elaborate preparation of political
programmes : the issue was of the simplest—the electors
voted for war or peace, and the result was overwhelmingly
in favour of peace.   It was not only a complete rejection of
Gambetta's policy of war to the knife, but it also appeared
to endanger the existence of his Republic, for the majority
of the new deputies had monarchist leanings, but not Bonapartist.   The results showed how much he had over-
estimated the power of his old enemies, and how unnecessary
was the ineligibility decree.   He seemed utterly to have
failed, and it looked as though all that was left of his work
would soon be undone.   The result of the elections still
further widened the breach between him and his Parisian
colleagues ; [4] they were furious against the man whom they

---

[1] FREYCINET, *Souvenirs*, I, 249.

[2] *Rapport* DE SUGNY, 187, cit. letter of GAMBETTA to GENT.

[3] *D.T.* II, Int. to pref. Lille, Feb. 8.

[4] Ferry was an exception, he could still write to Gambetta as " amatissimo
mio " (J. FERRY, *Lettres*, Feb. 8).

held to be chiefly responsible for the Republican defeat, and
who yet had emerged as the dominant figure in the Republican party. For, despite his failure, Gambetta still possessed a prestige sufficient to cause his election in nine departments. To the people of Alsace and Lorraine, threatened
with annexation, he was above all others the champion of
national resistance and the integrity of French territory, and
he was returned by all four eastern departments.[1] Cleverly
and effectively he showed his fidelity to that role by choosing
to represent the most important of them, the Bas-Rhin.
But of the uncongenial National Assembly he did not long
remain a member, and nothing became him like the leaving
of it. On March 1 a large majority ratified the preliminaries of the peace which Gambetta had so strenuously tried
to avoid. The announcement of the voting was followed
by an impressive scene : Jules Grosjean, deputy of Haut-
Rhin, rose to read the moving protest of the surrendered
provinces against their abandonment, and then, in a silence
broken only by the sounds of stifled emotion, Gambetta and
the other representatives of the lost departments left the
Assembly. He at once resigned his seat as deputy for a
district which was no longer to be part of France, and his
last act at Bordeaux was to pronounce the funeral oration
of Küss, the mayor of Strasbourg, who after a long illness
had succumbed to the strain and griefs of the past six
months. In that speech he sounded for the first time the
note of revenge which was to be echoed, sometimes loudly,
sometimes so faintly as to be almost inaudible, through forty
years to come.[2] This championship of Alsace and Lorraine
was Gambetta's most effective defence of the policy which
a nation had condemned, the policy of war to the knife in

[1] Bas-Rhin, Haut-Rhin, Meurthe, Moselle.
[2] Cp. P. DESCHANEL, *Gambetta*, 126 ff.

defence of a France one and indivisible.   Then, the gesture
made, the note sounded, the "Dictator" withdrew.   A
private citizen once more, he saw nothing now to detain
him in Bordeaux, and Thiers, it is said, fearful lest his
continued presence might be a pretext for disturbance or
cause difficulties with the Germans, appealed to his patriotism
to leave the city for a time.[1]   He did more, and in need of
a thorough change and rest,[2] foreseeing only too clearly the
troubles ahead which were to break out with the Commune,[3]
he wisely withdrew not only from Bordeaux but from France.
The Italian grocer's son, who for four long, strenuous,
tragic months had been master of France, went into close
and humble retirement in Spain.   Men asked themselves
whether this fiery southern meteor was not for ever extinct.

---

[1] Cp. H. Pessard, *Mes petits papiers*, II, 147, confirmed from other sources
by R. Dreyfus, *Revue de France*, Jan. 1, 1933.

[2] A. Tournier, *Gambetta, Souvenirs anecdotiques*, 147.

[3] Mme Adam, *Mes angoisses et nos luttes*, 26 ; Freycinet, *Souvenirs*, I, 265.

XVII

CONCLUSION

THE most spectacular period of Gambetta's career was over, and yet the man who now withdrew to retirement in Spain was only thirty-two years of age. His reputation was never so low as during the time of conservative reaction which followed the war. His enemies bitterly attacked the Government of National Defence and all its works ; they rejoiced in the belief that the Dictator had fallen never to rise again, that the career of the " Carnot of the Defeat " was ruined. Now his unhappy victim, France, no more disturbed by his sonorous trumpetings, would, under the guidance of her resurrected notables, have leisure to repair the havoc wrought by the " Dictatorship of Incapacity," and to replenish the treasury emptied by the " Government of National Expense ".[1] Such were the nicknames found for Gambetta and his colleagues of September 4 ; while the judgment of the majority of the National Assembly upon the policy of war to the knife was vividly reflected by Thiers' famous condemnation : " They prolonged the defence beyond all reason ; the means they employed were the worst conceived in any war at any time. We were all revolted, I like you, by this policy of raging madmen which placed France in the greatest peril."

[1] The extreme Left was also denunciatory : cp. e.g. MARX's reference to " a Government of National Defection " (*Civil War in France,* 16).

265

But the men who thus sought to discredit Gambetta and affected to believe that he was now a nullity in French politics, a man who had never been more than a vulgar demagogue, a bubble quickly pricked, gravely misjudged his character, and under-estimated his achievements. Their hopes were soon to be disappointed, and theirs was not to be the final verdict upon the Government of National Defence. The Assembly which listened to Thiers' denunciation set up a Commission of Inquiry into the acts of its predecessors ; that in itself was an act of censure—but its reports had no political effect, for by the time the Commissioners had completed their great task the Assembly, their creator, was no more, and the Republican Constitution had been voted. Gambetta's fame with his star was again on the rise, and the adverse criticism of some of the greatest of contemporary writers, Renan, Flaubert, George Sand, was powerless to prevent a new reading of his role in 1870-71. The legend of the raging madman was supplanted by the legend of the great-hearted hero who had but to stamp his foot and armies sprang forth from the soil, and when Gambetta died in 1882 the part he played in the Franco-German war was reckoned his greatest claim to undying glory. The detractors had greviously miscalculated. The triumph of the Republic had been largely the work of the fallen Dictator, and the Republic rewarded him by the cultivation of a legend which shed lustre both upon it and upon its founders. The government of the National Assembly and the presidency of Marshal MacMahon had provided admirable opportunities for the use of talents which he had already displayed in the earlier part of his career.

This new Mirabeau had shown himself very much the child of his age, and that age was a new era in the history of French Republicanism. The triumph of Liberalism in the

Europe of 1848 had been as fleeting as it was widespread ;
nowhere did the abundance of virtue and lofty principles
compensate for lack of practical genius and political experience. The age of Realpolitik followed that of Idealism,
and while the great Realpolitiker of Prussia was the arch-
enemy of Liberalism, practical opportunism was by no
means necessarily the monopoly of reactionaries. The un-
scrupulous Cavour won a brilliant victory for Liberalism
where Mazzini had failed, and in France the young Republican from Cahors was to be one of the most conspicuous
exponents of the new Liberal realism. Much has been
written of Gambetta, the anti-clerical, opportunist, statesman
of the Third Republic, but the statesman of the Third
Republic was merely the politician of the Second Empire
ripened by experience. The generation of Republicans to
which Gambetta belonged had come under the influence of
Comte rather than of Lamartine ; it was positivist, realist,
and anti-clerical, and for the " superstitions " of religion and
faith in the unseen it substituted superstitions of its own, a
naive belief in the omnicompetence of science and in the
miracles of education. Thus the realist, Gambetta, proclaimed the bankruptcy of the ideas of 1848 : henceforth
expediency not principle was to be the guiding factor in
Republican policy, and with expediency as his compass,
Gambetta founded his political fortunes, won a place as a
Republican leader, and sought to inspire his party with a
new vitality, if not with a greater moral strength.

A barrister, like so many of the leading Republicans—
in the Panthéon he has been called " le grand mort de la
République des avocats "—Gambetta had the ambition to become a great parliamentarian. The Baudin trial assured his
opportunity, and the Belleville election gave a perfect opening to his opportunist tactics. Once a deputy, he sought to

be leader of a strong and compact, well-disciplined party, and the story of Gambetta before September, 1870, is in great part the story of the evolution of the Republican opposition. The manner of his rise to fame and influence made him suspect as a mere adventurer and a demagogue : he was thought to be " vox et præterea nihil ". But in the Chamber he soon surprised by his moderation and good sense. A consummate tactician, he made it a rule to be moderate in action however violent he might be in electoral speeches, and while he continued to assert his uncompromising hostility to the Empire, he persistently disclaimed all sympathy with the men who worked for revolution by violence. The tribune of Belleville had a constructive theory of Republicanism and developed the idea that the Republic could come into being without any revolution merely as an expression of the wish of universal suffrage : in the meantime, he desired the Republican Left to be fit to govern. It was an attractive theory, but its prospects of realisation were sadly blighted by the plebiscite which seemed to re-establish the authority of the Empire more firmly than ever. The realist Gambetta betrayed a certain naivety in his hopes of universal suffrage, and now that he was disillusioned, his attitude was a matter for interesting speculation. Would the irreconcilable remain irreconcilable ? His evident opportunism could lead even friends to suggest that he would rally to a Liberal Empire in time. But that time never came, and his opportunism before the outbreak of war had always been opportunism within Republican limits. If Gambetta had believed in anything, the word Republic was the alpha and omega of his creed ; it represented the ideal goal which he must make every effort to attain ; not merely a form of democratic government, but the only true form and a whole political, social, and moral system. If his faith wavered for an instant after the plebiscite, and there is no evidence that it did, it was soon to be confirmed beyond doubt, for the declaration of war two months later was to prove the Empire's death sentence.

The plebiscite had seemed to check the development of the Republican opposition : the war swiftly altered its prospects. The crushing military defeats took all parties by surprise, and the deputies of the Left attained a sudden significant and wholly unexpected importance. The Republic appeared to be within grasp, yet under conditions far other and less auspicious than those dreamed of by Gambetta, and there is no reason to doubt the sincerity of the Republican deputies when, after Sedan, they wished to secure a " legal " transference of authority to a committee of the Legislative Body and to share the responsibilities of office at such a time of crisis. Gambetta remained true to his condemnation of revolution by violence, although he may have hoped that the invasion of the Chamber would influence the votes of his fellow deputies in the way he desired. But at the Palais Bourbon on the momentous day of September 4 he over-estimated his ability to control a vast, excited crowd. He was able only to guide and not to govern it, and he became a revolutionary *malgré lui*. Yet it was he, a newcomer and the Benjamin in the ranks of the Republican deputies, who played a dominant part in the events of that day, and he did so not as a revolutionary conspirator but as a leader of natural authority coming forward to exert a restraining influence at a critical moment. His quick intuition and adaptability to changing circumstances were perhaps decisive for the establishment of the Government of National Defence.

Thus far, in the foundation of his political career the eloquent southerner who now became Minister of the Interior had shown marked ability. His opportunism

placed him on a lower moral level than many of his older
colleagues, but not lower than many of his Bonapartist
adversaries, and it had had the effect of quickening the life-
blood of the Republican party, even though it strained its
quality.   Within a year of his appearance in the Chamber
he had been hailed as the greatest of its orators, a worthy
successor to Mirabeau and Royer-Collard.   By clever
tactics he had won an independent position ; he had created
a following of his own ; he had the fascination, self-confidence and consciousness of power which assured him a
position of authority ; he had proved that he was neither a
mere orator nor a demagogue ; he had brought with him
a definite and exclusively Republican programme which
testified both to his moderation and to his practical sense,
and in questions of foreign policy his realistic conception of
the nation's interests had been in strong contrast with the
romantic illusions of many of his Republican colleagues ; he
had shown himself more nationalist than they ; he was
patriot as well as partisan—it is difficult to imagine him
openly wishing, like Peyrat on the morrow of the plebiscite,
that an invasion would come to sweep the Empire away,[1] or
rejoicing, like Quinet, in " the joyful sound of the cannon of
Sedan ".   Eloquent and masterful as he was, this realist
had throughout shown his realism by condemning the use of
violence as a political weapon.   There·was no hint of a
" man of blood anc. iron " in the parliamentarian who so
deliberately set himself to lay the spectre of revolutionary
terror by which the Republic was haunted.   The new
Minister of the Interior, however, was by no means all
powerful in the Government which he had helped to establish.
His advice was often rejected by his elders, and after the
complete severance of communications between Paris and

[1] Mme ADAM, *Mes sentiments et nos idées*, 439.

the provinces he saw himself virtually deprived of control over the most important sphere of his administration. There can be little doubt that he welcomed the opportunity to go to Tours, where he would have much wider scope for his activity. But it was as Delegate of the Government at Paris that he went, and he always asserted his loyalty to the Central Government in the city which had made the Revolution. He advocated a policy of thorough republicanisation which his colleagues hesitated to approve, but it was not until December, when no answer came to his urgent appeals, that he began to apply it fully upon his own responsibility.

Dictator in fact, he was all absorbed in the grand twin task of saving country and regime, and was ready to share his authority in the provinces with Favre, the most distinguished of his imprisoned colleagues. As an administrator he showed a vast knowledge of the political atlas of France : he was supple or firm as need be, sometimes perhaps more supple than firm ; yet he did succeed in restoring a relative order throughout the country, and the reputed anti-clerical discouraged anti-clerical excesses.

But his great task was the conduct of the national defence, and his most unexpected role that of Minister of War. Much that was obscure had become clearer by the time that Gambetta left Paris on his mission to cancel the elections and to rouse the spirit of resistance in the provinces. The Government of National Defence had taken office, ignorant of the dispositions of Prussia, and hoping for peace on moderate terms. Ferrières dispelled such illusions. It had been expected that the Germans would easily capture Paris by assault, or that the Parisians would be unable to endure a siege of any length. But the city had held out three weeks, and there was every prospect that it might continue to hold out for as many months. This being so, the provinces acquired a new and vast importance, not merely from the point of view of a Republican Minister of the Interior concerned for the political opinions of his " administrés et contribuables," but from the point of view of an organiser of the national defence. It was the fortune of war rather than any merits of their own which had carried the Republicans to power, and the future of their Republic was likely to depend as much upon their conduct of the war as upon their conduct of internal administration. The Republican problem was overshadowed and complicated by the war from the outset. Partisan, Gambetta saw clearly that the salvation of the regime was inseparable from that of the country, and his patriotism was all the more ardent, if not the more disinterested, because in organising a national resistance he was fighting for both. It was his great merit to perceive the possibilities of provincial defence, and not merely to perceive them but to develop them as far as he could. The intervention of new armies in the provinces might save Paris, snatch victory from the jaws of disaster, and quite change the colour of the enemy's " fragile fortune ". The " might " was a big " might " ; but Gambetta had the vision to see that it was within the bounds of possibility, and the courage to make the attempt to realise it. He, indeed, did not improvise all the weapons of defence ; it is indisputable that the War Office at Tours had made considerable progress in the organisation of an army of the Loire before his arrival. But what mattered greatly was the spirit behind the organisation, and that spirit before his arrival was very far from optimistic. It was true that irresponsible Republican enthusiasts spoke glibly of a repetition of 1792, but until Gambetta came there was no one who had a practical conception of operations on a grand scale, and no one who had the authority and compelling power to arouse the spirit of enthusiasm necessary to carry them through. It is this all-important factor of morale which is ignored by those who would destroy Gambetta's claims to greatness merely by the production of statistics, and by those who criticise the idea of operations on a grand scale as fundamentally false. For the vast majority of Frenchmen, both within and without the city, Paris was the obvious objective ; there was a categorical imperative to attempt its relief, a moral obligation which could not be disregarded. But it was a task which required speed and the employment of large and well-trained forces. Gambetta recognised the obligation, and made valiant efforts to meet the requirements. Thus, the first phase of " la grande guerre en province " was concerned, and rightly concerned, with the attempt of the army of the Loire to relieve Paris. It did not succeed ; but there is abundant and striking German evidence to show how near it was at one time to success, and that evidence is, I consider, full justification of Gambetta's strategy. The attempt was worth while : the Germans actually contemplated raising the siege, and the moral effect of such a confession of failure on their part would have been truly prodigious.

Yet the venture not only failed but also ended in severe defeat, and the defeat coincided with the failure of the sortie from Paris. The relief of Paris could never again be essayed under such favourable conditions, and still Gambetta set to work with indomitable energy to repair his losses, and to plan new campaigns. Was this, indeed, the policy of a raging madman, the prolongation of the defence beyond all reason as Thiers declared ? Was early December, the moment of Moltke's overture to Trochu, the obvious moment for peace ? It was true that the provincial armies never again came so near great success as at Coulmiers, but it was by no means obvious that they were doomed to constant

and inevitable defeat.   They were clearly bound to continue
their efforts while Paris still held out—and the Parisians had
without any reference to Gambetta rejected Moltke's overture and determined on resistance to the bitter end.   He and
they were in fact in complete agreement upon a policy of
war to the knife : but whereas war to the knife for them
meant above all resistance as long as Paris could stave off
starvation, for him it began to take the form of resistance
even after the fall of Paris.   Even here his reasoning was
not the folly Thiers represented.   He argued correctly that
Prussia could scarcely demand more than Alsace-Lorraine
and an indemnity, and that as she asked for them already,
France would have nothing to lose as far as peace terms
were concerned by continuing the war ; on the contrary,
she might yet gain considerably, wear the invader out, and
force him to reduce his conditions.   While the armies of the
Loire, the North and the East were still unbroken, the
cogency of this argument must be admitted.   But the success
of these armies was essential if the country was to survive
such a catastrophe as the fall of Paris, and, instead of success,
there came defeat upon defeat, so that the morale of the
country was already rapidly declining before the city fell.[1]
Gambetta's policy, reasonable at the end of December, was
quite unreasonable at the end of January.   The capitulation
of Paris was closely followed by the internment of the army
of the East ; it was impossible for a people which had already
suffered so much to continue resistance after these two
crowning disasters. In the earlier stages of the war, Gambetta
had shown a keen sense of the fundamental importance of
the moral factor ; but when even after the fall of Paris, he
still urged the continuance of the war " until complete
exhaustion," it was evident that his reluctance to admit the

[1] Cp. Appendix XV, pp. 320 ff.

failure of a policy on which he had founded such great hopes, on which so much depended, and of which he himself was the personification, had blinded the realist's sense of reality. When a Gambetta could no longer kindle enthusiasm for a national cause, that cause was hopeless indeed. When he continued none the less to preach war to the knife, he threatened France with deeper ruin the Republic with final extinction.

Yet one of his most discriminating critics has judged him hardly not because he proclaimed this policy of war to the knife, but because, having proclaimed it so often and so loudly, he did not persevere and carry it through at all hazards. If Gambetta was convinced that Paris had no right to conclude an armistice for the whole country, argued von der Goltz, then consistency demanded that he should continue the struggle at all costs, and " not retire with a grumbling protest " : such conduct showed lack of energy and courage.[1] But would there have been any advantage or nobility in the courage of a man who adhered blindly to his policy, even at the risk of civil war ? He had obligations to the Government at Paris, from which he had received his mandate, and to the Parisians, who had made the revolution of September 4. By his electoral decree he made, without resorting to violence, every effort to ensure that his policy should be carried through. When those efforts failed, he had the wisdom to acknowledge his defeat. In such circumstances, discretion was not merely the better, but also the more patriotic, part of valour. By nothing could he have more justly earned the name of " raging madman " than by provoking civil war in the presence of the enemy, and in a country already distracted by so many misfortunes.

Gambetta has often been called the Carnot of the national

---

[1] *Gambetta und seine Armeen*, 228.

defence ; but the comparison is misleading, for there was an all-important difference between the organiser of 1870 and the organiser of 1793 : Carnot was a military engineer, a professional with long experience, while Gambetta was a complete amateur. In this, and in his whole character and the sort of influence he exercised, Gambetta resembled Danton far more closely than Carnot. The Carnot of 1870 was rather the mining engineer Freycinet ; for although he, too, was an amateur, it was upon him that the chief burden of organisation fell. Gambetta, like Danton, was first and foremost the man of energy, the eloquent tribune who kindled the spirit of national resistance, and supplied an indispensable moral driving force. He, Minister of the Interior as well as of War, was, like Danton, Minister of Justice, concerned with the general direction of policy as well as with the conduct of the war, but in the conduct of war he exerted a much more direct and extensive control. Thus Danton influenced the choice of officers : Gambetta did more, and chose many himself. Danton concerned himself with the political aspects of the war : Gambetta did more, and the lawyer of 1870 was strategist as well as politician.

Gambetta, however, failed, while Danton was to a great extent successful. And Gambetta's failure seemed to mean the ruin of all his hopes, of all that he had stood for, of his country mutilated by the loss of two fair provinces, of the Republic jeopardised by the result of the elections, and of his own future. " Had Mirabeau never existed," wrote one of his biographers, " the French Revolution would probably have run the same course ; had his life been protracted, the event would have been the same, the ruin of the Monarchy not less tragic and complete." Had the new Mirabeau, Gambetta, not existed, Paris would none the less have put up a stubborn resistance, and clung to its policy of war to the knife, and the terms of peace would probably not have been materially different from those which were actually imposed. What, then, was the significance of his work ? Had it no permanent value ? Was it merely a ruinous waste of blood and treasure ? I have tried to show the injustice of judgment merely by the immediate practical result.[1] The legends of the raging madman, and of the heroic creator of armies, are almost equally removed from the truth. Juster is the dry verdict of Clemenceau : " He had conducted the war—both well and badly, but more badly than well—but he certainly did conduct it, and as well as he could ".[2] And I would add that there was no one else at the time who could have done it as well, no one who had the confidence, the energy, and the prestige necessary to carry the country with him as did Gambetta. Badly, indeed, he did conduct the war in many ways : the blunders and blots in the national defence were very numerous : there were Gambetta's own blunders and miscalculations, the failure to undeceive Trochu about compliance with his plan, the Epinay despatch, the condemnation of D'Aurelle, the misjudgment of Bourbaki, the interference with the progress of operations, the ineligibility thesis ; and there were the general blots, such as the confusion of command at critical moments, strategical misdirection, the constant friction between the civil and military authorities, ineffective armament, and camps like Conlie and Les Alpines. But, despite all this, and despite its apparent fruitlessness, Gambetta's work had a real significance ; for, in so far as it was conducted well, it

---

[1] And, even judging by material effects, the prolongation of the war had not been so ruinous as Thiers implied : witness the quickness with which France recovered and the over-subscription of the indemnity loan.

[2] *Clemenceau, the Events of his Life, as told by Himself to his Former Secretary,* JEAN MARTET (London, 1930), 280.

revealed new possibilities, and it had a genuine moral value. " It is impossible to govern against Paris, it is impossible to govern without Paris," was a saying later attributed to Gambetta.[1] But Thiers had soon disproved the first half of the sentence while Gambetta himself, by his government in the provinces, had disproved the second half, and amply demonstrated the falsity of the saying that Paris was France. He raised the dignity of the departments, and despite the return of centralised administration to Paris, the capital was never completely to regain its absolute political supremacy.[2] If, as Renan said, he destroyed the legend of 1792, nevertheless, despite the defects of his administration, he showed the immense possibilities of a well-organised national defence, and of the systematic resistance of a whole people to a foreign invader. And Europe, and, most important of all, in Europe Germany, was impressed by that demonstration. There was no more eloquent tribute to its effectiveness than the wish expressed by von der Goltz that should Germany ever suffer such defeat as France in 1870, she should find a man like Gambetta to kindle resistance to the uttermost.[3] Despite Rathenau's advocacy of a *levée en masse*,[4] that wish was unfulfilled when Germany's hour of humiliation came in 1918. The Supreme Command rejected the idea, and after the collapse of the Empire the Socialists and Republicans did not attempt to revive it. It is interesting to note that Adolf Hitler constantly reproached them with their failure to do this, and that he, in his turn, reinforced the homage of

[1] Cit. L. ANDRIEUX, *A travers la République* (Paris, 1926), 224.

[2] Though all is centralised in Paris, the deputies of the provinces play a very important part in legislation and government-making ; cp. A. THIBAUDET, *La République des professeurs* (Paris, 1927), 110.

[3] *Gambetta und seine Armeen*, 231.

[4] Count HARRY KESSLER, *Walther Rathenau, his Life and Work*, 256, 257 (London, 1929).

von der Goltz : " The war was waged with fresh energy. . . . The French national honour was restored by the Republic. What a contrast with our Republic ! " [1] Whatever the interpretation of the war scare of 1875, that incident was indirectly a tribute to Gambetta's display of the resources and powers of endurance of the French nation, and to the force of the idea which he voiced at once after the ratification of the peace preliminaries, the idea of revenge. The power of Gambetta the man, as Dilke said, was more a physical than a moral power, but the work and policy of the man had a real and vital moral importance. He had helped to restore the self-respect of the French people, to save its honour, and by identifying every citizen with the national defence to revive the idea of the " Patrie " in all its full significance. Even after his programme of war to the knife had proved impracticable, the idea had value. By it and by his protest against the treaty of Frankfort, Gambetta personified the conception of the essential unity and indivisibility of France.

Despite his failure and the obloquy heaped upon him by his enemies, he emerged the only great man of the Government of National Defence : he was energetic and optimistic : he was clear-sighted, although he exaggerated the power of the Bonapartists, and was loth to recognise the collapse of morale ; he was courageous, although he hesitated to assume responsibility for the defeat at Orléans ; he adhered consistently to a determined policy of war to the knife, although he allowed armistice negotiations to interfere with operations. What he accomplished only an amateur could have done, but as an amateur he had also many of the defects of an

---

[1] ADOLF HITLER, *Reden* (1933). Speeches of April 17, 1923 ; March 23, 1933 ; and Sept. 12, 1933. I am indebted to Herr Felix Gilbert for these references.

amateur, defects which appeared all the more glaring when such great issues were at stake. He had some sound military instincts, but not the genius which circumstances required ; nor, unfortunately, did he discover it in his commanders. For Gambetta's adversaries this want of genius was an unpardonable crime.

APPENDIX I

(P. 11.) GAMBETTA AND THE ORLEANISTS

1. In the elections of 1863, Gambetta supported the candidature of Prévost-Paradol.
2. In 1865, " when pleading against Delescluze he seems to have treated the Republicans and greybeards of 1848 harshly enough ". (H. Dutrait-Crozon, *Gambetta et la défense nationale, 1870-71*, 40.)
3. In the same year he paid his only visit to England ; accompanied by his friend Laurier he visited Twickenham, where the head of the House of Orléans, the Comte de Paris, resided in exile.

These circumstances, and especially the visit to Twickenham, gave rise to all kinds of gossip, and excited suspicion among certain Republicans.[1] Gambetta and Laurier were charged with desertion to the Orleanists. They were suspected of having betrayed Republican principles, and at the time of the Affaire Baudin it was said that Delescluze made the Twickenham visit a pretext for refusal to take Laurier as his counsel. It was odd, then, that he should have chosen Gambetta, Laurier's companion, to conduct his defence.[2]

What, in fact, was the significance of the Twickenham visit ? Does it, in conjunction with the other incidents mentioned above, justify the conclusion of Dutrait-Crozon that the needy adventurer from Cahors was "feeling his way "[3] and the inference which

[1] H. PESSARD, *Mes petits papiers*, I, 128 ff., gives the story as it went round the cafés. But he does not really throw any light upon the incident.
[2] But cp. A. TOURNIER, *Souvenirs anecdotiques*, 71-73, for an explanation.
[3] Op. cit. 40.

naturally follows that he would not have hesitated to change his allegiance had the prospects of the Orleanists seemed brighter than those of the Republicans ?

The actual circumstances of the visit to Twickenham, and what happened there, are obscure. Gambetta's latest biographer, M. P. B. Gheusi,[1] makes no mention of it. J. Reinach says that Thiers provided Gambetta with a letter of introduction to the princes.[2] Deschanel (*Gambetta*, p. 22) dismisses the visit in a brief paragraph, which implies that it was undertaken at Laurier's initiative, and suggests that Gambetta agreed to accompany him for the same reasons for which he had supported Prévost-Paradol in 1863 : " he knew that agreement between Legitimists, Orleanists, and Republicans was indispensable ". Deschanel adds that his first words at Twickenham were : " I am a Republican ".[3]

When Gambetta was directly charged with Orleanism at an election meeting in 1869, he skilfully diverted the attack without offering any enlightenment : " It is true, I was invited to dine at the Comte de Paris, but owing to circumstances not of my willing I did not dine there and I am sorry for it. . . . (Loud exclamations. Signs of general astonishment.) Why ? . . . I will tell you : because the cooking there ought to be excellent." The audience roared with delight, and no more was said of the visit to Twickenham.[4]

Many years later, Gambetta told Dilke of his only journey to England. " That was on a curious mission," Dilke noted in August, 1876, " for he came under the Empire as the representative of the Republicans to enter into consultation with the Orléans princes for the overthrow of Louis Napoleon." [5]   But if

---

[1] *La vie et la mort singulières de Gambetta.*

[2] *Récits et portraits, Monsieur Thiers* (Paris, 1915), 29.

[3] His source presumably being A. TOURNIER, *Gambetta, Souvenirs anecdotiques*, 71 ff.

[4] R. DREYFUS, " Les premières armes de Gambetta," *Revue de France*, Jan. 1, 1933 ; cp. A. TOURNIER, op. cit., loc. cit.   The detailed story of the supposed dinner is given by H. PESSARD, *Mes petits papiers*, I, 128, 129, and anecdotes of a "déjeuner" are also related by PAUL BOSQ, *Souvenirs de l'Assemblée nationale, 1871-5* (Paris, 1908), 151 ff.

[5] GWYNN and TUCKWELL, *Life of Dilke*, I, 434.

Dilke heard the details of the Twickenham visit, he did not record them, and certain questions still remain, and perhaps always must remain, unanswered : 1. What authority had Gambetta to go to England as a negotiator ? 2. What happened at Twickenham? Were definite proposals made for Republican-Orleanist collaboration ? 3. If so, did anything come of them, or were they rejected then and there, and, if they were rejected, by whom and why ?

I think Gambetta's own account, such as it is, should be accepted, and Deschanel's explanation of his motives, unless first-hand evidence emerges to disprove them, or unless the other indications of Orleanist leanings produce an overwhelming conviction that that account is false. These indications, however, appear to have very little weight. 1. Although, in the 1863 elections, Gambetta was the only Republican to support the Orleanist Paradol against Guéroult, the editor of the democratic *Opinion nationale*, the Orleanist Paradol was by no means the only candidate in whose favour he canvassed. He was no less vigorous in championing the Cinq, the radical Jules Simon, and the proletarian Tolain ; in fact, he supported all those whom he thought likely to prove the most effective opponents of the Empire. 2. Contempt for the naïve idealism of the men of 1848 was one of the characteristics of the young Republican group, of which Gambetta was a leading member. Gambetta's references in the 1865 trial were therefore not at all inconsistent with adherence to a Republican programme. They merely marked the difference between the realism of " les jeunes " and the idealism of " les vieux ".

Of Gambetta's ambition and readiness to take advantage of any connections which might be useful to his career there is no doubt. But these were not incompatible with adherence to Republican beliefs. I can find no evidence strong enough to prove that he was contemplating a change of allegiance in 1865. The explanation of his conduct given by Deschanel is wholly consistent with his character and general outlook. Moreover, there was generally a marked increase of intimacy between Republicans and Orleanists after 1863, and Gambetta was by no means the only Republican of note to come into personal contact

with the Orleanist princes.   Jules Simon was acquainted with
the Comte de Paris, and in the same year as Gambetta's visit to
Twickenham, Jules Ferry and Georges Coulon were presented to
the Duc de Chartres at Berne.[1]

[1] M. RECLUS, *Jules Favre*, 246 ; cp. I. TCHERNOFF, *Histoire du parti républicain
au coup d'état et sous le second Empire*, 431.   He speaks of a meeting between
Gambetta and the Comte de Paris at Vienna, but I have been unable to learn
from him when this took place.   It is one of several striking instances he gives
of the close relations which obtained between Orleanists and Republicans.   I
can find no reference to it elsewhere : it attracted none of the attention which
attached to the Twickenham visit.

APPENDIX II

(P. 17.) TEXT OF THE BELLEVILLE MANDATE

The following is the text of Gambetta's Belleville Mandate, as quoted by Ollivier (*L'Empire libéral*, XI, 497) : " Au nom du suffrage universel, base de toute organisation politique et sociale, donnons mandat à notre député d'affirmer les principes de la démocratie radicale et de revendiquer énergiquement : l'application la plus radicale du suffrage universel, tant pour l'élection des maires et conseillers municipaux, sans distinction de localité, que pour l'élection des députés ; la répartition des circonscriptions effectuée sur le nombre réel des électeurs de droit, et non sur le nombre des électeurs inscrits ; la liberté individuelle désormais placée sous l'égide des lois, et non soumise au bon plaisir et à l'arbitraire administratifs ; l'abrogation de la loi de sûreté générale ; la suppression de l'article 75 de la Constitution de l'an VIII et la responsabilité directe de tous les fonctionnaires ; les délits politiques de tout ordre déférés au jury ; la liberté de la presse dans toute sa plénitude, débarrassée du timbre et du cautionnement ; la suppression des brevets d'imprimerie et de librairie ; la liberté de réunion sans entraves et sans pièges, avec la faculté de discuter toute matière religieuse, philosophique, politique et sociale ; l'abrogation de l'article 291 du Code pénal ; la liberté d'association pleine et entière ; la suppression du budget des cultes et la séparation des Églises et de l'État ; l'instruction primaire laïque, gratuite et obligatoire, avec concours entre les intelligences d'élite pour l'admission aux cours supérieurs, également gratuits ; la suppression des octrois, la suppression des gros traitements et des cumuls, et la modification de notre système d'impôts ; la nomination de tous les fonctionnaires publics par l'élection ; la suppression des armées permanentes,

cause de ruine pour les finances et les affaires de la nation, source
de haine entre les peuples et de défiance a l'intérieur ; l'abolition
des privilèges et monopoles, que nous définissons par ces mots :
' Prime à l'oisiveté ' ; les réformes économiques, qui touchent
au problème social, dont la solution, quoique subordonnée à
la transformation politique, doit être constamment étudiée et
recherchée au nom du principe de justice et d'égalité sociale.
Ce principe généralisé et appliqué peut seul, en effet, faire disparaître l'antagonisme social et réaliser complètement notre
formule : *Liberté, égalité, fraternité.*"

Gambetta replied :—[1]

" Citoyens électeurs,

" Ce mandat je l'accepte.

" A ces conditions, je serai particulièrement fier de vous
représenter parce que cette élection se sera faite conformément
aux véritables principes du suffrage universel ;

" Les électeurs auront librement choisi leur candidat.

" Les électeurs auront déterminé le programme politique de
leur mandataire.   Cette méthode me paraît à la fois conforme
au droit et à la tradition des premiers jours de la Révolution
française.

" Donc j'adhère librement à mon tour à la déclaration de
principes et à la revendication des droits dont vous me donnez
commission de poursuivre la réclamation à la tribune.

" Comme vous, je pense qu'il n'y a d'autre souverain que le
peuple et que le suffrage universel, instrument de cette souverain-
eté, n'a de valeur, n'oblige et ne fonde qu'à la condition d'être
radicalement libre.

" La plus urgente des réformes doit donc être de l'affranchir
de toute tutelle, de toute entrave, de toute pression, de toute
corruption.

" Comme vous, je pense que le suffrage universel, une fois
maître, suffirait à opérer toutes les destructions que réclame votre

[1] This " Réponse au Cahier de mes Electeurs " is printed in full in
J. REINACH's edn. of GAMBETTA's *Discours et plaidoyers politiques*, I, 422, whereas
OLLIVIER gives only a fraction of it, XI, 498.

programme et à fonder toutes les libertés, toutes les institutions dont nous poursuivons l'avènement.

" Comme vous, je pense que la France, siège d'une démocratie indestructible, ne rencontrera la liberté, la paix, l'ordre, la justice, la prosperité matérielle et la grandeur morale que dans le triomphe des principes de la Révolution française.

" Comme vous, je pense qu'une démocratie régulière et loyale est par excellence le système politique qui réalise le plus promptement et le plus sûrement l'émancipation morale et matérielle du plus grand nombre et assure le mieux l'égalité sociale dans les lois, dans les faits et dans les moeurs.

" Mais, comme vous aussi, j'estime que la série progressive de ces réformes sociales dépend absolument du régime et de la réforme politiques et c'est pour moi un axiome en ces matières que la forme emporte et résout le fond.

" C'est d'ailleurs cet enchaînement et cette gradation que nos pères avaient marqués et fixés dans la profonde et complète devise en dehors de laquelle il n'y a pas de salut : Liberté, Egalité, Fraternité. Nous voilà donc réciproquement d'accord. Notre contrat est complet. Je suis à la fois votre mandataire et votre dépositaire.

" Je fais plus que consentir. Voici mon serment : Je jure obéissance au présent contrat et fidélité au peuple souverain."

And yet, on November 15 of the same year, the chosen of Belleville could sign a manifesto containing the following condemnation :—

" On a essayé de réhabiliter la théorie du mandat impératif, on a repété que le député, mandataire de ses électeurs, leur restait incessamment subordonné, et qu'il devait les consulter sur ses desseins et sur ses votes. On a même ajouté qu'il leur était justiciable ; que cité devant eux, il pouvait y être jugé et condamné. Les députés soussignés repoussent cette prétention comme fausse et dangereuse. Ils sont décidés à la combattre résolument. Le mandat impératif fausserait radicalement le suffrage universel en livrant l'élu, c'est à dire la majorité des électeurs, à la merci d'une minorité."

APPENDIX III

(P. 20.)   WAS GAMBETTA A JEW?

The story that Gambetta was a Jew gained some plausibility from his appearance.   It would seem to have been popularised, if not invented, by E. Drumont who, in his book, *La France juive*, gave this account of Gambetta's ancestry :   " Un Juif wurtembergeois, A. Gamberlé, se fixa à Gênes au temps du blocus continental, fit le commerce de cafés et la contrebande, épousa une Juive du pays, dont un des parents avait été pendu, et italianisa alors son nom en s'appellant Gambetta.   Le fils ou le petit-fils vint en France, s'établit à Cahors et nous donna le grand homme " (p. 207, popular edn.).   The unscrupulousness of this author, and the vagueness of the genealogy (" le fils ou le petit-fils ") lay the tale open to suspicion at once, and its falsity has been completely demonstrated by the authors who write under the name of H. Dutrait-Crozon, royalist supporters of the anti-Semitic *Action française*.   In their book, *Gambetta et la défense nationale, 1870-71* (an elaborate attack upon Gambetta and his conduct of the war), they printed the birth and death certificates of Gambetta's grandfather, Giambattista.[1]   Giambattista Gambetta, 1764-1842, was born and buried at Celle in Liguria ; he was baptised into Holy Church and departed this life fortified by the rite of extreme unction.   Léon Gambetta's mother was of Aquitaine stock, his grandparents were Ligurians, and all were practising Catholics. His most persevering enemies have so far failed to produce any trustworthy evidence of Jewish descent.   But it is to be noted that Drumont's book has been widely read in France.   Its excellence is still periodically proclaimed by the *Action française*, and its account of Gambetta's ancestry has been widely accepted,

---

[1] Appendix B, 528, 529.

and often repeated (e.g. in a lecture given by Mgr. Delmont to the Catholic faculties on Feb. 28, 1921).[1]

Appearance alone is no absolute proof of Jewish blood, although the combination of a Hebraic nose and dark curly hair would suggest the presence of a Jewish strain. Gambetta's hair, however, was straight, and his nose, according to Deschanel and M. Gheusi, who were acquainted with the Ligurian coast, was of a type commonly seen in that region among men supposedly of " Saracen " or Phœnician origin.

[1] Cp. also BUSCH, *Count Bismarck, Some Secret Pages of His History*, II, 423 ; and ROCHEFORT, *Les aventures de ma vie* (Paris, 1896-97), II, 250.

APPENDIX IV

(P. 30.) GAMBETTA AND THE EMPIRE

Madame Adam expressed the opinion that Picard, Ferry, " et même Gambetta étaient prêts à prendre part aux essais de cette transformation (i.e. the new Liberal Empire) avec Emile Ollivier, lorsqu'il aurait quelque peu essuyé les plâtres ; et sans la guerre, on les eût vus, comme bien d'autres personnalités de notre parti, être impérialistes libéraux après avoir été sermentistes ".[1] She also quotes a letter from Cernuschi (" qui a connu Gambetta chez nous et le voit beaucoup ") to Edmond Adam, apparently written at the time of the formation of the Ollivier ministry : " Il y a à gauche un tas de gens qui ne demandent qu'à se mettre en selle, tous prêts à succéder à Ollivier quand il aura sauté le fossé. Il y aura maintenant peu d'assermentés capables de rester irréconciliables jusqu'au bout. . . . Nous verrons, mon cher Adam, si Dieu prête vie à l'Empire, après Ollivier, Picard ; après Picard, Jules Ferry ; après Jules Ferry, Gambetta. Ce sera le pont d'Avignon ! " [2] H. Pessard's memoirs show that many people thought it possible that Picard and his followers would rally to a Liberal Empire ; even the irreconcilable historian Taxile Delord wrote in the *Siècle* prophesying that the next General Elections, in 1875, would lead to the formation of a Favre-Picard ministry.[3] But the probability of Gambetta's rallying was anyhow much less immediate, and the indications of

---

[1] *Mes sentiments et nos idées avant 1870*, 372.

[2] Ibid. 425 ; cp. also LUDOVIC HALÉVY, *Carnets*, II, 130, 141 ; KARL MARX, *Civil War in France*, 18.

[3] *Mes Petits Papiers*, I, 1860-70, 301 ff. ; but cp. OLLIVIER, *L'Empire libéral*, XIII, 463, for Picard's denial, et TCHERNOFF, *Le parti républicain au coup d'état et sous le second Empire*, 574 ; ANATOLE CLAVEAU, *Souvenirs politiques et parle mentaires*, I, 349 ; LOUIS ULBACH, *Misères et grandeurs littéraires*, 287.

its likelihood were still less clear. Madame Adam's opinion, recorded much later, may possibly have been influenced by feminine jealousy and by what she regarded as his betrayal or abandonment of the policy of " la revanche ". Ambitious and opportunist he had, indeed, shown himself to be before the war of 1870, but it is fair to point out that his opportunism had always been within Republican limits, and if he believed in any ideals, they were the ideals which, for him, were summed up in the word Republic. The plebiscite had shown how much must be done to educate the electorate to share his apparent enthusiasm for those ideals ; it was a great task, and one not unsuited to a man of his energy and ability as an " homme d'opposition ". On the other hand, he had shown himself to be a realist and a believer in policies which would bring speedy and tangible results, and the realism of his outlook would be likely to increase rather than diminish with the increase of his political experience.[1] If the Liberal Empire clearly gained strength, I can quite well conceive that he would have abandoned his irreconcilability as being as unpractical as the abstentionism of elder Republicans,[2] and have proclaimed his acceptance of Liberal Empire as a necessary stage in the transition to the Republic ; and once the Empire was accepted, even with such reservations, the accession of the Republic, like the execution of

[1] J. REINACH (*Récits et portraits contemporains*, 165) quotes an interesting passage from a copy of Prévost-Paradol's *France nouvelle* which Gambetta had annotated. The second chapter, " Du chef de l'Etat," ended thus : " J'appelle expressément bon citoyen le Français qui ne repousse aucune des formes du gouvernement libre, qui ne souffre point l'idée de troubler le repos de la patrie pour ses ambitions ou ses préférences particulières, qui n'est ni enivré ni révolté par les mots de Monarchie ou République et qui borne à un seul point ses exigences : que la nation se gouverne elle-même, sous le nom de république ou de monarchie, par le moyen d'assemblées librement élues et de ministres responsables." And Gambetta wrote in the margin : " Bonne conclusion ".

[2] The only alternative being to join forces with the extremists Blanqui, Flourens and Co. (and acceptance of the Empire would be much more congenial to a man of Gambetta's moderate temperament) for even Gambetta might have found it hard to keep alive a moderate Republican party when men like Favre and Picard had rallied to the Empire.

" la revanche," might well have been postponed indefinitely.
Principles certainly would not have deterred him from such an
acceptance. The question is whether the intensity of his Republican faith would have proved stronger than the realism which
inclined to acceptance, and so have made the abandonment of
irreconcilability impossible ; this I very much doubt. Important
political decisions often depend upon personal relationships :
perhaps the deciding factor in his future attitude to the Liberal
Empire would have been the effect upon him of personal contact
with the Emperor. Would Napoleon III have fascinated Gambetta as he had fascinated Ollivier ?

APPENDIX V

(P. 71.) TEXT OF GAMBETTA'S FIRST DESPATCH FROM THE MINISTRY OF THE INTERIOR

The following is the text of Gambetta's first " ministerial " despatch, sent at 6 p.m. on September 4 :—

" RÉPUBLIQUE FRANÇAISE.
" MINISTÈRE DE L'INTÉRIEUR.

" A MM. les préfets, sous-préfets, généraux, gouverneur général de l'Algérie et à toutes les stations télégraphiques de France.

" La déchéance a été prononcée au Corps législatif.

" La République a été proclamée à l'Hôtel de Ville.

" Un gouvernement de défense nationale composé de onze membres, tous députés de Paris, a été constitué et ratifié par l'acclamation populaire.

" Les noms sont :

" Arago (Emmanuel), Crémieux, Favre (Jules), Ferry, Gambetta, Garnier-Pagès.

" Glais-Bizoin, Pelletan, Picard, Rochefort, Simon (Jules).

" Le général Trochu, investi des pleins pouvoirs militaires pour la défense nationale, a été appelé à la présidence du gouvernement.

" Veuillez faire afficher immédiatement, et au besoin proclamer par le crieur public, la présente déclaration.

" Pour le gouvernement de défense nationale,
" Le ministre de l'intérieur,
" LÉON GAMBETTA.

" Paris, ce 4 septembre 1870, six heures du soir." [1]

---

[1] *D.T.* II, 209, cit. J. CLARETIE, *Histoire de la Révolution de 1870*, 71, 249.

The sentence about Trochu apparently reveals the position which the new rulers had naturally intended Trochu to fill. When Gambetta despatched this message to the departments, he can neither have known nor expected that the general would make conditions ; but he seems to have taken his entry into the Government for granted. The important thing was to impress the provincials by the announcement that the Republic was backed by the name and prestige of Trochu, and this Gambetta did not hesitate to do without further verification.

APPENDIX VI

(P. 72.) THE VOTING ON THE MINISTRY OF THE INTERIOR

There is disagreement as to the majority by which Gambetta gained the Ministry of the Interior. Simon says that he had a majority of one ;[1] Favre[2] and Picard[3] declare that he had a majority of two. I accept their version, for surely Picard, if anyone, would be likely to know by how much his rival had defeated him. Picard also explicitly says that Gambetta obtained five votes in all. Thus eight members of the Council voted out of the twelve [4] who were present at the meeting. Of these twelve, the two persons most interested, Gambetta and Picard, clearly did not vote. The remaining ten were Trochu, Jules Favre, Crémieux, Garnier-Pagès, Jules Simon, Pelletan, Emmanuel Arago, Rochefort, Jules Ferry, and Glais-Bizoin,[4] I suggest that Trochu, whose acquaintance with his new colleagues was so slight, was one of the two of these who abstained from voting : the other is less easy to determine ; possibly it was Pelletan whose rôle in the Government was to be singularly inconspicuous. None of the Council was a member of Picard's " gauche ouverte," so there is no obvious clue to the way in which the votes were cast : but I suggest the following distribution :—

For Picard (3).

> Jules Simon, who expressly stated that he gave his vote thus.[5]

> Jules Favre, who ten days later proposed that Picard should accompany him to the provinces.

> ? Garnier-Pagès, who firmly adhered to the old Liberalism of 1848.

---

[1] *Souvenirs du 4 septembre*, II, 5, accepted by J. REINACH.
[2] *Gouvernement de la défense nationale*, I, 90.   [3] *Dép.* I, 477.
[4] DRÉO, *Procès-verbaux*, Sept. 4.   [5] *Dép.* I, 504.

For Gambetta (5).

 Jules Ferry, a " jeune " and an intimate friend.

 Crémieux, Gambetta's old patron.

 Rochefort, Gambetta's successor at Belleville ; much
more likely to prefer the radical Gambetta to the
moderate Picard.

 ? Glais-Bizoin.

 ? Emmanuel Arago (or Pelletan).

APPENDIX VII

The following curious passage from Glais-Bizoin's book, *Dictature de cinq mois*,[1] though written later, probably gives an accurate reflection of the contradictory state of mind of the Delegation at this moment : " Un tiers de la France était occupé par l'ennemi. Le vote y serait-il possible ? Les deux autres tiers se partageraient, plus ou moins également, en abstention-nistes et en partisans du vote. Quel serait le crédit d'une Assemblée élue dans de pareilles conditions ? Nul, à coup sûr ; tous le reconnurent en disant, comme Crémieux, l'amiral et moi, fatal ballon !

" Oui, fatal, car si les élections avaient eu lieu le 16 octobre, elles auraient été toutes républicaines. Comme il n'y avait eu qu'une voix dans le pays pour acclamer la République, il ne serait tombé dans les urnes électorales que des votes républicains. Et comment ne pas penser qu'une Assemblée sortie ainsi des entrailles du pays n'aurait pas été plus puissante pour sa défense ? Cette conviction me restera toujours : jamais elle n'aurait souscrit au traité de paix si facilement accepté à Bordeaux par l'Assemblée de Versailles." M. Glais-Bizoin did not explain how an Assembly whose credit was nil could be either more powerful for the defence of the Republic or of much advantage to the Republic, even if it were composed entirely of Republicans.

But would elections on the 16th October have produced a Republican Assembly ? This is by no means as certain as Glais-Bizoin pretended. There is no evidence, as far as I can discover, to suppose that other parties intended to abstain from voting, and although the purification of the municipalities was mostly complete by the end of September, this in itself was not enough

---

[1] P. 85.

to convert the rural populations to Republicanism.   If they were ceasing to be Bonapartist they were not yet Republican,[1] and, while the result of elections in October, 1870, would indubitably have been more favourable to the Republicans than in February, 1871, the agitation of prefects over the proposals to hold municipal elections, the doubts of Republicans themselves and the opinions of observers such as Thiers, Prince Metternich, and George Sand all show that there was no absolute certainty of a Republican majority.   Thiers had told Lord Granville that the elections would return " a majority of Liberal conservatives, determined, as I am, to support the Government ".[2]   (This may, of course, have been in part a diplomatic forecast.)   Such an Assembly would have been far from what the Government itself desired : but, whatever the composition of an Assembly, its election at this time, in despite of the wishes of the Government at Paris, would have created a situation of peculiar interest.   It was this which Gambetta's safe coming prevented.

[1] Cp. G. SAND, *Journal d'un voyageur*, 97.
[2] Cit. J. SIMON, *Souvenirs du 4 septembre*, II, 72.

APPENDIX VIII

(P. 119.) TEXT OF GAMBETTA'S INSTRUCTIONS ON HIS MISSION
TO TOURS

The document in which the terms of Gambetta's mission to
Tours were drawn up began with a brief statement of the circumstances which had led to the establishment of a Delegation of the
Government of National Defence in the provinces. The following
is that main part of the text relative to Gambetta's departure :— [1]

" . . . S'ignorant respectivement l'un l'autre, Paris et la
province peuvent, à leur insu, donner lieu à un conflit.

" Or, ce qui importe avant tout, c'est le maintien énergique
de la pensée, c'est à dire de la direction politique.

" C'est dans ce but que le Gouvernement ordonne à M.
Gambetta, l'un de ses membres et ministre de l'intérieur, de se
rendre auprès de la délégation et de concourir avec elle à l'administration et à la défense du pays.

" M. Gambetta a pour instructions précises de faire connaître
et exécuter les volontés du Gouvernement.

" Il s'attachera à maintenir l'unité d'action et, en cas de
partage aura voix prépondérante.

" De concert avec eux, il fera exécuter le décret par lequel
les élections à la Constituante sont ajournées jusqu'au moment
où les circonstances de guerre permettront de consulter le pays.

" Comme ministre de l'intérieur, il est revêtu de pleins pouvoirs
pour le recrutement, la réunion et l'armement de toutes les forces
nationales qu'il conviendrait d'appeler à la défense du pays.

" En ce qui touche l'organisation et l'action militaires, les
résolutions prises par la Délégation seront exécuteés par le ministre
de la guerre et de la marine.

[1] From *Dépêches, circulaires*, etc., I, 34, 35.

" La Délégation continuera à représenter le Gouvernement de la défense nationale dans les termes qui viennent d'être indiqués.   Elle suivra les négociations diplomatiques, à la charge d'en référer au ministre des affaires étrangères ; mais elle ne pourra prendre sur ce point aucune décision, le Gouvernement de la défense nationale ayant seul qualité pour en arrêter une."

APPENDIX IX

(P. 124.) GAMBETTA'S KNOWLEDGE OF MILITARY MATTERS
BEFORE HE BECAME MINISTER OF WAR

1. Though he had a Corsican friend who was a captain in the
Imperial Guard, and sometimes entertained him in the officers'
mess,[1] there is no evidence that, as a young man, Gambetta was
particularly inquisitive about army life and organisation, or that
he made any study of military theory.

2. He certainly had no personal experience of the French
army, for he never did military service. He appeared before
the " Conseil de révision " in May, 1860, but was rejected by it as
unfit on account of his bad eye.[2]

3. Where he is to be found showing interest in military
questions, it is as a Republican seeking an opportunity to criticise
the Imperial Government :—

(1) by interference in debates upon military expenditure ;

(2) by articles in the *Revue politique et littéraire* (1869),
one on the pay of officers and another on the War Budget
for 1869. But the latter, which is the more important,
though signed by Gambetta, was written, not by him, but
by a certain Captain Jung, who, as an army officer, could
not publish his criticisms under his own name. However,
the fact that Gambetta lent his name was proof of his
sympathy with the criticisms, whether it be true or not,
as Reinach suggests, that he also introduced arguments of
his own into the article. The chief points were that an
army career was excessively expensive, that a really national

---

[1] Mme ADAM, *Mes angoisses et nos luttes*, 263.
[2] P. B. GHEUSI, *La vie et la mort singulières de Gambetta*, 55.

French army should be drawn from the whole nation, and not rest upon certain classes, that the victory in modern war lay (as was soon to be demonstrated) with the best-trained troops, that modern wars were too short to produce experienced generals—" ce qu'il faut ce sont des hommes jeunes, des chefs jeunes se renouvelant souvent "—that the hierarchic system of command was incompetent, and the decorations were too abundant.   In short, it was a plea for a democratic reorganisation of the army in accordance with the traditions of the great Revolution.   A third article upon General Grant showed that Gambetta had a slight acquaintance with the American Civil War.

4. The mere absence of evidence that Gambetta had made any close study of military organisation, or of the theory of war, is not in itself conclusive, although the silence of such witnesses as Lavertujon, Ranc, Spuller, Laurier, Freycinet, and Challemel-Lacour is very significant.   But the conclusion to which it points is, I think, confirmed by what happened when the time came for him to put such knowledge as he might have acquired into practice. Then the slightness of his military knowledge was apparent, apparent first of all in the organisation of the National Guards, and then in the kind of utterance he made on arrival at Tours. " War to the knife ! " [1] he proclaimed.   " We must put into motion all our resources, which are immense, rouse the countryside from its torpor, react against foolish panics, intensify guerilla warfare, set traps for an enemy so fertile in ambush and surprise, harry his flank, surprise his rear, and in a word begin a national war."   However just these counsels and resolutions, they were the words of an eloquent civilian, not of a military expert.   As Gambetta himself admitted later, he was not a specialist, but " a will supplying an impulse ".[2]

---

[1] Cit. J. CLARETIE, Histoire de la Révolution de 1870-71, 306.
[2] Annales de l'Assemblée Nationale, VI, annexe 59.

APPENDIX X

(P. 137.) Points of Comparison with the American Civil War

Freycinet had been a keen student of the American Civil War, and is said to have contributed articles upon it to the *Journal des Débats*.[1] The influence of these studies was to be seen in the war of National Defence, and some of the most important measures passed after his appointment as Delegate to the Minister of War, notably the creation of the auxiliary army and the establishment of regional training camps, were conscious adaptations of North American institutions.[2]

" Notre armée auxiliaire," he wrote later, " malgré les incontestables services qu'elle a rendus, n'a pas jeté le même éclat que celle des États-Unis. La raison en est simple : la guerre en Amérique a duré plusieurs années, tandis que notre effort a duré quatre mois. Or, c'est seulement après avoir été vaincus pendant trois ans que les généraux du Nord ont appris à vaincre à leur tour. Cela seul explique notre inferiorité apparente." [3] But in fact that alone by no means suffices to explain the whole difference, and, while Freycinet did well to borrow the methods for training civilian armies which had been adopted by the Northern States, it is doubtful whether he ever realised how incomplete was the analogy of the war he was waging with that fought in America. In reality, the general conditions were

[1] Gen. Thoumas, *Paris, Tours, Bordeaux,* 100. If this is so, they must have been unsigned, for the Director of the *Journal des Débats* informs me that the name of Freycinet does not appear at all in the register of the newspaper.

[2] The example of the Northern States at the time of the Civil War was also used as an argument by Laurier in favour of an issue of paper money in France ; J. Durieux, *Le Ministre Pierre Magne*, II, 262.

[3] *Souvenirs*, I, 151.

303

wholly dissimilar : 1. The field of operations in America was infinitely vaster, the country much less thickly populated, and good roads and railroads were few and far between. As a result, the progress of the war was much slower than in France, and there were often long intervals between battles and campaigns. In France, on the other hand, with its well-cultivated soil, good road and rail system, and comparatively dense population, the grave problems of transport and commissariat with which the Americans were so often confronted did not play nearly such an important part. The strategy of the American generals, so closely dependent upon local geography and upon the nature of their troops, was, as von der Goltz said, more reminiscent of the Thirty Years War than of a modern European war.[1] 2. Not only was the enemy whom the French had to face free from the difficulties of provisioning and communications which hampered American commanders, but he was in possession of an infinitely more powerful, better disciplined, and better trained fighting force than ever the Confederate States had had. That force was directed by a soldier of great experience, whereas the operations of both American armies were, for the greater part of the time, under the control of the respective Presidents, Abraham Lincoln, a civilian without any previous military experience, and Jefferson Davis, who was not a soldier by profession, although he had been educated at West Point Academy, and had seen service in Mexico. The length of the American Civil War was, then, due to many circumstances besides the one mentioned by Freycinet. And he omitted to observe that it was not until the civilian President, Lincoln, had resigned his direction of the Northern forces and entrusted the chief command to a general, Grant, that the career of victory properly began.

But, while the general character of the Franco-German War was thus markedly different from that of the American Civil War, there were many particular points of resemblance, e.g. :—

  1. The inexperienced civilian Lincoln, like the inexperienced civilian Gambetta, showed a prompt and firm grasp of the magnitude of the task with which he was confronted.

---

[1] *Gambetta und seine Armeen*, 27.

At an early stage he recommended the increase of the army and navy to the great total of 400,000 men ; while Gambetta at once addressed himself to the business of raising a big army to relieve Paris, and prepared to wage war on a large scale.

2. The senior officers in the regular armies, both of the Northerners and of the French provinces, were for the most part unfit for active service.

3. In France and in America civilian administrators showed the same disregard for military experience, and the same impatience for results, which was generally shared by public opinion. The Northern Secretary for War, Stanton, was far from being the exact counterpart of Freycinet, but in general his attitude corresponded to that of many French Republican officials : " Utterly ignorant of military matters ; despising, from the bottom of his soul, what is known as military science ; making no secret of his general distrust of educated officers ; rarely if ever lending an intelligent support to any general in the service ; treating them all in the way in which the Committee of Public Safety treated the generals of the first French Republic ; arrogant, impatient, irascible. . . ." [1]

Like Freycinet and Gambetta, Lincoln and Stanton often failed to realise the difficulties of organising and manœuvring citizen soldiers, and harshly blamed their generals for inactivity or faintheartedness when they complained of the condition of their troops.

Public impatience led the Northerners to defeat at the first battle of Bull Run, and in the same way governmental impatience for results and desire to gratify public opinion led in France to the first loss of Orléans in October, 1870, and to the unfortunate Pithiviers diversion in November.

4. Mistrust of their generals eventually led the civilian directors of operations to take important decisions without consulting them, and to hint at the inefficiency or disobedience of officers in a way which was both unjust and

[1] J. C. ROPES, The Story of the Civil War (London, 1894), 225.

impolitic. Thus, Lincoln's first General Order of January 27, 1862, issued without the knowledge of the Commander of the Potomac army, McClellan, though very different in tone, did, in effect, by its last command, resemble Gambetta's proclamation after the fall of Metz. Again, his third General Order, which betrayed unmistakable distrust of the Commander-in-Chief, without whose knowledge it was published, resembled Gambetta's circular concerning D'Aurelle, and the loss of Orléans ; while its indirect attempt to put pressure upon McClellan, and to induce him to change his plans, resembles the indirect methods employed in November by Gambetta and Freycinet to put pressure upon D'Aurelle. Lincoln, in this published order, introduced a new objective, apparently hoping thereby to force McClellan to modify his plans. Gambetta and Freycinet withheld full information as to their plan for an advance upon Paris, because they feared D'Aurelle's objections and consequent delay ; instead, they proposed a diversion against Pithiviers as the objective, hoping that when this movement was launched the Commander-in-Chief would find himself committed to a general supporting offensive which he might well have refused to sanction, had he been consulted as to the whole plan.

At the same time as he issued his third General Order, Lincoln promulgated, again without McClellan's knowledge, another order dividing the army into corps, and assigning to each its commander. Although McClellan had spoken with him of the subject, this was the first intimation he received that any decision had been reached, and it was another example of the President's lack of confidence and of ordinary courtesy. No less brusque and inconsiderate was the first communication to D'Aurelle concerning the diversion towards Pithiviers. The general had not been consulted as to any new movements, and was counting on some days' respite for his troops to concentrate and recondition at Orléans, when an envoy from Freycinet brought him a single sheet of notepaper on which was written a curt " Avis," signed Freycinet, and beginning without explanation or introduction : " 1. Départ de Des Paillères (*sic*) avec une 30ᵉ de mille hommes dans la direction de Pithiviers jeudi 23 ct." Such a document, as von der Goltz pointed out, showed scant respect for the Commander-in-Chief of an army of 180,000 men.[1]

5. If there were thus similarities in the treatment of Generals McClellan and D'Aurelle by the civil authorities under whom they served, there were also points of resemblance in the attitudes of the generals themselves. Both as professional soldiers were insistent on high standards of drill and discipline, and both were reluctant to undertake any offensive movements with troops whom they considered insufficiently trained. In consequence, both provoked the displeasure of civilians who were impatient for results, and objected to their seeming inactivity. Both, too, were prone to consider merely the interests of their own army and to ignore the general requirements of the political situation as matters with which they were not concerned. Thus, D'Aurelle never appeared to appreciate the political urgency for a bold attempt at the relief of Paris, and McClellan would not realise the importance of leaving an adequate garrison in Washington. Again, both generals, cautious by nature, much over-estimated the strength of their enemy; for instance, D'Aurelle greatly exaggerated the numbers of the German forces which lay between him and Paris immediately after the battle of Coulmiers, and McClellan doubled the strength of Johnston's army at Manassas.

[1] *Gambetta und seine Armeen*, 56, 57.

APPENDIX XI

The recruitment of the army in 1870 was fixed by a law of Feb. 1, 1868, which modified a former law of 1832, and in addition, instituted the Garde Mobile.[1] This law of 1868 was an object of constant attack by the Republicans. Thus, the manifesto of Nov. 15, 1869, signed by Gambetta, laid down as an aim of Republican policy the abrogation of " la loi militaire. Cette loi, qui renferme une double menace contre la paix et contre la liberté, épuise le pays en le privant de ses plus fécondes ressources. Elle doit disparaître et faire place à un système armant la nation pour la défense de la nation et de ses libres institutions." [2] According to the law, all Frenchmen were, in principle, liable to serve five years in the active army and four in the reserve. In practice, the numbers of the contingent to be recruited each year were fixed annually by law : thus the 1870 contingent was 100,000, but as a pacific gesture the Ollivier Government proposed that the next year's contingent should be reduced by 10,000. The report upon this proposal was debated in the Legislative Body on June 30, 1870, and gave the Republicans a new opportunity to denounce the whole of the actual system of recruitment. Gambetta, however, took no part in this debate.

The composition of the annual contingent was determined by lot, but those who drew a number which obliged them to serve were permitted to find substitutes if they wished. Naturally enough, the tickets of exemption came to be known as " les bons numéros," and military service was regarded as an irksome *corvée* rather than as a patriotic duty. All those who were not

[1] Cp. H. Dutrait-Crozon, *Gambetta et la défense nationale*, Introd. 19, and Appendices A.

[2] Gambetta, *Discours et plaidoyers politiques*, I, 94 ff.

called up by lot, were enrolled in the Garde Mobile, which was intended to form a kind of reserve for service in the interior, while the active army was employed against the enemy. The Gardes Mobiles were organised by departments, and were expected to undergo a short period of training each year.

When war broke out, the Imperial Government took various measures to increase its effectiveness ; amongst others, calling up the Garde Mobile, and the result was, according to Dutrait-Crozon, that by September 4 there was in the provinces an available effective of combined regulars and Gardes Mobiles numbering some 750,000 men : " on voit que la délégation n'eut pas à lever un seul homme de l'armée régulière ou de la mobile et qu'elle ne put même pas épuiser les forces mises à sa disposition ".[1] These figures seem to be a fair estimate (cp. Dutrait-Crozon's detailed appendix, pp. 505 ff., and *Revue d'Histoire, La guerre de 1870-71, Mesures d'organisation . . . et situation des forces françaises au ler septembre*, 83 ff.), but what exactly was the significance of an effective ? It appears to be nothing more than an estimate of the number of men who, in accordance with certain legislative dispositions, were at the disposal of the military authorities. The figures themselves convey no information as to the military efficiency of these men. The Imperial Government had passed laws and issued decrees, but the mere issuing of decrees was not in itself enough to produce an army, and most of these laws depended for their complete application and execution upon the Government of National Defence. According to the *Revue d'Histoire*, about 100,000 of the young soldiers reckoned in this effective had done less than a month's service ; [2] while a large proportion of the Garde Mobile had yet to be both equipped and trained.[3] Should all the honour be given to those who passed decrees, and none to those who attempted to give them practical effect ?

But the credit for the organisation of the regular troops, maintains Dutrait-Crozon, was due not to the Government of

---

[1] *Gambetta et la défense nationale, 1870-71*, 508.

[2] *Mesures d'organisation . . . jusqu'au 4 septembre*, 91.

[3] FREYCINET, *La guerre en province*, 37 ; LAVISSE, *Histoire de France Contemporaine*, VIII, 226.

National Defence, but to the " administration militaire, qui d'ailleurs, comme on l'a déjà vu, avait, dès l'arrivée de Gambetta et de Freycinet, constitué les 15ᵉ et 16ᵉ corps presque entièrement ".[1] It was thanks to the " bureaux " that " la France a pu continuer la lutte ". " L'œuvre de la délégation consista surtout à envoyer au feu des gardes nationaux sédentaires, dit ' mobilisés ' à tâcher de les pourvoir d'armes et d'effets. Les efforts tentés dans ce sens eurent pour résultat d'opposer des hommes dépourvus de tout esprit et de toute instruction militaire, à peine vêtus, mal armés et qui, à part de très rares exceptions, tournérent le dos a leur première apparition sur le champ de bataille." [2]   Now, there is truth in all this—the " bureaux " evidently do play an important part in military organisation, particularly under modern conditions of war ; and Gambetta and his colleagues clearly did attach undue importance to the mobilisation of the National Guard, an experiment which, so far as it was completed, was scarcely justified by the results—but is it the whole truth ?   If the organisation of the regular army depended upon the bureaux, yet it was upon bureaux which, after October 12, were extended and reorganised by Freycinet (although Dutrait-Crozon would make out that the work was carried on despite their extension and reorganisation which, he argues, was intended partly to create places for adherents of the regime, and often led to confusion rather than to increased efficiency [3]).   The bureaux, it is true, had achieved the organisation of the 15th and 16th army corps, so far as they were complete,[4] before the civilians took over the control of the War Office.   But the Gardes Mobiles were a not unimportant part of the effective actually used—according to the *Revue d'Histoire* there were 97,727, according to the *Rapport de Mornay* 135,735, on active service at the time of the armistice [5]—and the equipment of these men depended, not upon the bureaux of the War Office, but upon the prefects of the departments in which they were enrolled.[6]

---

[1] P. 20.   [2] P. 20.   [3] Cp. 113 ff., *L'organisation du ministère.*

[4] D'AURELLE found there was still much to be done ; cp. his book, *La 1ᵐᵉ armée de la Loire.*

[5] DUTRAIT-CROZON, *Gambetta et la défense nationale,* 507.   [6] Ibid. 498.

Moreover, however indispensable the part played by the bureaux in any administration, bureaux are not everything. They are seldom inspired, never inspiring. The knowledge that the War Office was engaged in executing the military measures passed by a fallen Government was not in itself sufficient to rouse great enthusiasm in the French provinces, and General Lefort, the head of the Tours War Office and a typical military bureaucrat, himself said that he never expected that the troops he was organising would be called upon to take any active share in operations.[1] If the second period of the Franco-Prussian War was characterised by greater bitterness, if large cities no longer surrendered to a handful of Uhlans, if there was a general will to resist such as had never manifested itself in August, this surely was not due to the permanent officials of the War Office. When Gambetta came to Tours, the outlook was as black as it could be ; there was disorder in the south, and the new armies on the Loire and in the Vosges were both defeated in their first serious encounters. France seemed beyond the power of recovery. But the coming of Gambetta largely offset the serious effect of these reverses upon the general morale of the country. Gambetta no doubt could not continue the struggle wholly without the bureaux, but could the bureaux have continued the struggle without Gambetta? Would the armies they were organising have been allowed to take any further active share in operations if Lefort had been in supreme control ? And would the imperturbability of the bureaux have enabled the country to bear the blow of Metz ? These questions seem to me to be very pertinent, however important the actual work of organisation achieved by the bureaucrats.

Dutrait-Crozon has powerfully exploded the legend that the whole of the armies of the National Defence was improvised by the civilian genius of Gambetta ; he has vividly shown up the drawbacks of civilian interference in military matters, and the defects of what was intended to be the great military achievement of the Republic, the mobilisation of " universal suffrage ". But he fails to convince when he assigns all the credit for the organisation of the defence to the " bureaux " of the War Office.

[1] *Dép.*

Moreover, while it may have been true that it was unnecessary for Gambetta to issue a single decree in order to obtain more regular soldiers or Gardes Mobiles, that part of the available effective of these men was still unabsorbed in his armies by the time of the armistice, and that from a military point of view it would no doubt have been better to use up these reserves before the still less experienced National Guards were brought into action, it must be remembered that it was not in accordance with Gambetta's policy that the war ended when it did.   Had he been able to continue the struggle to the knife, many more men would have been absorbed in the armies : the *levée en masse* itself would, he told Favre, provide a reservoir of nearly 2,000,000 men " dans lequel on pourra puiser des soldats pendant un laps de temps bien supérieur à celui pendant lequel la Prusse espère prolonger la guerre d'invasion ".[1]   In accordance with his policy of waging a war of exhaustion, it was a prudent, long-sighted measure ;   only in the actual circumstances of the time it was short-sighted, for it was of little use to call up many more men than could be properly armed or trained.   Gambetta deceived himself when he thought that the *levée en masse* would provide an inexhaustible reserve of " soldiers ".   The citizens affected by the decree could not become soldiers until they had been well trained and well armed, and the shortage of arms and of competent instructors was one of the serious disadvantages under which the national defence laboured before ever the decree was issued.   Gambetta's idea was sound, but the conditions were unsuited to its immediate and profitable application.   This and not the fact that he did not use up the whole of the effective of the Garde Mobile is the real criticism of Gambetta's mobilisation of universal suffrage.

[1] *Dép. circ.* I, 124.

APPENDIX XII

(P. 177.) UTILITY OF AN ASSEMBLY IN NOVEMBER

While it is certain that elections, had they been held in the middle of November, would have produced an Assembly very different from that of February, 1871, it is by no means certain that they would have led, as Thiers hoped, to the immediate conclusion of peace. The historian, Sorel, who was working under Chaudordy at Tours, thought not,[1] and whereas Lord Lyons considered that it was " hardly doubtful " that an Assembly would " in any case displace the men now in power," [2] Metternich believed that if it could meet before civil war broke out in the south it would probably acclaim the provisional Government " at least in the persons of Trochu, Jules Favre, and Gambetta ".[3]

If, then, the Assembly was not to conclude peace, it is pertinent to inquire of what advantage it would have been for the prosecution of the war. There is no reason to suppose that its support would have been of much practical benefit to the organisers of the defence or that, assuming responsibility itself, it would have proved an " improviser of armies " any more effective than Gambetta and his lieutenants. Its intervention would have been far more likely to have made confusion worse confounded. An Assembly, as the Royalist De Falloux pointed out, " est impropre à la rapidité et à l'énergie des mesures qu'exige un péril tel que celui de Paris et de la France entière ".[4] Its formal procedure and its desire constantly to

---

[1] *Histoire diplomatique de la guerre franco-allemande*, II, 83.

[2] *F.O.* 146, 1482, LYONS to GRANVILLE, Oct. 31.

[3] *H.H.u.S.A.*, Nov. 5, to BEUST.

[4] *Mémoires d'un royaliste*, ch. xxix.

assert its control would probably have led to innumerable delays. The permanent session of the Chambers in the Great War was to show how the valuable time of Ministers could be wasted by the obligation to render constant account of the most trivial details.[1] In a situation of emergency, too much democratic control may be a serious obstacle to the realisation of the true interests of the democracy.

[1] L. MARCELLIN, *Politique et politiciens pendant la guerre*, passim.

APPENDIX XIII

(P. 200.) THE IDEA OF CONTINUING THE WAR EVEN AFTER THE
FALL OF PARIS

The idea of continuing the war, even after the fall of Paris,
first appears in a despatch from Gambetta to Jules Favre on
November 26. He developed it most fully in another despatch
two months later : " Le printemps viendra, et ils n'auront pas
réalisé le fruit de leur conquête et, au milieu de l'Europe inquiète
et jalouse, ils n'auront pas obtenu de sanction pour l'œuvre de la
force. Nous les condamnons à une occupation aussi ruineuse
pour eux que pour nous, et nous n'aurons pas compromis l'intég-
rité de la France, et à la première occasion de trouble ou de
conflit européen, nous serons l'allié nécessaire de tous ceux qui
auront à se venger des prétentions germaniques." [1] This view of
the possibilities of war to the knife was shared by General Chanzy;[2]
while on the German side Bismarck recorded that the anxiety to
put an end to the war in military circles at Versailles was " as
great as the uneasiness at home concerning the slow progress.
. . . The thought disturbed me . . . whether the prestige
gained and the political impression made upon the neutral
Courts by our first rapid and great victories would not be en-
feebled by the apparent inactivity and weakness of our position
before Paris and whether the enthusiasm, in the fire of which a
lasting unity might be forged, would hold out." [3]
But was there any real likelihood that German prestige would
diminish so far as to lead neutral powers to active intervention in
favour of France ? Was there any real substance in Gambetta's
hope that some European trouble would bring France an ally ?

[1] Cit. J. CLARETIE, *Histoire de la Révolution de 1870-71*, 543.
[2] A. CHUQUET, *Le Général Chanzy*, 163 ff.
[3] *Reflections and Reminiscences*, I, 120.

Austria was bound hand and foot by fear of Russia, and the Russian and Prussian courts were on terms of the most friendly intimacy. Although opinion in England was far more sympathetic to France than at the beginning of the war, the Gladstone Ministry was essentially pacific, and a break with Prussia was the last thing desired by either Queen or Ministers. There remained only Italy, and here the French had thrown away their best bargaining counter by the evacuation of Rome. The new Mediterranean kingdom had no incentive to back a losing cause, or to support the patrons of Garibaldi. It was not, indeed, wholly impossible that some incident should occur which would lead to the generalisation of the war, but the probability of this was very small.

Moreover, if German morale was weakening, French morale had already weakened, and the signs of war weariness were more and more numerous as January drew to a close.[1] With the dis. aster to the army of the East, the chief instrument with which Gambetta had designed to continue the war to the knife was broken in his hands. Lavertujon recorded a conversation on February 2 in which Gambetta now seemed to be contemplating a guerrilla war like the Spanish War of 1810-12.[2] But, apart from the dissimilarities of the country, habits, and temperament of Frenchmen and Spaniards, guerrilla war could rouse little enthusiasm when so many greater enterprises had failed. A systematic guerrilla warfare might have been very effective in October and November : February was too late.

It was, indeed, true that France still possessed considerable resources : numerically they were impressive. Jauréguiberry's report upon the state of the military forces presented to the National Assembly on February 26, showed that there were 888,000 men doing service ; but of these 534,000 only could be incorporated in the active army, and half of them were unreliable *Mobilisés*. This left 220,000 infantry " capables d'opposer

[1] Cp. Appendix XV.

[2] A. LAVERTUJON, *Gambetta inconnu*, 76 ; cp. P. B. des VALADES, *Martial Delpit, député à l'Assemblée nationale, Journal et correspondance* (Paris, 1897), 230, for von Manteuffel's opinion of the futility of attempting a guerrilla war.

quelque résistance ". But to the question whether there was any chance of their resistance being successful, Jauréguiberry replied : " Nous n'osons même pas l'espérer, car il ne faut pas se le dissimuler, pour vaincre des armées aussi nombreuses, aussi bien organisées que le sont, à tous égards, celles contre lesquelles nous sommes appelés à lutter, il est indispensable que nos troupes soient, non-seulement instruites et bien armées, mais surtout animées d'un esprit de ténacité indomptable, d'un mépris du danger, d'un sentiment exalté de patriotisme que malheureusement toutes ne possèdent plus."[1] The question of morale was vital, and it was this, the want of spirit of the troops and the war weariness of the civil population, which more than anything else made Gambetta's policy wholly impracticable.

[1] Cit. J. CLARETIE, *Histoire de la Révolution de 1870-71*, 566 ; cp. the statistics and discussion of the whole question in G. HANOTAUX, *Le Gouvernement de M. Thiers*, I, 74 ff.

APPENDIX XIV

(P. 202.) Eugène Spuller

The closest of Gambetta's companions throughout his ministry was Eugène Spuller, a friend with whom he had been intimately acquainted for about ten years. Spuller had no official salaried post, but in effect he was Gambetta's personal secretary, the man who arranged Gambetta's receptions and audiences, interviewed petitioners, reminded him of urgent business, saved him from interruptions, and drafted certain despatches.[1] He enjoyed Gambetta's complete confidence, and was clearly in a position to exercise great influence. Freycinet said that Spuller's opinion was for Gambetta " un des éléments de sa résolution " ;[2] and Dalloz declared that at Bordeaux Spuller and Ranc together with Laurier were the only persons to exercise any influence over Gambetta.[3] It is difficult to determine exactly how great that influence was, and I have not discovered any instance of a decision made by Gambetta which was quite obviously the result of Spuller's advice. Gambetta was not at all the man to be a mere puppet in the hands of his advisers,[4] but it is true that he listened readily to the arguments of people in whom he trusted, or which appealed to his own Republican convictions and prejudices. The influence of Spuller, however, is likely to have been exercised in the interests of moderation rather than otherwise. This faithful Achates was a very different person from his enthusiastic, highly intelligent,

[1] Spuller, *Dép.* IV, 346, " Je me suis appliqué soit . . . soit aux correspondances qu'il pouvait entretenir avec les différents fonctionnaires ".

[2] *Souvenirs*, I, 163.   [3] *Dép.* IV, 397.

[4] Cp. *D.T.* II, 466, for a despatch in which Gambetta reproved Laurier, Ranc, and Steenackers for giving him advice and attempting to direct his movements.

temperamental southern Aeneas ; he was not the stupid fellow
Dilke took him for,[1] but he was slow and deliberate with a
Germanic cast of thought,[2] calm and unruffled, free from sudden
impulses and fits of temper ; also, unlike his patron, he was a
firm believer in organised religion.   Madame Adam's memoirs
show that he had an enormous admiration for Gambetta.   There
is nothing to suggest that at Tours and Bordeaux this man
deliberately set out to play the part of an " Eminence grise."

[1] Dilke often met him later, cp. GWYNN and TUCKWELL, *Life of Sir Charles
Dilke*, I, 299, 407.
[2] His father came from Baden.

APPENDIX XV

(P. 274.) THE CURVE OF MORALE IN THE PROVINCES

In a " people's war " such as that of national defence in France, the maintenance of the morale of the country was all important. This fact was fully appreciated by Gambetta, and throughout his ministry he did his utmost to rouse enthusiasm for the war and to keep alive the spirit of resistance.

There were two principal sources from which Gambetta himself was able to judge the state of public opinion in the provinces :

(A) The press.

(B) The reports of his prefects and sub-prefects. There is a considerable collection of these in the parliamentary Commission of Enquiry's two volumes of *Dépêches Télégraphiques*, but they do not give a complete picture of French opinion, for the postal archives of some of the departments were entirely destroyed or lost during the war, and from some others very few telegrams were preserved. Moreover, the authors of the telegrams were for the most part thorough-going Republicans, ardent supporters of Gambetta's policy, who more often than not seem to reflect their own opinions and those of their immediate entourage rather than of the general public. Hostile currents of opinion they tend to describe as due to " la réaction " and it is not always easy to determine what lies behind this vague word ; whether " the intrigues of the reactionaries " refer to the activities of a few anti-Republican politicians, or whether they imply a real war weariness and lack of enthusiasm among a considerable section of the population.

Nevertheless, it is possible to obtain a fair estimate of the general trend of opinion, and of the popular reaction to the most momentous events of Gambetta's four months' rule in the provinces,[1] and the evidence which is known to have been available to Gambetta can be reinforced or corrected from the observations of others than prefects and journalists.

In OCTOBER the two chief events were (1) the arrival of Gambetta in the provinces, and (2) the fall of Metz.

Official evidence as to the good effect of (1) is almost unanimous ; prefects are agreed that the decree cancelling elections was well received, and Gambetta himself confidently reported to Favre that the war was now the one preoccupation of the departments.   But he was under no illusion as to the effort necessary to rouse the provincials from their inertia : " La vérité est triste.   Les campagnes sont inertes, la bourgeoisie des petites villes est lâche, l'administration perfide et passive, ou d'une désespérante lenteur," [2] and two days later, October 16, he repeated " malgré l'animation des villes les campagnes sont toujours très passives." [3]   Four days later Lissagaray, a journalist, and for some time Laurier's secretary, wrote from Tarn that no one at Tours, " not even Gambetta," could have any conception of the lifelessness (atonie) of the provinces.[4]

Certain private observers were more critical of the new impetus imparted to the national defence by the advent of Gambetta.   Thus the Duc de Broglie wrote to Thiers on the 14th that the Republicans had good intentions but that they were incapable, and brought disorder into the public services, and alarmed the populations whose enthusiasm they wished to kindle : confusion and discouragement were universal.[5]   But it was still early, as Prince Metternich recognised, to pronounce definitely upon the effect of Gambetta's arrival and of his first

---

[1] Gambetta's own estimate is best discovered from his despatches to Favre ; but it must be remembered that he tends sometimes to be unduly, and perhaps deliberately, optimistic in order to maintain the spirit of the Parisians.

[2] *D.T.* II, 272.   [3] *Dép. circ.*, etc., I, 83.

[4] *D.T.* II, 124 ; cp. A. DÄNZER, *Mit den badischen Truppen, 1870-71, nach Frankreich* (Freiburg i. Br., 1912), 40, for spirit of prisoners of 16th Chasseurs battalion, Oct. 22.

[5] D. HALÉVY, *Le courrier de M. Thiers*, 417.

acts, for " il se trouve en présence d'une désorganisation complète et sa tâche n'est pas facile ".[1]

(2) The fall of Metz. This was bound to have a very grave effect upon the morale of the country, and Gambetta defended the proclamation in which he announced the capitulation and at the same time denounced the " treachery " of Bazaine and the generals, on the ground that morale would have collapsed had he not uttered " the cry of vengeance ".[2] The event and the proclamation both made a deep impression, and the reaction to them is vividly reflected in the prefects' telegrams. The proclamation certainly had the effect of exciting the patriotism, at least of Republicans, almost to frenzy. In general, there was indignation but not despair, and disaster only increased the demand for energetic measures for the prosecution of the war, for a plebiscite [3] (this was encouraged by the example of Paris), for Gambetta to assume dictatorship,[4] for a levée en masse,[5] and for the rejection of an armistice.[6] But it also led to exasperation against the generals, and the good effect of this upon morale was much more doubtful. " On se défie de tous les chefs," wrote the prefect of Saône et Loire on November 3, " et il est difficile de secouer le découragement qui naît de la défiance." [7] In the Var the prefect thought it prudent to place certain officers under arrest in order to save them from the fury of the populace,[8] at Perpignan there was a riot,[9] at Grenoble there were demonstrations against army officers, in Cher and Haute Garonne the removal of various generals was demanded.[10] Thus, what good effect Gambetta's proclamation had in maintaining the courage of the civil population was partly offset by the bad effect upon discipline. However, from one department only came any word of peace : the prefect of Nord declared that after the news of the events at Paris on October 31 " les populations déjà si

---

[1] H.H.u.S.A., METTERNICH to BEUST, Oct. 14.
[2] Dép. circ. I, 157, Nov. 26.
[3] Tarn, Vaucluse, Landes, Basses Alpes, Cantal, Hérault.
[4] Var, Landes, Toulouse.
[5] Vienne, Haute Vienne, Gard, Haute Garonne, Mayenne, Gironde.
[6] Tarn, Saône et Loire, Landes, Morbihan.
[7] D.T. II, 58.   [8] D.T. II, 136.   [9] D.T. I, 555.   [10] D.T. I, 197, 288.

découragées exigeront la paix à tout prix ".[1] Private observers like Metternich and George Sand confirm the general spirit of exaltation which prevailed throughout the week following the fall of Metz.

NOVEMBER.—Various events, however, combined to ease the situation and to calm public opinion (and particularly Republican opinion). Gambetta acceded to the demand for the *levée en masse ;* the Paris plebiscite was a triumph for the Government of National Defence ; and finally the army of the Loire was victorious at Coulmiers. On November 13 Gambetta reported to Favre that " toute l'effervescence excitée par l'abominable trahison de Bazaine, dont nous avons aujourd'hui l'irrécusable preuve, est maintenant calmée sur tous les points du territoire ".[2] During the three weeks November 10–December 4, in which the French remained in possession of Orléans, the morale of soldiers and civilians alike was at its best. As the first victory won by the provincial armies, Coulmiers was of very real moral importance ; every one rejoiced at the success, and hopes of the relief of Paris were high, and were encouraged by Gambetta's proclamations. From one department, however, Saône et Loire, come some hints of discontent ; hardship was being felt in the towns owing to unemployment and loss of trade, and the decree calling up all married men between twenty-one and forty was much resented in the country districts.[3] On the whole, prefects are very silent as to the success of this measure, which Republicans had demanded so eagerly at the end of October, and it is very probable that Saône et Loire was not the only department in which it caused irritation rather than enthusiasm among the peasantry.[4]

Gambetta's despatches, however, speak no more of the inertia of the provincial populations. He freely admits the shortcomings of his armies, the shortage of officers and munitions, but he no longer complains of the morale of the people.

[1] *D.T.* I, 497.   [2] *D.T.* II, 303.   [3] *D.T.* II, 64.
[4] Cp. *D.T.* II, 165, 480, 516, desp. from Pref. of Morbihan and Orne and Vendée, which show that they had misgivings about its effects ; cp. *Rapport de la* BORDERIE, *Dép.* BIDARD, 25.

DECEMBER.—Enthusiasm reached its peak on December 2, after the news of a successful sortie from Paris had been triumphantly telegraphed by Gambetta to all the departments. Joy was " indicible, débordante, frénétique ".[1] But the news was false, and disillusionment was all the more bitter because it coincided with the defeat of the army of the Loire,[2] which was followed by the loss of Orléans and the removal of the Delegation to Bordeaux. Reports of the activity of " la réaction " are now more frequent, and various incidents, of which the principal was the affair at Lyons on the 19th, when a demonstration organised to prevent the departure of *Mobilisés* for the front resulted in the murder of a National Guard commandant, indicated that morale was on the decline. Gambetta, however, never wavered in his determination to wage war to the knife and, despite the activities of M. Thiers and his friends, there were many Orleanists and Legitimists, as well as Republicans who, however much they eschewed the Republic, could still admire the energy and approve the policy of the Republican Minister.[3] But close observers could not but discern a change in the general attitude : " We should not deceive ourselves," wrote Duvergier de Hauranne to Thiers on January 1, " in spite of the resistance of Paris and some partial successes, war to the knife is hateful to France, and everywhere there is a desire for peace. My recent passage through Bourbaki's army has convinced me. Newspapers and public meetings may proclaim that this army is full of enthusiasm ; that is no longer true. A month ago, at the time of the combined movements of Paris and the army of the Loire, it was quite different. Then, in fact, there was a large measure of enthusiasm and hope. Since the failure of the great sortie from Paris, and the retreat of the army, there is discouragement

---

[1] Cp. e.g. *D.T.* I, 64, 136, 169, 204, 267, 332, 346, 371.

[2] Thus, in a despatch to prefects dated December 6, Gambetta referred to " les bruits les plus alarmants (sont) répandus sur la situation de l'armée de la Loire," and bade them " Démenez hardiment toutes ces mauvaises nouvelles apportées par la malveillance, dans le but de provoquer le découragement, la démoralisation," *Murailles politiques françaises*, 555.

[3] E.g. Guizot, Marquis de Castellane ; cp. E. SCHLUMBERGER, *Mes Souvenirs*, I, 133.

everywhere, and enthusiasm will not revive unless there is a great success to raise people's spirits."[1] This judgment is strikingly confirmed by von der Goltz, who describes from his own experience how considerable numbers of the young French soldiers used to allow themselves to be taken prisoner simply in order to escape the hardships of campaigning.[2]

JANUARY-FEBRUARY.—The decline of enthusiasm for the war which had thus set in in December increased rapidly in January. " A great success " was, indeed, necessary to arrest it ; but, instead of victory, there came a series of defeats. Even Government circles were dispirited,[3] and on the 19th Ranc went so far as to speak to Gambetta of the " discouragement of the army ". The numbers of deserters from Chanzy's army during the retreat from Le Mans were enormous : Lord Lyons thought the conduct of the French soldiers " an unmistakable sign that a large proportion of the new levies go into action without hope and without enthusiasm ".[4] The judgment was borne out by several reports from the departments concerning the condition of the new citizen soldiers ; there were mutinies among the *Mobilisés* of Gers and Vendée ;[5] the *Mobilisés* of Vienne left well-equipped, but ill-armed, and without confidence ;[6] all the departures from Gard were alike : " Ils manquent d'ordre et laissent de nombreux réfractaires ".[7] The town officials of Laval, like the population of Laon at an earlier stage in the war, implored Chanzy not to attempt to defend the place ;[8] they had no ambition to emulate the heroic resistance of Châteaudun. The inhabitants of Creuse rejoiced at the fall of Paris, because it must, they thought, mean the end of the war,[9] and the English Consul at Marseilles reported on February 4

---

[1] D. HALÉVY, *Le courrier de M. Thiers*, 420 ; cp. A. DÄNZER, *Mit den badischen Truppen, 1870-71, nach Frankreich*, 82, December 4, " In town and country people hereabouts (nr. Dijon) long for peace ".

[2] *Gambetta und seine Armeen*, 31 ; cp. G. SCHLUMBERGER, *Mes Souvenirs*, I, 132.

[3] *H.H.u.S.A.*, METTERNICH to BEUST, Jan. 13.

[4] *F.O.* 146, 1520.   [5] *D.T.* II, 164, 165.

[6] *D.T.* II, 170.   [7] *D.T.* II, 193.

[8] CHUQUET, *Le Général Chanzy*, 170, 171.

[9] *Frazer's Magazine*, Nov. 1872, *Six Months of Prefecture under Gambetta*.

that the population in general sighed for peace.[1] Cathelineau might assure Feilding a little earlier that the greater part of the " real gentry " were still anxious for the continuance of the war until favourable terms could be obtained from the Germans,[2] but the real gentry were a small minority of the French people. The great majority was unmistakably to express its whole-hearted desire for peace in the elections of February 8. All Gambetta's eloquence was unavailing to counteract the effect of a series of defeats which culminated in the fall of Paris and the disaster to the Army of the East.

The curve of morale thus shows a rise from the date of Gambetta's arrival at Tours to the fall of Metz ; between Metz and Coulmiers it fluctuates rather uneasily, to rise again after the recapture of Orléans, and to reach its zenith on December 2 ; almost immediately there is a sharp drop, and thenceforward the descent is uninterrupted, gradual at first, during the rest of December, rapid after the first fortnight of January.

[1] *F.O.* 146, 1561.

[2] Cp. G. SCHLUMBERGER, *Mes Souvenirs*, I, 134, 135, letters written from Paris on January 22 and 27 suggest that, as often happens, the people who were most bellicose were the farthest from the front. The following passage is also illuminating : " On ne peut se figurer combien l'esprit public s'est relevé partout. Des nouvelles comme celles de l'armée de Chanzy et celles de Paris, qui autrefois nous eussent démoralisés, sont considérées maintenant comme de purs accidents."

INDEX

(The more important references are, for convenience, printed in heavier type.)

327